# Law Without Future

# Law Without Future

*Anti-Constitutional Politics and the American Right*

Jack Jackson

**PENN**

UNIVERSITY OF PENNSYLVANIA PRESS

PHILADELPHIA

Published by
University of Pennsylvania Press
Philadelphia, Pennsylvania 19104-4112
www.upenn.edu/pennpress

Printed in the United States of America
on acid-free paper

10 9 8 7 6 5 4 3 2 1

Library of Congress Cataloging-in-Publication Data
ISBN 978-0-8122-5133-3

*For Wendy Brown*

# Contents

# The Pardon of the Sheriff

This is not a book about Donald Trump or the Trump presidency, although it is a book about the disintegration of constitutional norms and commitments on the American Right. Nevertheless, I want to begin with an incident from the early days of the Trump presidency to highlight the broad political condition the book explores: the paradoxical erosion of constitutional grounds via constitutional action, the discursive collapse of the rule of law with "the Constitution," and the uncritical embrace and celebration of the Constitution/rule of law by liberals with a simultaneous turn against the tumultuousness of politics (a turn sometimes explicit, sometimes implicit). In some sense, we begin with Trump to think past and move beyond him to properly think the present.

In the whirlwind of President Trump's first years in office, the administration's approach to the law has flickered between treating it as merely advisory, narrowly instrumental, mercilessly enforceable, or utterly irrelevant (depending on the political context and population in question). Against this chaotic political backdrop, one action stands out as perhaps paradigmatic of the president's orientation toward constitutional government in general and the constitutional principle of equality more specifically: his theatrical pardon of Joe Arpaio, the sheriff from Arizona. To the extent that the pardon represents the particular occupant of the executive office, the sheriff represents the ethos and energy of the political movement that ushered him into power.

Joe Arpaio came to power in Maricopa County, Arizona, in 1992. "Sheriff Joe," as his admirers tend to call him, imposed a policing regime in his jurisdiction that trafficked in anti-immigrant politics, and he implemented a harsh order of racial profiling to further this anti-immigrant policy. As sheriff, his signature was cruelty and humiliation. Most notoriously, he housed prisoners in an outdoor cage under the blazing sun of the southwest desert where temperatures frequently soared into triple digits. Prisoners slept in old army tents and were compelled to watch the Food Channel while eating meals the prisoners described as "slop."[1] When some nativist constituents asked why there were no concentration camps for the "illegals," the sheriff assured them that in fact there *was* a concentration camp in Maricopa County.[2] Under the sheriff's watch, all Latinos (citizens or not) lived and labored under the suspicion of being "illegal," and all immigrants without legal documents became figured as public enemies and grave threats to the polity even in the absence of any actions that constituted violations of the state's criminal law.

After years of governing with near impunity, Latino victims of his rule successfully challenged him in federal court. In 2011, a district court judge issued a preliminary injunction against the sheriff and ordered a halt to racial profiling; subsequently in 2013, a district judge found the Maricopa County sheriff's office to have been engaged in practices that violated both the Fourth Amendment's prohibition against unreasonable search and seizure as well as the Fourteenth Amendment's guarantee of equal protection of the law.[3] As a result, the court ordered a permanent cessation of the discriminatory policing practices. In response to the sheriff's refusals to yield to federal court orders, a federal judge found Joe Arpaio guilty of criminal contempt in 2017. Arpaio faced up to six months in jail for his crimes. However, this potential sentence was rendered null by President Trump's preemptive pardon issued in August 2017 prior to sentencing.

The ongoing violation of the constitutional rights of others, coupled with contempt for the courts that sought to defend those rights, earned the sheriff broad support and acclaim on the American Right. As the *Wall Street Journal* editorial board noted, "Sheriff Joe" stands as "a hero to many conservatives."[4] By issuing a full and unconditional pardon weeks before Arpaio even faced a sentencing for his crime, President Trump recognized and affirmed the heroic status of the sheriff, whose heroism ultimately consisted of nothing more than his perpetual disregard for the constitutional principle of equality. The symbolic weight of the pardon is heightened by the fact that this was the *first* pardon of Trump's presidency. But this was not the first time American conservatism has found such behavior pardonable. Corey Robin, in his illuminating exploration of conservative thought, reminds us that during the period of massive resistance in the South to desegregation on the heels of the Supreme Court's decision in *Brown v. Board of Education of Topeka*, the editorial board of William F. Buckley's *National Review* penned editorials that inquired "whether the White community in the South is entitled to take such measures as are necessary to prevail, politically and culturally, in areas in which it does not predominate numerically?" Reflecting upon their principles, the editors of the flagship journal of modern conservatism answered, "The sobering answer is Yes— the White community is so entitled because, for the time being, it is the advanced race."[5]

In pardoning this assault on constitutional equality, Trump also bypassed the normal procedures established by the Department of Justice to field and process requests for presidential pardons. Of course, these procedures are discretionary and not stipulated anywhere in the Constitution. Article II's language is sparse, and the power is mostly unencumbered: "The President shall . . . have Power to grant Reprieves and Pardons for Offenses against the United States, except in Cases of Impeachment."[6] The pardon power thus excludes violations of state laws from its reach as well as cases of impeachment. Unlike most of the other enumerated powers in Article II, it requires no action from either house of Congress to go into effect and is immune from being overturned by any action of Congress. Although the Supreme Court has emphasized that this "power of the President is not subject to *legislative* control,"[7] it remains an enumerated constitutional power within a broader constitutional structure rather than a power exterior or above or prior to the Constitution.

Presidents issue pardons for a variety of reasons. President Abraham Lincoln offered pardons to rebels during the Civil War on the condition that they would swear oaths to the Union. President Andrew Johnson issued pardons to numerous Southerners after the Civil War concluded; President Jimmy Carter provided mass pardons to those who resisted the draft to fight in Vietnam. In these instances, the pardon power was deployed to repair divisions in the polity. It is, in this way, a tool of governance.[8] Presidents have also granted pardons to relieve unduly harsh sentences or to demonstrate human sympathy for an individual and the particular circumstances of their case. The Supreme Court, in the case of

*Ex Parte Garland*, explained that the "benign prerogative of mercy" rests at the heart of the pardon power.[9] In practice, of course, the power to pardon is not immune to petty corruption, and the distribution of mercy can degenerate into something resembling the sale of indulgences. President Bill Clinton's pardon of the financier and party donor Marc Rich for tax fraud illustrates this most clearly.

Trump's pardon of Arpaio breaks with these various traditions. The pardon does not forgive a rebel; it instead affirms the revolt. Arpaio's transgression of the fundamental constitutional rights of others is rechristened as a political good by the pardon. The White House issued a statement in conjunction with the pardon. Nowhere in the statement does it mention either the violation of rights or the conviction for criminal contempt. Nowhere does it speak of either contrition or apology by the pardoned. Nowhere does it gesture to some larger sociopolitical good being measured against the crime and being vindicated by the pardon. Instead, the president represents Arpaio's tenure as sheriff as a "life's work of protecting the public from the scourges of crime and illegal immigration."[10] As such, his decades of "admirable service" make him a "worthy candidate for a Presidential pardon."[11]

It is enlightening to contrast this with perhaps the only other modern pardon that rivals it for raising such widespread constitutional controversy: the 1974 pardon of Richard Nixon by President Gerald Ford. Nixon committed crimes during his presidency that exposed him to criminal liability and prosecution after he resigned in disgrace. In the proclamation granting the pardon, President Ford noted the votes in the House Judiciary Committee recommending impeachment and also admitted candidly that Nixon's "acts or omissions" would likely lead to a "trial for offenses against the United States."[12] By pardoning Nixon, Ford did not seek to celebrate the "acts or omissions" that set in motion the wheels of impeachment, the resignation, and the potentiality of a criminal trial. The president instead sought to calibrate the punishment with the crime and thus implicitly acknowledged wrongdoing. Ford argued that Nixon had "already paid the unprecedented penalty of relinquishing the highest elective office in the United States."[13] In addition, Ford believed that the "tranquility to which this nation has been restored" by Nixon's resignation would be "irreparably lost" by the trial of Richard Nixon.[14]

In contrast to the case of Ford/Nixon, in the case of Trump/Arpaio, the crime itself not only disappeared from record but also was refashioned into a badge of honor or reimagined as service to the country well rendered. Lawyers challenging the constitutionality of the pardon zeroed in on this radical and unprecedented dimension of the case: "No President till now has proclaimed that a public official who violated the Constitution and flouted court orders was 'doing his job.'"[15] Organs of the legal establishment and liberal opinion quickly condemned the pardon. The ACLU denounced Trump's action as a "presidential endorsement of racism."[16] The president of the cautious and staid American Bar Association worried about an erosion of judicial power and prestige, castigating the president for exhibiting a "blatant disregard for the authority of the judiciary."[17] Conservative opinion split: editors at the *Wall Street Journal* warned that "pardoning Mr. Arpaio sends a message that law enforcers can ignore court orders and get away with it,"[18] and the editors at the *National Review* criticized the pardon for endorsing "the sheriff's lawlessness."[19] Nonetheless, the editors at the *National Review* were compelled to acknowledge that "Arpaio remains a hero to the populist Right."[20]

One may succinctly state the thesis of these critiques as this: the "rule of law" has yielded to the "lawlessness" of the president and his sheriff. Yet this critique circles back into something of a paradox: the so-called lawless pardon emanated from an enumerated constitutional power. Thus, we confront a vexing anti-constitutional situation in which constitutional power undermines constitutional government. As the *New York Times* described it, the president "used his constitutional power to block a federal judge's effort to enforce the Constitution . . . [this] excused the lawlessness of an official who had sworn to defend the constitutional structure."[21] Some of those lamenting this perfectly legal lawlessness (as they tended to phrase it) interpreted it as a "depressing sign of our hyper-politicized times."[22] Politics allegedly cracked the rule of law open, and a crisis of lawlessness emerged from its splintered shell. A leading constitutional scholar sounded the alarm of constitutional crisis: "Trump has pulled the republic into uncharted waters. Our best guide home is the Constitution."[23]

The book ahead charts the waters. But it maps the political present in the United States in a manner that displaces the centrality of the current presidential administration. For this movement toward anti-constitutionalism did not spring forth from the election of 2016; rather, that election and this current regime were born out of an anti-constitutional movement that was already under way. Trump and Arpaio did not pull the republic to some new place; they simply shined a light on our present location. And neither do the sheriff and the president represent some new moment of "hyper-politicized" times. Instead, they signal a time when a *particular kind* of politics is ascendant on the American Right, a politics ill-suited for and unmoored from constitutional governance.

Only political action can offer a different vision of the future, and the first effort of political resistance requires naming and claiming the future as a horizon of constitutional vision. It will require a political thinking long neglected in everyday political life and a constitutional reimagining long absent in the body politic—both by constitutional design, it should be noted. The disintegration of constitutional norms should thus emancipate us from longing only for a return "home" to "the Constitution." As Bonnie Honig has helpfully reminded us, there "are many varieties of constitutionalism, including popular constitutionalism, many of which were casualties of [the constitutional convention of 1787 in] Philadelphia."[24] Rather than return "home" by way of Philadelphia, this book invites the reader to consider the possibility of setting sail for new shores.

# Politicization, Lawlessness, and Anti-Constitutional Times

> *To stamp out world Communism I would be willing to destroy the entire*
> *universe, even to the furthest star.*
>
> —L. Brent Bozell Jr.

Imagine: "You are an American. You love your country. You think it is the greatest nation on Earth." Then: "One day, quite by accident, you are shocked out of your complacence." The communist tide has risen, quietly but certainly. As an example: "You pay a visit to your son's schoolroom, his teacher is expounding to the class—including your son—some theories that sound strangely alien to you. They *are* alien to sound American thinking, but this teacher doesn't label them as such." The shock of the red tide rising compels you into action. You visit the principal of the school to demand the firing of this teacher who "sounds like a communist" or "at least a fellow traveler." Yet you discover that you and your community are blocked from this action. What force enables the red menace and hobbles the true patriot? The Supreme Court of the United States.

The examples begin to multiply: you need an attorney and select one who is accredited by your state. However, you "aren't talking to him long before you realize that if you give this man your case, you will have a communist representing you. You leave his office in a rage and go to your State Bar association." You issue a demand for answers: how is it that "this young man, only just out of law school, can be an accredited attorney in your state—particularly in the face of all we know about the communist conspiracy?" You learn that the local State Bar had in fact disallowed bar membership to communists, but the U.S. Supreme Court invaded the sovereignty of the states and invalidated this prohibition.[1]

At this point, "your mind is in a whirl." What, you ask, "is happening to us—to me, to my country? Surely something is wrong somewhere." Again and again, your determined inquiry leads you to a Supreme Court that has limited the means by which real Americans may fortify their country "against tyranny from within and without." These nine men who stand against America must be studied. We must know: "What makes them tick?" What is it about these men that enabled them to push the republic to the brink of extinction? How shall we combat them? What reforms are needed to wipe out all the changes they have wrought since the New Deal? What will ensure that after this resistance and return, we will be safe from a relapse into such despotic madness? We "must know the answers to these questions, because the future of our country—the country we love is at stake."

These observations and questions emerged from the fevered world of the John Birch Society in the late 1950s. In *Nine Men Against America*, a book unknown and unremembered outside that cloistered Bircher world of conspiracy making and treason hunting, Rosalie Gordon offers a central thesis about the Court and its deeds since the presidency of FDR.[2] The Court decisions she decries, in the cause of a liberty to suppress, are purportedly the result of political machinations rather than legal thinking. The communist conspiracy infiltrated the jurisprudence of the United States because the modern justices have been overwhelmingly drawn from the ranks of "politicians rather than jurists." Justice William O. Douglas, as example, was a "darling of the radicals," but even worse, he lacked "judicial experience" when named to the Court.[3] Another Roosevelt appointee, Justice Frank Murphy, likewise had no "previous judicial experience."[4] And of course Earl Warren, the embodiment of all that was amiss, moved directly from the governorship of California into the seat of chief justice of the United States. In response, Rosalie Gordon endorsed a reform measure that would require Supreme Court appointees to possess at least ten years of judicial experience.[5] It remained unexplained how and why "politicians" were more likely to turn against "Americanism" or how and why judicial experience would inculcate and fortify a devotion to "Americanism." Even more, when Gordon accused Justice Douglas of writing opinions designed to propel him toward the Democratic nomination and the White House, clearly it was not nine men against America that so frightened her but instead the possibility of a majority of Americans against Americanism. In so many ways, this John Birch pamphleteer was ahead of her time.

The crux of Gordon's argument is this: when the world of politics and the world of law blur together, when the line between them wavers, the consequences are catastrophic for both. The law opens itself up to becoming a plaything of the communists, and consequently, political life is devoured by the rogue legality of the communists and their fellow travelers. Communism was the particular political movement, but its capacity for movement was only enabled by the breakdown of the more general jurisprudential order of things. This argument has been updated more recently by Robert Bork. Still nursing the wounds of the Senate's rejection of his nomination to the Supreme Court, Bork wrote a book in 1990 entitled *The Tempting of America: The Political Seduction of the Law*. The opening line of the book picks up where the subtitle leaves off: "In the past few decades American institutions have struggled with the temptation of politics."[6] Bork elaborates, "Politics invariably tries to dominate another discipline, to capture it and use it for politics' own purposes, while the second subject—law, religion, literature, economics, science, journalism, or whatever—struggles to maintain its independence. But retaining a separate identity and integrity becomes increasingly difficult as more areas of our culture become . . . politicized."[7] It is of note here that the seductress of the law is not liberalism or leftism or communism or nihilism or any of the other familiar specters haunting the right-wing imagination. Rather, the temptation is "politics" as such.

One might at this moment issue a charge of hypocrisy against Robert Bork. Who, after all, has done more to "politicize" the precincts of American law than Bork, the neoconservatives, the Federalist Society, and all of their fellow travelers? And such a charge would no doubt score points in a variety of liberal legal circles today as the Court stands at most one vote away from a root and branch assault on fifty-plus years of constitutional development. Such point scoring, however, presumes rather than challenges the mechanism by which the argumentative score is tallied. That is, it too accepts the deployment of "politics" as a rightful charge, a just accusation, a seduction to be resisted, and a temptation to be thwarted. Consider Columbia University president (and former Michigan Law dean) Lee Bollinger's observation in the wake of Justice Sandra Day O'Connor's retirement from the Supreme Court: "Everybody knows that there's a difference between acting within a body of jurisprudence and acting politically. . . . It's a question of degree, and I think many sensible people fear a distortion of that balance. That's what the Bork nomination was all about. And that's why the O'Connor replacement is like the Bork issue, because it's a critical decision point."[8] Here we have at once an opposition to Bork and a perfect agreement with Bork. Jurisprudence in the Bollinger schema is marked by its difference from politics. The threat is not conservatism or right-wing fanaticism or reactionary illiberalism. Rather, the difference making the difference is "politics" as such.

A distinction is often made between something called "law," on the one hand, and something called "politics," on the other. Sometimes the move to distinguish is driven by a hope to defend the former from the incursion of the latter, to keep the "law" safe and sequestered from the supposed unprincipled tawdriness of "politics." It's the juridico-political equivalent of seeking the separation of church and state (the Bollinger-Bork position). At other times, the distinction is rendered hierarchically as law over politics: the latter must submit to the requirements, demands, rules, methods, and style of the former.[9] This is represented in the familiar assertion about the necessity and primacy of the "rule of law" over the "rule of men." Similarly, law is sometimes presented as the frontier or boundary of politics; law keeps politics bounded and halts the political from transforming and transgressing into pure violence or arbitrary force. Here the law guards politics from its extremes; when and where law is suspended or absent, we have *nothing but* politics (this is often what people mean with the charge of "lawlessness").

The "law is law because it is not politics" thesis has been under assault for quite some time. To many observers, this move to distinguish law from politics has seemed misguided at best and disingenuous at worst. For instance, Marx first described the birth of the modern constitutional state, and the emergence of the "rights of man" concordant with it, as the bifurcation of human existence into civil society and the state. The location of political life in the state and the realization of rights against it only served to depoliticize powers coursing through civil society. As such, the legalities and ideals of liberal constitutionalism worked *politically* in relationship to those powers of property and religion and "egoism" by presuming, securing, and enabling them.[10] In Marx's words, "The consummation of the idealism of the state was at the same time the consummation of the materialism of civil society."[11] To place this in the vocabulary of contractualism for purposes of illustration, the theoretical equality of public law's social contract and the material inequality undergirding private law's contracts (labor contract, tenancy contract, marriage contract, futures contract, etc.) were bound in a co-constitutive bond. So indeed, "a state may be a *free state* without man himself being a *free man*."[12]

Another strand of Marxist thought viewed the law more precisely and narrowly as instrumental for capital, as a superstructural reflection of the capitalist economic relations underneath. In the *Manifesto of the Communist Party*, Marx and Engels argued that to members of the proletariat, "[l]aw, morality, and religion are to him so many bourgeois prejudices, behind which lurk in ambush just as many bourgeois interests."[13] The vision of the law wavers here. The prejudices at first appear plain, easy to see, and matter-of-fact, but then the law becomes or perhaps is at the same time something that obscures, conceals, hides an ambush: direct instrumentalism, on the one hand, and class interests determining in the "last instance," on the other. Both: class utility and ideology; ideology as class utility. Bourgeois law *is* bourgeois politics.

Critical legal theorists in the American legal academy have extended and complicated Marxist inquiries and explanations. They have excelled in showing the "radical indeterminacy" of the law, an indeterminacy rendered determinate by political calculations at odds with the popular perception of what constitutes proper methods of adjudication.[14] Indeterminacy and contingency challenge reductionist readings of legal doctrines but also affirm the primacy of politics and struggle in the law. Meanwhile, in the behavioral social sciences, the assault on the division between law and politics is offered through grids of quantification and scientific measurement: judicial votes are tallied, opinions are coded as "liberal" or "conservative," party identifications of the judges are marked, and the perhaps disconcerting conclusion is reached: "[T]he behavior we find do[es] not support [C. Herman] Pritchett's statement 'Judges make choices, but they are not the "free" choices of congressmen.' Indeed, given the extraordinary constraints on representatives imposed by constituents and party, we would conversely argue that members of Congress make choices, but they are not the free choices of Supreme Court justices."[15] This unconstrained free choice for action thus means that "the decisions of the Supreme Court can be overwhelmingly explained" by the political attitudes and policy values of individual justices and that "traditional legal factors" are fictions exposed as such by science.[16]

These critiques need not overwhelm or even necessarily be positioned in opposition to the "law is law because it is not politics" claim. They could, at least in theory, operate as a lament, a hymn to loss and a call for a restoration. Louis Brandeis, for example, accepted several tenets of what today might be read as a quasi-Marxist critique but responded with a call for the fortification of law and lawyering from the temptations of capitalist domination, on the one hand, and unruly labor radicalism, on the other—to hover above and mediate between "political" antagonisms. Here is Brandeis: "Instead of holding a position of independence, between the wealthy and the people, prepared to curb the excesses of either, able lawyers have, to a large extent, allowed themselves to become adjuncts of great corporations."[17] Bollinger and Bork likewise could agree with the observations of the critical legal theorists, behavioral social scientists, and Brandeis but see in them a diagnosis of juridical malady and thus revive the Brandeisian call for recovering "a position of independence" for the law. In fact, this is precisely what Bork does.

By contrast, other critics are insisting, each in their specific way, that the law/politics distinction is fool's gold. Moreover, the longing and fantasy of a law/politics disjuncture is itself potentially a constitutive element of forms of sociopolitical domination. Mirroring Marx but displacing communism with feminism, Catharine MacKinnon presses this point when she argues that "the state is male in the feminist sense: the law sees and treats women the way men see and treat women . . . the state's formal norms recapitulate the male point of view on the level of design. In Anglo-American jurisprudence, morals (value judgments) are deemed separable and separated from politics (power contests), and both from adjudication (interpretation)."[18] Or from the entirely different direction of the behavioralists, the fantasy of disjuncture is a mystifying mechanism for an antidemocratic institutional triumph. Without the mystification, there is no deference, and without the deference, there is no triumph.[19] Each critique revels in exposing the power behind the apolitical facade: class for the Marxists, "sex" for the MacKinnonites, and individualistic, conscious, and calculable political desire for the behavioralists.

The most radical critique, in a sense, is the behavioralist one. It is also the most prominent and prevalent one in everyday political discourse. Thus, it bears pausing upon it. First, its radicalness. Whereas Catharine MacKinnon argues that the *specific* forms of jurisprudence embody and perform a masculinist epistemology and political rationality, the specificity of the discourse is not abolished—there is a call for feminist jurisprudence, not the abolition of jurisprudence as such: "Justice will require change, not reflection—a new jurisprudence, a new relation between life and law."[20] As noted, Marxist thought frequently acknowledges the "relative autonomy" of the law, and even if jurisprudence is ultimately reducible to class power, some differences remain intact: it is the very specificity of law that gives it such ideological power. By contrast, the behavorialist charge is not that the distinctness of law reflects or constitutes a mode of classed or sexed or raced power and domination; in fact, there's no logic underneath it at all. Further (and here's the radicalness), *there is no distinction*: "Traditional legal factors, such as precedent, text, and intent, [have] virtually no impact" on adjudication.[21]

This is the pivot around which the Bork-Bollinger position turns as well but in a counter-rotation to the behavioralists. That is, the porousness or perhaps borderless space between interpretation and partisanship constitutes a transgression for Bork-Bollinger while existing as a matter-of-fact norm made visible by science for the behavioralists. It is also what most commentators have in mind when they accuse an opinion, a judge, a court, or a juridical epoch of being "political." To be "political" is to abandon traditional legal factors for specific "policy ends" as judgment becomes severed from precedent, text, and intent. A clear illustration of this vision may be located in the strenuous and futile efforts by then senator Arlen Specter to extract a public oath of allegiance to existing "precedent" from Samuel Alito in the Senate confirmation hearings for President George W. Bush's final nominee to the Supreme Court. The desire for such unenforceable assurances was seen as that which would offer some protection for the "law" from the sharpened talons of "politics."[22] Neither the Senate nor many commentators at the time of the appointment openly acknowledged the fact that "traditional legal factors" might themselves be the carrier of an entire panoply of political investments or that political thinking was properly interior, rather than alien, to constitutional interpretation.

We must ask: Why does the charge of "politics" have purchase and bite when levied against legal interpretations and enactments? Why is *that* the term of reproach and disapprobation? What dangers and pitfalls inhere in such a justificatory-rhetorical regime? What limitations on political judgment does this enact? What confinements does this impose on political movements and constitutional imagination? What suffocations are potential in a desire to have law safe from politics when politics is itself legally saturated and oriented? What is produced and enabled by a "politics is politics is politics" debunking—illumination or occlusion? One aim of this book is to move against the presumption or hope of both legal difference without politics and an undifferentiated politics of law.

\* \* \*

Another vision of the law/politics borderland is one organized through the erection of legal barriers *around* political movement; the law as a daywatchman on the frontiers, keeping things in rather than out. Whereas anxiety about politicization aims to keep politics from invading the law, here the walls of law enclose political life to prevent a deterioration of politics back into an imagined Hobbesian state of nature. The trump move in the former case is the accusation of being "political," but the trump move in the latter instance is the accusation of being "lawless." Benjamin Barber summarizes this Hobbesian perspective: "The anarchy of the state of nature is literal: a condition of lawlessness where there are no governors, no agreements, no contracts . . . the remedy is not power, which men have in the state of nature, but law and contract which they lack."[23] Here the content of the law is less important than its presence and force.

But political movements exterior to extant legal forms and practices need not lead the polity into a Hobbesian state of nature. Walls may need to be breached, agreements may need to be broken, governors may need to be ignored: all of this may be a *life source* for the law. This position perhaps converges with Lida Maxwell's effort to revalue and center the "unpredictability of political action" as the condition of law's grounds.[24] Indeed, lawless action finds shelter within the U.S. constitutional-legal tradition, as that tradition is one of multiple revolutionary ruptures and reconstructions. Thinkers as diverse as Edmund Burke and Hannah Arendt have minimized this aspect of the U.S. constitutional order (often in stark contrast to the French experience),[25] but one should recall that colonial assemblies and declarations existed in tandem with purges and expulsions of loyalists to the Crown; in the shadow of Independence Hall sits the ransacked home of loyalist Massachusetts Governor Thomas Hutchinson. When apologists for the Crown expressed fury and contempt at "mob violence" during the struggle for independence, they were not lost in delusion or trafficking in hyperbole. Gordon Wood observes that "mob action would become, as the Tories pointed out, 'a necessary ingredient' in fomenting the American

Revolution. 'Mass violence,' Arthur M. Schlesinger reminded us in 1955, 'played a dominant role at every significant turning point of the events leading up to the War for Independence.' "[26]

Not just origins, but tradition: the Thirteenth, Fourteenth, and Fifteenth Amendments did not arrive in the South via free deliberation and the normal means of constitutional ratification. They are, after all, collectively referred to as "the Civil War Amendments." Although Bruce Ackerman has sought to rescue this history from the category of lawlessness, he, unlike many constitutional lawyers, has at least confronted it directly: "Were it not for the purge of Southern Senators and Representatives, the 'Congress' meeting in June [1866] would never have mustered the two-thirds majorities required to propose the Fourteenth Amendment."[27] And the promise of those amendments would find no reality absent extralegal theorization and practice, a point on which those on different sides of any violent/nonviolent theoretical divide agree.[28] Some civil rights lawyers, including future Supreme Court justice Thurgood Marshall, "disapproved of 'lawless' direct action, even if nonviolent," but in retrospect, it is difficult to disagree with Professor Charles Ogletree's conclusion that the boycotts, sit-ins, and unauthorized marches in fact "benefitted the legal battles" being waged on behalf of civil rights.[29] The end result of direct action was the establishment of a regime of just laws. Notwithstanding this history, "lawlessness" (much like "politicization") increasingly serves as both a diagnosis and critique of the present. In rendering lawless action as necessarily antagonistic to both the rule of law and the possibility of justice, a revolutionary tradition renounces its legitimacy, erases its history, and announces its end: the tradition recedes at precisely the moment when its lessons might be thought to be most timely.

These twin specters, politicization and lawlessness, that so agitated critics of post–New Deal jurisprudence in the twentieth century now haunt the political imaginations of many on the Left in the twenty-first. What historical forces or political events generated such an unexpected turning of the tables? One may be tempted to point to the multitude of dislocations produced by the "War on Terror." This ill-defined yet omnipresent war—with the bombing, invasion, and occupation of Iraq; the rapid proliferation of torture camps across the planet; the spread of drones beyond numerous national frontiers with neither consent from impacted nations nor a proper declaration of war from the U.S. Congress—has in fact incited a resistance that aims its fire at the imagined dual menace of the politicization of law and the lawlessness of politics. Phillipe Sands has concluded that the War on Terror heralds nothing less than the emergence of a "lawless world,"[30] and critics of the U.S. torture camps in Guantanamo Bay imagine within them the logical end of law's politicization. Torture is the branch, but politicization is the root: it is "political legal thinking" that marks the "trail to the field of forbidden legal and moral fruit" of torture.[31] And many legal scholars understand 9/11 as ushering in a "new era in American law," a period in which the law is weakened, besieged, or endangered, when "unconstitutional policies" cease to be aberrational and have instead "taken on a life of their own."[32] In response, the ideal of the "rule of law" is held forth as a beacon in dark times.

This book offers a series of dissents in response to this narrative. First, the ongoing crisis of constitutionalism in the United States predates 9/11, emerges in locales and situations neither reducible nor tethered to the petrol-theological crusades in the Middle East, and operates as a new mode of right-wing governance far beyond the exertions of executive power in an imperial context. Second, this crisis is not born of the politicization of the law and can, in fact, only be confronted by the mobilization of political action and thinking both inside and outside the law. Third, an insistence upon a "return" to the rule of law in conjunction with the expulsion of politics from its realm serves to reinforce if not legitimate systems and practices of injustice that are partially constitutive of the constitutional order. Fourth, the identification of the crisis as one of lawlessness negates the revolutionary tradition and misidentifies the corruption of constitutionalism as being exterior rather than interior to law and legal practice.

\*   \*   \*

A crisis of constitutionalism has developed in the United States from a widening fissure between a waning of traditional conservatism, on the one hand, and an ascendant radicalized illiberal Rightist ethos, on the other. This latter phenomenon is not marginal, and despite the inclination of many in the media and some in the academy to narrate it as such, one finds no comparable movement that mirrors it in content, form, or impact on the Left. None of this is to suggest that liberals and leftists are constitutional saints nor deny that the issue of constitutionalism is one that has divided liberals and leftists across generations since at least the writings of Marx. But it is simply an inaccurate reading of U.S. political life in recent decades to claim that the major center-Left party is infused with a similar energy and constituency that eschews basic constitutional commitments and conventions. Quite the contrary, as this book will show, many on the political Left have increasingly embraced constitutionalism in response to right-wing radicalization, often in a manner that leads to conservative-to-reactionary conclusions or implications. So, this book explores a double break on the Right with the emergence of an anti-constitutional politics: a break from both conservatism and constitutionalism. As well, this book tracks and engages with a twofold flight on the Left: to apolitical legality and to a studiously lawful politics, both figured as fidelity to the rule of law. A central aim of the book is to think beyond this impasse.

What makes contemporary anti-constitutionalism so perplexing is the open-ended articulation of legal transgression within the field of law itself. It rules most intensely in the name of that which it simultaneously dismembers. It cannot do without that which it so relentlessly undoes. Jurisprudential paradoxes govern, and while there may be some theoretical and political connections to theories of sovereign exceptionality, the paradox of anti-constitutionalism is not simply interchangeable with Carl Schmitt's sovereign "monopoly to decide" where the decision departs "from the legal norm, and (to formulate it paradoxically) authority proves that to produce law it need not be based on law."[33] In contrast, the paradox of anti-constitutionalism springs forth as a *law that is no law but which is not lawless*, in that it is neither exterior to the law nor capable of discounting or suspending the law. Anti-constitutionalism rules without producing a new juridical norm or legal order but instead generates a show and shadow of legality that becomes the claimed basis of authority—law thus governs at the precise moment it withdraws. In this withdrawal, the temporal underpinnings of constitutional politics disappear: futurity evaporates.

As an introductory illustration, the structure and logic of anti-constitutionalism may be glimpsed far "off in a corner of habeas corpus doctrine."[34] In the wake of the Supreme Court's decision in *Teague v. Lane* (1989),[35] Professor Linda Meyer observed a troubling dimension of the Court's opinion. The Court, in attempting to draw a distinction between new rules, on the one hand, and rules dictated by precedent, on the other, sought to severely limit situations representing the latter so as to make it more difficult for prisoners to bring habeas cases to court. The holding in

*Teague* advanced the political project of restricting the rights of prisoners, a central plank of post–Warren Court conservative jurisprudence. But it did more than that. Meyer notes that the Court in *Teague* began "wearing away the power of precedent itself, stripping all prior cases of all persuasive force beyond their particular factual contexts. Limited to its facts, a case will guide future cases only in the extraordinary event that history repeats itself. The analogical links forged between past and present, from one case to the next stand broken."[36] Legal scholar Susan Bandes also highlights this aspect of the case: "[T]he courts are in fact precluded from using the normal common law tools to decide cases before them or to set precedent for the future."[37] Justice William Brennan explained in his *Teague* dissent that " 'as every first-year law student learns, adjudication according to prevailing law means far more than perfunctorily applying holdings in previous cases to virtually identical fact patterns. . . . A judge must thereby discern whether the principles applied to specific fact patterns in prior cases fairly extend to govern analogous fact patterns.' "[38] Narrowing precedent to the point of perfunctoriness would constitute, in Meyer's words, "self-destructive legal analysis."[39]

To return to the idiom of this book, we can translate "self-destructive legal analysis" as "anti-constitutionalism." The nullification of futurity present in the *Teague* case is not confined to habeas corpus doctrine. It is exemplary of a broader crisis of futurity on the Right. Constitutionalism both presumes and requires future-oriented commitments. The substance of those commitments may be varied, but the commitment itself is substantive too. Looking back, one is struck by the centrality of the temporal question in the eighteenth-century ratification debates over the U.S. Constitution. Alexander Hamilton believed that the vison of law included not just the present but rather the horizon of constitutionalism oriented toward "posterity." On this point, Hamilton's foes in the anti-Federalist camp stood in perfect agreement with him. The celebrated anti-Federalist essayist "Brutus" framed the constitutional debate as one upon which hung "the happiness and misery of generations yet unborn." Thus, it is not surprising that the preamble of the Constitution states its aim as securing justice, tranquility, liberty, and the general welfare for both "ourselves" and for "our posterity." Before any particular arrangement of power and beyond deployment of any specific set of rights stood an orientation toward the future and a commitment to secure it, a security on which all other securities rested.

Against the future there stands today a radicalized politics of apocalyptic orientation and, in some instances, longing. Some political actors consciously embrace this turn against the time of the world (which is also coterminous with the time of the law), but self-consciousness of action is not a prerequisite for identifying events that emanate from and/or reinforce a political ethos. For example, L. Brent Bozell Jr.'s eagerness to destroy the universe even out to the furthest star to achieve victory in an anticommunist crusade might fulfill a religious eschatological desire or simply represent a secular fanaticism that converges with an apocalyptic hope. Whereas the constitutional age began with a willingness for self-sacrifice of life to secure a new future—and here we can turn to Patrick Henry's "liberty or death" speech and to the closing lines of the Declaration of Independence where the signatories mutually "pledge to each other our lives"—the anti-constitutional impulse or drive happily sacrifices the prospect of a future for a present-tense "victory" or redefines the sacrifice of the future as victory itself. I would like to suggest that this split between a worldview represented by Patrick Henry, on the one hand, and a worldview represented by L. Brent Bozell Jr., on the other, is an unbridgeable chasm structuring the political present in the United States.

Political theorist William Connolly has diagnosed the latter half of this split as being defined by an "ethos of existential revenge," an ethos that increasingly infuses political rhetoric, informs cultural production, structures political desire, and ultimately "becomes *embedded* in a variety of institutions."[40] Connolly traces the emergence of a sensibility that cuts across theocratic conservatism and libertarian conservatism and yet also emerges from, binds, and reinforces the sensibility of both. Whereas Connolly writes of "*affinities of spirituality*,"[41] my aim is to track "*affinities of temporality*" that are coordinated with and constitutive of an apocalyptic ethos. Today, we are witnessing its deepening manifestation in the institutions of law: an ethos antithetical to the life of law burrows itself into legal thought and practice.

If this paradox existed only in the minutiae of habeas corpus doctrine, it would be perhaps of interest only to legal scholars, the criminal defense bar, and the condemned dwelling in America's vast prison system. But anti-constitutionalism is not confined to the stony fields of U.S. constitutional criminal law. Instead, as this book will show, this jurisprudential auto-negation has moved far beyond a narrow dispute in habeas doctrine (and to be clear, habeas doctrine here serves as only an introductory example and not an imagined origin); it has determined a presidential election, irrigated and informed a vast transnational torture regime, suspended fundamental constitutional rights long thought implicit in the very idea of Anglo-American liberty, and successfully negated the enumerated power of the president to appoint Supreme Court justices. Thus, a political urgency attends the effort to understand the anti-constitutional turn: it marks and makes the political present.

The brief example from habeas corpus not only introduces the temporal/logical structure of anti-constitutionalism but also exposes the analytical and political limits of denouncing the politicization of the law. Limiting habeas appeals by prisoners constituted a true political triumph of the Rehnquist Court over the legacy of the Warren Court. It is a victory for the police state buttressed by the law: "*Teague* can be fully understood only as a part of the current Court's relentless campaign against habeas corpus and the constitutional protections underlying it . . . the Court thinly disguises its hostility and impatience towards habeas claims in the language of formalism and inexorable reason: The Court seeks to present its value choices as value free."[42] Political commitment is inescapable: judgment may fall on the side of order and finality, *or* the decision may tilt toward a recognition of judicial fallibility and revulsion at the possibility of an innocent man being incarcerated. Constitutional judgment cannot escape politics or political thinking. Politicization of the law in this case is nothing more than tracking the circulation of value in value-free formalism and contesting it with a countervalue. In her discussion of mid- twentieth-century political trials, Judith Shklar posed the issue thusly: "The question, in short, is not, 'Is law political?' but 'What sort of politics can law maintain and reflect?' "[43]

The example of *Teague* also shows the limits of envisioning lawlessness as the sign of anti-constitutionalism and/or as that which is by definition antagonistic to justice. To turn again to Linda Meyer's phrasing, *Teague* may represent "self-destructive legal analysis," but the critical point is that it originates within legal vocabularies and practices while nonetheless turning against their foundations; it is destructive, but it is *self*-destructive. As to the question of justice, who can tell the unfairly condemned that there exists no political life beyond the four corners of the law when the law conspires with such injustice? Marx said that "revolutions are not made by law," but he was only saying what the eighteenth-century revolutionaries of Boston and Paris knew to be true before him. The revolutionary assertion of a new constitutional order differs not in degree but in kind from a "law that is not law" erosion of a constitutional order. From this perspective, the path is not a *return* to the rule of law but the institution of a new law worthy of rule.

In summary form: the emergence of an energetic and empowered anti-constitutionalism has produced increasing calls for a mobilization to defend the "rule of law" against lawlessness and politicization. This mobilization and its attendant discourse unwittingly carry forth a reactionary political project. With respect to "politicization," idealizing the rule of law against politics insulates the law from critique and transformation by freezing the current jurisprudential order in place or envisioning its most immediate past as a place of return. In an epoch when the law increasingly entrenches the power of private wealth, legitimates structures and practices of racial domination, and reinscribes patriarchal norms within its reasoning, struggles for political freedom necessitate the politicization of the law. Judith Shklar's warning still rings true: "[I]t cannot be repeated often enough that procedurally 'correct' repression is perfectly compatible with legalism."[44] With respect to "lawlessness," the Left severs itself from the rich revolutionary tradition it inaugurated and (until recently) inhabited. The result is an erasure of the past, a misreading of the present, and an enfeebled ability to chart a different future.

In a broad sense, this book inhabits a space wary of, if not antagonistic to, *both* end-of-history celebrations of contemporary liberal constitutionalism *and* critiques of constitutionalism that fold it entirely into the horizon of contemporary liberalism. This book invites the reader to inhabit a set of theoretical tensions and to wrestle with a variety of cross-cutting political visions. The aim here is less to set forth a rule or defend a doctrine and more to nurture a practice of thinking politically and rendering judgment within the contingencies of historical time with an eye toward and commitment to posterity.

\*    \*    \*

Chapter 1 begins with the judicial power and analyzes the Supreme Court's decision in *Bush v. Gore* to halt the recount of ballots in Florida. Much of the critical response to that extraordinary ruling castigated it as either a decision marred by "politics" or as a lawless decision (or, in the alternative, a legal decision made by a lawless Court). This chapter explores the politics always present in the law with a turn to the jurisprudential doctrines that expanded the Bill of Rights to the states in the twentieth century and the establishment of judicial review in the nineteenth century. Foregrounding the politics of these two regimes of precedent enables us to see that the departure from the norms of jurisprudence in *Bush v. Gore* was not the surprise appearance of "politics" but instead a politics of law against the idea of precedent in U.S. constitutional law. *Bush v. Gore* shows the vital importance of futurity in the articulation and realization of constitutional principle—a futurity curiously lacking in the decision.

Although many scholars and activists highlighted this dimension of the case when they offered a democratic critique of the Court's decision, they quite frequently offered a narrative that situated the rule of law as interchangeable with the rule of democracy as a matter of practice, a joint rule allegedly only suspended by the ruling in *Bush v. Gore*. Consequently, this story also posited the return of the rule of law as the return of the rule of democracy. However, this narrative excludes the systematic hostility to democracy irrigating U.S. constitutional law and electoral practice and, in particular, the racial exclusions and subordinations that delimit the electorate in any election. True justice thus demands more than the return of the law; it requires a politicization of the laws of democracy.

Chapter 2 turns to the inflation of executive power during the "War on Terror" and offers a sustained consideration of the "torture memos" that emerged from executive branch legal departments soon after September 11, 2001. The colonial violence facilitated by these legal memoranda is now well documented. However, in describing that violence as being fundamentally "outlaw" in nature, many critics of the violence of empire obscure the centrality of systematic forms of racialized violence that have defined American law from the beginning and continue into the present day.

The abnormality of the torture memos is not in the precise acts they produced but instead is in the paradoxical relationship of the legal memos to the legal tradition and practice in which they operated: the turn toward the law (these appeared on their surface to be ordinary legal memos) by the authors of the memos occurred in a manner that simultaneously undermined the basic tenets of legal interpretation and counsel (the memos simply ignored leading cases and disavowed the shared norms of interpretation). That paradox is a defining feature of contemporary anti-constitutionalism. And mirroring the response to *Bush v. Gore*, leading liberals criticized the legal memos for being either "political" or for enacting and enabling a regime of injustice that they saw as originating in the memos rather than in ordinary legal rationality and prison practices long preceding them.

Chapter 3 looks at the federal legislative power in the response to the case of Terri Schiavo. In the spring of 2005, the U.S. Congress passed emergency "culture of life" legislation in an attempt to prevent the removal of feeding tubes keeping the brain-dead Schiavo "alive." Congress passed this law to address only the case of Terri Schiavo, and this law abridged Schiavo's (and only Schiavo's) well-established constitutional rights. The singularity of the law echoed the temporal logic found in *Bush v. Gore* and the torture memos. Here, the precedential force of landmark cases acknowledging and securing a fundamental constitutional right disappeared, and the transgression of rights (reconceived as a "rescue" of life) applied to this case only.

Linking the tenuousness of the future of the law in the case with the paradigmatic subjects of the "culture of life"—the fetus and the vegetative patient—the chapter argues that anti-constitutional political orientations may best be situated within an apocalyptic imaginary that has come to structure New Right politics in the United States since the conclusion of World War II. Apocalypticism migrates from the realm of faith into the political sphere, and a commitment to the future of historical and earthly time is no longer the shared ground of politics but a point of political contestation. A new sensibility and temporality incompatible with the idea of a constitution is revealed in the schisms of the culture wars, a sensibility and temporality in no way quarantined to them.

Chapter 4 opens with a consideration of the popular maxim that "the Constitution is not a suicide pact" and unpacks what life or vision of life, precisely, is protected by this assertion. To facilitate this inquiry, the chapter turns back to the Revolutionary period in American history and explores the confused and contradictory concept of the "rule of law" in relationship to the sovereign power of the people. On the one hand, the rule of law stood against despotic discretion under the monarchy and thus became nearly coterminous with the idea of "the people" and their newfound political power. On the other hand, the rule of law slipped quite quickly into a force outside of and even against popular politics generally. In the latter case, a new equation began to emerge: the people = politics = lawlessness —an unholy trinity. The law, the object of the people's politics, turned against them: now as a guarantor of individualism that drained democracy of its collective force (see Thomas Paine) or as an aristocratic tutor in the art and science of republicanism (see Alexis de Tocqueville) or as a structural barrier against the capacity of the people to self-represent as a majority class in a class-ridden society (see James Madison). Thus, the Constitution is in some sense constituted against itself.

The Coda confronts two simultaneous events of 2016: the Senate's refusal to hold any hearings or schedule any votes on any Supreme Court nominee nominated by the popularly elected President Obama and the ascendancy of Donald Trump to the presidency after losing the popular vote. Political observers across the ideological spectrum have warned of the potential threat to constitutional norms presented by the latter event, but the Senate's refusal to grant even a hearing to Obama's nominee, Judge Merrick Garland, in some ways poses the more fundamental challenge to constitutional government. Moreover, viewing the Senate majority's actions in the case of Judge Garland in conjunction with the other cases in this book should give one pause in assuming that American legal institutions and constitutional norms are in robust enough condition to weather the challenges posed by a president who sees constraints on power as obstacles to winning that must be overcome.

How does the Senate's great refusal in the Garland case fall into the orbit of anti-constitutional politics? At first glance, the Senate majority appeared to be developing a new principle for selecting Supreme Court justices: "the people" should decide. Such a principle constitutes an elemental break with conservative principles of traditionalism and originalism but nonetheless is legible as a principle. However, as the presidential election of 2016 approached and it appeared most likely that the Democratic nominee would win, key senators declared this newfound principle to be no principle at all and began laying the groundwork for blocking any nominee from any popularly elected Democratic president. In the place of constitutional principle now stood nothing more than the duration and endurance of willpower. And yet again this willpower triumphed, at least in part, because a fear and loathing of politics saturated the response to the anti-constitutional gambit.

All of these cases or events have contoured U.S. political life in the twenty-first century in profound ways. The clashes in all of them radiated far beyond courtrooms or legal offices and consequently generated a broad discourse on and about "the politics of law," a discourse that itself partially constituted the meaning and scope of the events. And while an anti-constitutional logic binds together these cases, I have permitted the full particularity and peculiarity of each case to bloom rather than shear all facts that do not fit neatly into a predetermined theory. In so doing, I have sought to find theory in both vine and flower of this strange garland.

## Chapter 1

# The Judicial Power: This Is Not a Decision

*To be a surrealist means barring from your mind all remembrance of what you have seen.*

—René Magritte

## Bush v. Gore: *Without Precedent*

As the 2000 decision by the U.S. Supreme Court to effectively deliver the Electoral College votes of Florida to George W. Bush (and hence the presidency) recedes in time, its real meaning comes closer into view. If an immediate critique of the Court was that it had altered the rules of democracy after the fact, the perspective of distance permits us to see the fact that the rules were, in some sense, not altered at all. This too was an immediate critique of the Court, but the political question of the assumption of the presidency blotted it out beyond the precincts of constitutional scholarship, and even there it receded into memory and something more like a bitter taste than a pressing political problem of first rank. But in retrospect, the selection of a particular candidate for the presidency in 2000 is the least interesting element of the case, although it is no doubt that fact which is most remembered. What is of far greater consequence, in the long run, is that the Supreme Court issued a landmark decision that marked the land not at all. So, the rather banal point that the best way to look at the impact of a case is from the vantage point of its future trajectory and elaboration becomes less matter of fact when it is the absence of a future trajectory that we must consider.

The post–election day legal contest between Bush and Gore over Florida's disputed electoral votes transpired in a variety of institutional settings across a period of five weeks, from the election day of November 7 to the Supreme Court's *per curiam* decision on December 12, 2000. The entirety of the political contest, of which the legal was a constitutive component, ended when Vice President Gore conceded the election on the evening of December 13. Two primary constitutional questions came to the fore during the litigation struggle: (1) What governmental power or decision point within the state of Florida properly adhered to the Article II provision that "[e]ach State shall appoint, in such Manner as the Legislature thereof may direct, a Number of Electors, equal to the whole Number of Senators and Representatives to which the State may be entitled in the Congress"? and (2) Did the ballot recount standards in the state of Florida after the election meet the requirements of the Fourteenth Amendment's Equal Protection Clause?

Three justices of the U.S. Supreme Court argued that the entry of the Florida Supreme Court as arbiter of the recount, rather than the Florida secretary of state (who had certified Bush's victory prior to entry of the Florida courts into the matter), violated the express provision that it is the *legislature* of the state that controls the selection of electors. According to them, the election scheme devised by that state's legislature privileged the secretary of state in election decisions. In addition, these justices—Rehnquist, Scalia, and Thomas—hemmed in the Florida court, even presuming it had authority to order the recount, to an (alleged) legislatively intended remedy date of December 12, the federal "safe harbor" date for electors. This date would be impossible to reconcile with a recount given that the Court issued its decision on December 12. The need for a remedy without the time to remedy, a time made absent by the Court itself,[1] also held in the holding that managed to gather the five votes needed for a majority in the case, and now nothing less than the temporal arc of law itself had begun to buckle.

On December 8, 2000, the Florida Supreme Court had ordered a manual recount of all ballots in all counties that had not yet conducted such a recount. A machine recount had already occurred in keeping with the Florida election code, a recount triggered by the exceptionally small difference of votes separating each side (less than 1,800 votes out of approximately 6 million cast in the state). Manual recounts offered an assurance that all "legal votes" would be counted. Mechanical recounts could not always ascertain the "clear intention of the voter," especially in counties that used punch-card ballots. As even the *per curiam* opinion of the U.S. Supreme

Court acknowledged, "punch card balloting machines can produce an unfortunate number of ballots which are not punched in a clean, complete way by the voter" and thus remain uncounted by mechanical techniques.[2] Nonetheless, the *per curiam* opinion ruled that the recount ordered by the Florida Supreme Court was unconstitutional. Ultimately, it was a failure to provide explicit "uniformity" in the standards of the manual recount that doomed it.

The *per curiam* opinion of the Court rested upon equal protection analysis. The Court held that the lack of uniformity in ascertaining voter intent across different counties in Florida violated the Fourteenth Amendment. The state may not "value one person's vote over that of another."[3] However, by that standard, the very fact that different voting mechanisms operated across the different precincts of Florida on election day appear to make the entire Florida vote constitutionally suspect. As Akhil Amar has asked, "If the Florida recount was constitutionally flawed why wasn't the initial Florida count—which the Court's judgment reinstated—even more flawed? The initial count . . . featured highly uneven standards from county to county."[4] The vote, rather than the recount, stands in violation of equal protection under the Court's analysis.

Equally puzzling, the traditional subjects of equal protection analysis, "classifications, such as those based on race, ethnicity, or gender, that systematically disadvantage various social groups,"[5] simply disappeared in the analysis and in its place stood the "individual" in relationship only to other individuals. Yet, the lack of uniformity in the election (not the recount) tracked along precisely those traditional categories and classifications of equal protection: "[M]inority voters were roughly *ten times* as likely not to have their votes correctly counted in this election as were non-minority voters."[6] So, the Court's temporal framework severed itself from the past in two senses: it generated an apparent principle at odds with its previous equal protection jurisprudence, *and* it limited the timeframe of inquiry into potential violation of the newly discovered principle to the recount rather than the initial vote itself, where both the old and new principles were most severely transgressed.

As already noted, the future-tense time of remedy also disintegrated into an institutionally self-imposed present tense. The U.S. Supreme Court issued its opinion on December 12, 2000, and remanded the case back to the Florida Supreme Court with the instruction that any recount in accordance with the newly minted principle of individualized uniformity be completed by the legislatively determined deadline of December 12, 2000. As this would be impossible, the recount ordered by the Florida Supreme Court was moot. An opinion that began by stating that when, pursuant to Article II, the "state legislature vests the right to vote for President in its people, the right to vote as the legislature has prescribed is fundamental; and one source of its fundamental nature lies in the equal weight accorded to each vote and the dignity owed to each voter"[7] concluded by deferring to a legislatively determined calendar that nullified equality. The inequalities of the count and the recount of "legal votes" were constitutionally frozen into place, and the candidate who had lost the popular vote nationwide was installed into the executive power by five right-wing Supreme Court justices.[8]

If the December 12 deadline blocked the flow of principle into a future fact of remedy in the particular case, there was still the potential emergence of an equal protection holding that might serve as a basis for further constitutional articulation. But the future was lost not once but twice in the decision. From the *per curiam* opinion: "Our consideration is limited to the present circumstances" in the "special instance of a statewide recount under the authority of a single state judicial officer."[9] The lack of applicability of the newly imagined doctrine of "uniformity" was hinted at earlier in the decision as well: "[A]fter the current counting, it is likely legislative bodies nationwide will examine ways to improve the mechanisms and machinery for voting."[10] The newfound doctrine of uniformity would seem to militate against the deference to the legislatures of the different states. If uniformity establishes a constitutional necessity of avoiding the "arbitrary and disparate treatment of the members of [the state's] electorates," then surely something more than a likely examination of the already acknowledged disparity in vote tabulation would be required of the states. The future was thus lazily thought about, on the one hand (and seemed implicitly undisturbed by the decision itself), and on the other hand, the future was diligently attended to by the opinion and was deliberately barred by the explicit effort to limit the rule to "the present circumstances."

Under normal conditions, disputes over constitutional rulings are centered on the fact of their future effect. Under extraordinary conditions, such as with a sharp break from precedent or the emergence of a novel precedent-setting case, the future contours of the law and political life are even more illuminated as the terrain of contestation. If this was not the case, then the very logic of precedent would disintegrate into nothing other than "the present circumstances." Thus, it comes as no surprise to hear contemporary legal scholars praise Chief Justice John Marshall for his greatness as a judicial "prophet" because "prophets are the servants of the future."[11] And critically, those less than stellar justices, such as Chief Justice Taney, may be viewed as "false prophets" rather than as antiprophets even as their opinions form an "anticanon" of constitutional thought.[12] The future abandoned them; they did not abandon the future.

By contrast, leading constitutional scholars in the legal academy insisted that the significance of the Supreme Court's *per curiam* opinion in *Bush v. Gore* was precisely the "jarring combination of an almost unprecedented equal protection analysis, with a proviso that this approach should not be presumed to apply to future cases."[13] However, the exceptionality of *Bush v. Gore* is rendered entirely unexceptional by prominent social scientific readings of the case. For the behavioralists in political science, judicial decisions, even or especially at the level of constitutional interpretation, are nothing more than the particular "preferences" of this or that judge binding on nothing and no one afterward. The decisions rendered by the Supreme Court are individualized as merely "attitudinal," and politics is reduced to a question of tastes and instant outcomes. As such, "traditional legal factors, such as precedent, text, and intent, [have] virtually no impact" on interpretation.[14]

At stake in this disagreement between behavioral social science and the legal academy is the configuration of the "past and future" as the "usual terrain" of the rule of law.[15] To understand how vital precedent is to the rule of law in the United States' legal order, we should perhaps try to locate the past in present legal disagreements and decisions.

### The Politics of Precedent: Incorporation and Marbury v. Madison

For precedent to govern as a force and as something other than a ruse for the force of individualized free-form preference, behavioralists have established the following test: "[I]f factors such as precedent can be used to support any position that a [Supreme Court] justice could take, such that one could not predict *a priori* how precedent might influence a decision, then precedent is *completely meaningless* as an explanation of the Court's decision."[16] If this narrow criterion is the criterion for analyzing the force of precedent, then the facts organized under this inquiry might indeed confirm and conform to the premise. However, precedent does not simply contour the decision of a case; precedent structures the very path of litigation from which a particular case and decision might emerge. Most questions never reach the Court, and this is determined in part by precedent and the imagined "plausibility" of a claim in light of it.[17]

As example, if today there was a push to raise the minimum wage, at either the state or federal level, how might a libertarian political opponent respond? She will organize against it with appeals to business pragmatism and effect. The arguments against the wage legislation will be that it will "dampen the economy" or "hurt profits" or "weaken business" or "raise unemployment." That is, the claims will be ones of utility in the electoral realm rather than assertions of right in the constitutional realm. Why is this? Certainly there are those who imagine that the primary injustice of the minimum wage law is that it violates a fundamental freedom of the individual to enter into contractual agreements.[18] Yet it is unlikely that the opponents of the wage floor would assert a violation of liberty in the courts. Quite simply, the libertarian would have no argument as the Supreme Court many decades ago abandoned a theory of due process liberty that protected the contractual relationship from state regulation.[19] Even if such a case arose in the lower courts, it is unlikely that one would find the votes necessary on the Supreme Court to even hear the argument.[20] The past then governs the present, and the force of precedent appears as something other than "completely meaningless" in constitutional law.

Precedent shapes and binds even those right-wing justices whose interpretative commitments apparently undercut vast swaths of American law. There are three related, yet distinct, commitments that these justices have articulated in opinions, speeches, and articles. They are, in no particular order, (1) textualism, (2) originalism, and (3) neo-federalism.[21] Textualism finds meaning within the "four corners" of the text. Originalists may or may not be textually bound but in either case look to the time-bound meaning of the Constitution. Justice Antonin Scalia combined textualism and originalism: "[W]hat I look for in the Constitution is precisely what I look for in a statute: the original meaning of the text."[22] However, a critical concession is made by Justice Scalia: "Originalism, like any other theory of interpretation put into practice in an ongoing system of law, must accommodate the doctrine of *stare decisis*; it cannot remake the world anew."[23] This constraint on generating a purified jurisprudential tabula rasa helps explain why most originalist justices do not launch a full assault on each and every edifice of modern constitutional law. If they were simply unbound actors of individual preference as the behavioralists imagine, then we would expect a central tenet of modern U.S. constitutionalism, the doctrine of "incorporation," to be under severe stress in their decisions. Incorporation is the doctrine whereby the Bill of Rights slowly created applicable checks on the power of state governments vis-à-vis their citizens. Today, most of the Bill of Rights have been incorporated, including the First Amendment.[24]

The First Amendment begins, "Congress shall make no law . . ." and for most of the history of the United States, its prohibitions were so confined. The textual door through which the incorporation of the First Amendment (as well as others) occurred is the Due Process Clause of the Fourteenth Amendment. Here is the relevant text: "No State shall make or enforce any law which shall abridge the privileges and immunities of the United States; nor shall any State deprive any person of life, liberty, or property, without due process of law; nor deny to any person within its jurisdiction the equal protection of the laws" (1868). The fact that "freedom of speech" now applies with equal force to, say, the state of California as well as the Congress of the United States is today taken for granted. At both the level of common sense in everyday political knowledge and within the conceptually dense political world of constitutional law, it is merely a given. But there is nothing at all *necessarily* given about it. In fact, it cuts against many of the premises and aims of the current right-wing majority on the Court.

There is thin textual support for an expansion of the First Amendment's protective zone via incorporation. After all, the Due Process Clause speaks explicitly of process: liberty may be deprived so long as there is due process of law. The textual case is further weakened by the existence of the exact same text within the Bill of Rights. Here is the relevant text of the Fifth Amendment: "Nor shall any person be . . . deprived of life, liberty, or property without due process of law" (1791). As John Hart Ely has noted, "There is general agreement that the earlier clause [the Fifth Amendment] had been understood at the time of its conclusion to refer only to lawful procedures. What recorded comment there was at the time of the replication of the Fourteenth Amendment is devoid of any reference that gives the provision more than procedural connotation."[25] So, the committed textualist and originalist confronts a puzzle in affirming incorporation: how does the text of the Fifth Amendment stand as distinct from the First Amendment when the exact text of the Fourteenth Amendment is presumed to include the First? If we are to be bound by the "original meaning of the text," then there is almost no support at all for applying the First Amendment to state action beyond Congress.

Yet in all contemporary cases involving the First Amendment, the disagreements do not center on this issue. As but one of innumerable examples, the flag burning case of *Texas v. Johnson* illustrates this.[26] In that case, the Court overturned a Texas law that made it a crime to desecrate the American flag. The majority opinion, authored by Justice Scalia, considers a series of constitutional questions: whether the conduct proscribed was within the orbit of "speech," whether Texas had an interest other than suppressing the "content" of the conduct forbidden by the law, and whether the law survives "strict scrutiny" if it was aimed at content. The Court split 5 to 4 in the case, with the majority overturning the conviction. Each side reached different conclusions on the questions just posed, but *all* sides in the case operated on the assumption that the First Amendment of the United States applied even to the proud state of Texas. It might seem "odd that a provision regarding 'process' has come to protect 'substance.' Nevertheless, history seems to have settled the issue."[27]

When "history" becomes capable of action, it is necessary to consider what political forces succeeded so absolutely as to permit the fiction of history speaking in the singular, of creating that which it allegedly only records. It is tempting to think that the politics of law are present only in the stated disagreements of differing judicial camps. One could have answered the questions of speech, content, and scrutiny in *Texas v. Johnson* in a plausible manner on either side. Five-to-four decisions almost by definition suggest the plausibility of incongruent correct answers. This is the crux of the behavioralist claim that "traditional legal factors such as precedent, text, and intent [have] virtually no impact."[28] Or to go further: neither side is bound by "law" and is engaged only in something called "politics." The questions posed in *Texas v. Johnson* were pure form, and form obscured substance. On this account, traditional legal factors have no impact on the politics of law precisely because they are imagined to have no political value. Since precedent is void of politics, politics may invoke precedent to carry on its masquerade in the theater of law.

Yet it is precisely in the traditions of law that the politics of law is most firmly present. The extension of most of the provisions of the Bill of Rights to the states is not a politically hollow formalism or a one-off adventure. In fact, it has slowly bound the law to one side in the dispute between which sovereign is sovereign in the American political order, a dispute born out first in Madison's constitutional concept of a "compound republic."[29] It is one of the great ironies of history that Madison defended the compound republic on grounds of "amity" (it was nonsensical by the "standard of theory").[30] His resolution simply sewed our constitutional fabric with the threads of perpetual discord. This original disagreement saw the polity divide into two camps in its early years, with Daniel Webster representative of the one side and John C. Calhoun of the other. In the twentieth century, the political currents informing the doctrine of incorporation reaffirmed that Calhoun had lost the battle and, more literally, lost the civil war.

Of course, justices may turn against precedent, but that turn will be to establish new precedent even as it involves distinguishing that which is turned against. In fact, it is only the possibility of precedent's future that makes the disagreement of any import at all beyond the facts of the individual case. The possible disjunction between the resolution of the individual facts of the particular case and the legal principle vindicated by a ruling irrespective of individual interests in the case at hand is nowhere more visible than in the most well-known case of American law, *Marbury v. Madison.*[31]

In the gap of time between President John Adams's defeat for reelection in 1800 and the inauguration of Thomas Jefferson, the Federalists hurried to pass new laws and fill positions of government. Adams appointed William Marbury as a justice of the peace for the District of Columbia, yet the actual delivery of the commission was not delivered prior to Jefferson assuming the presidency. Although Marbury's appointment had been confirmed by the Senate and his commission signed by Adams's secretary of state, President Jefferson refused to deliver the commission to Marbury. Marbury sought to compel the delivery of the commission by seeking a writ of mandamus from the U.S. Supreme Court. The Supreme Court, in an opinion by Chief Justice John Marshall, held that the Judiciary Act of 1789 granted original jurisdiction in the case to the Supreme Court but that this grant of jurisdiction conflicted with Article III of the Constitution. As such, the law was ruled unconstitutional, and the Court, for the first time, established itself as arbiter of constitutional meaning. This critical victory for a core Federalist value (judicial review) was won by sacrificing the commissions of a few Federalist appointees.[32]

The decision by Chief Justice Marshall has long been viewed as one of political genius. The Jeffersonians won the small prize of a handful of insignificant appointments, while the Federalists won the far more significant prize of the constitutional question. And because Jefferson "won" the case in the immediate sense, he could not easily turn around and attack the Court for the principle articulated in securing that victory. Marshall had outmaneuvered Jefferson and delivered to him a quintessentially pyrrhic victory. But the pyrrhic nature of that victory hinges ultimately on the force of precedent as a source of law. And to be clear, the precedent of *Marbury* was drenched in politics: the law was indeterminate on the questions in the case, and no mechanical judgment could resolve it. Rather, Marshall's opinion was a plausible one, and it was buttressed by a political desire to "establish the judiciary on solid ground and use the power to defend the cause of national union."[33]

Had the Marshall Court issued a writ of mandamus in the case on the basis of a newly discovered *anti*-Federalist principle that would hold only in the case of Marbury, then it is fairly safe to say that the Supreme Court would have imploded amid Republican laughter at the absurdity. The Republican-led impeachment of Federalist Justice Samuel Chase occurred in 1805 with far less provocation, and Chase's acquittal in no way disproves the intensity of the political currents swirling at the time. It is quite strange, then, to hear political scientists today argue that there is no difference between *Marbury v. Madison* and *Bush v. Gore*. Our analysis of *Marbury* must be turned inside out to accept that reading. If precedent has absolutely no value and no purchase on the future, then Chief Justice Marshall was a fool to abandon Marbury the individual for *Marbury* the decision. After all, why establish precedent, in this case the precedent of judicial review, if precedent does not matter? When the political scientists simultaneously acknowledge that the decision in *Marbury v. Madison* "gained sufficient acceptance among the American public to become the warp and woof of the constitutional fabric,"[34] we must note that it remains for the scientists to explain how precedent is irrelevant while at the same time speaking of the existence of a constitutional fabric woven of *precedent*.

It is the inversion of *Marbury*'s logic that renders the *Bush v. Gore* holding so anomalous. It will not suffice, either analytically or politically, to say of *Bush v. Gore*, "that's not law, that's politics."[35] Condemnation in these terms transforms the monumental decisions of constitutional law from first-rank political questions into depoliticized historical ones: "history

decides" is the removal of judgment from the possibility of political reconsideration, and such reconsideration is forbidden if and when "politics"
becomes the no man's land of constitutional inquiry and decision. If the
infirmity of the case is not one of politics as such, then perhaps the case
suggests an emerging lawlessness in political life. In fact, many castigated
the *Bush v. Gore* ruling as a "lawless opinion," and some have suggested
that the one potential norm emerging in response to the case is a "consensus against lawlessness."[36]

As a proposition, the accusation of lawlessness levied against the
Supreme Court's ruling must be, at least to some degree, nonsensical. As a
theoretical matter, it runs into the determinative fact of a jurisdictional and
jurisprudential hierarchy: the final word is with the Court, and the finality
of the word is, at least in part, what produces the law. Justice Jackson's
truism thus never rang truer: "[W]e are not final because we are infallible,
but we are infallible only because we are final."[37] Even more importantly
for law as a social fact, the fact is that this so-called lawless decision ruled
with the force of law. The ruling halted the Florida recount. It also forced
from Vice President Gore a political concession, a concession made in the
name of the law and by the force of the law. On the evening of December
13, 2000, Gore addressed the nation:

> Over the library of one of our great law schools is inscribed the
> motto: "Not under man, but under God and law." That's the ruling
> principle of American freedom, the source of our democratic liber-
> ties. I've tried to make it my guide throughout this contest, as it has
> guided America's deliberations of all the complex issues of the past
> five weeks. Now the U.S. Supreme Court has spoken. Let there be no
> doubt, while I strongly disagree with the Court's decision, I accept it.
> I accept the finality of this outcome. . . . And tonight, for the sake
> of our unity as a people and the strength of our democracy, I offer
> my concession.[38]

A decision that turns the law inside out nonetheless governs with the full
prestige and power of the law. We do not confront lawlessness; we have
instead entered into a self-negating yet force-making jurispolitical riddle.

As one scholar has rightly noted, "[I]t is as if the Supreme Court had
written an opinion, and then, in a bow to René Magritte, put as its last
sentence: 'This is not an opinion.'"[39] To trace the inner workings of an

emerging anti-constitutionalism in the case of *Bush v. Gore*, one should hold fast to the paradoxes of surrealist absurdity. It is a decision of the court, a rule of law, a juridical force ordering the political future; it is also and at the same exact time not a decision, an inversion of the rule of law, limited to the particular present-tense facts of the case. To simply call the case lawless or to see in the decision an invasion of the law by "politics" is to move too quickly along familiar lines for what will in the end turn into nothing more than a false exit. Even more, such a discursive regime in fact denies the very need for the real exit as it fails to give a proper account of the operative logic of the riddle we inhabit. Perhaps the most useful thinking on the matter comes from Michel Foucault, but not from his more widely cited works on power and governmentality. Instead, here is Foucault reading Magritte's painting, *Ceci n'est pas une pipe*: the "vague uneasiness provoked" by Magritte's masterpiece is produced by a sense of "being trapped in a double cipher" where each element of the riddle is "annulled as soon as it has been accomplished."[40] So, the seemingly inescapable conundrum of our anti-constitutional moment becomes how to break out of this trap born of a double annulment where the disconcerting play of paradoxes has merged with the official vocabulary of the state.

### Rule of Law Versus Rule of Democracy

The initial dissents from some in the legal academy against the ruling in *Bush v. Gore* understood clearly that a trap had been sprung, that a right-wing movement had seized the executive branch with a heretofore-unimagined turn within *and* against the law. So the surprising instance arose where the call for extraordinary resistance sprang from the very quarters of political and intellectual life that had historically tended most carefully to the nurture and defense of ordinary means, even without regard to the ends pursued. As example of the departure from the norm, Professor Margaret Radin expressed a desire to move beyond "conservative" modes of restrained legal commentary and shift to "protest in the streets."[41] Professor Kathryn Abrams also argued that "extraordinary" and "atypical" modes of resistance were required in response to the decision. Working against the exclusive resort to endless dialogue, Abrams insisted that it was the very destruction of the premises of normal disagreement that had to be resisted: "[W]hat is needed at this point is not simply more dialogue, but a frank objection to the truncation of dialogue, and an appeal to the importance of the social process that conventionally produces law."[42]

Whatever collective creative burst that was generated in response to the decision soon dissipated or devolved into private complaint or flowed back into the old and well-worn paths of normal disagreement. A potential movement was isolated and a moment of genuine possibility slipped away almost as quickly as it had appeared.[43] Even before the dust had settled and normality had returned, the turn to the streets had failed to move beyond the confines imposed by the paradox of anti-constitutionalism. Understanding the seriousness of the violation to the rule of law, the professoriate couched its demands in nothing less and nothing more than a return to the rule of law in contrast to the imagined "lawlessness" of the decision and the politicization of the law by the right-wing justices. Professor Bruce Ackerman stated that he "protest[ed] in the name of the rule of law,"[44] and the unprecedented petition of 500 + law professors protested under the organizational rubric of "Law Professors for the Rule of Law." Professor Radin, a leading voice in this movement, expressed some sense of surprise that "we had more of a commitment to the rule of law than we knew."[45] This recommitment to the law was envisioned as "speaking truth to power."[46]

It is one of the ironies of our time that the very moment of such radical engagements with the rule of law by those so intimately embedded in its practice was also the exact moment when critical sensibilities toward the rule of law took flight from the scene. This flight went largely unnoticed, in part, because the relationship between the rule of law and rule of democracy blurred in the particular political battle. This conceptual indistinction arose since the rule of law was called into question in the contested election of the executive power, with a primary dispute over vote counting. So, the battle for democracy marched under the banner of the rule of law, and those protesting for the return to the rule of law imagined that they were defending democracy as such. In this sense, they took Jürgen Habermas's normative and historical account of the relationship between modern constitutional law and democracy as a taken-for-granted fact of American political life.

Habermas has argued that an "internal relationship" developed between law and democracy beginning at the end of the eighteenth century.[47] Democratic methods conferred legitimacy on the coercive power of a law now shorn of divine sanction or natural right or ancient provenance: "[T]he positivity of law . . . is bound up with the demand for legitimation . . . positively enacted law should guarantee the autonomy of all legal persons equally; and the democratic procedure of legislation should in turn satisfy this demand."[48] The inner linking of the concepts and practices of law and democracy was necessary as a normative matter and also denoted a historical fact defining the "constitutional reality of Western societies."[49]

Some variation of this presumption circulated in the demands to count and recount "every legal vote" in Florida. The short-circuiting of the recount by the Supreme Court was thus seen by critics of *Bush v. Gore* as a short-circuiting of democracy. However, it is the accelerating disjunction of constitutional reality and democracy in the United States that must trouble any account of democracy being vindicated by the mere fact of a return to the rule of law, figured here in this case as counting every legal vote. The law professors for the rule of law arrived in the streets after December 13, 2000. Yet the rule of democracy endured extreme resistance from the law well before that date. So, the law professors who spoke truth to power by protesting in the name of the rule of law only obscured the truth that the power of the law had long been waging war against democracy in the United States. And this war of law against democracy was perfectly alive and active during the entirety of the campaign and election of 2000.

An obvious place to begin is with the Constitution itself. The curious fact that the winner of the majority of the popular vote could legally be denied the presidency highlights a theory of sovereignty where something other than the people as a people rule or, in more liberal terms, where each individual has equal value and voice. The determinative relevance in 2000 of an anachronistic institution such as the Electoral College served to remind that the inner links between law and democracy were less than certain in U.S. constitutional reality. Beyond the peculiar election mechanisms involved in selecting the executive, the nondemocratic organization of the U.S. Senate stands as an enduring refusal of democracy by the basic law of the republic.[50] Succinctly, "democracy" is not the first value or primary procedure of the U.S. Constitution.[51]

In addition to the structural provisions of the federal Constitution, we must consider as well antidemocratic practices that have secured constitutional sanction. More exactly, democracy has become beset by three principal exclusions, exclusions that ran riot in 2000 and continue to this day. These exclusions extend across every zone of democratic action: association, deliberation, and decision. Party association has been limited by legal rules designed to block multiple parties from the ballot. Deliberation has been confined to narrow bands of possibility by the privatization of the rules of debate within a First Amendment universe organized around the concept of "state action." And perhaps most critically, the ranks of citizens excluded from having any capacity to participate in electoral decision making via the vote have swelled to cataclysmic proportions from the perspective of democratic value. Concretely, these exclusions are exclusions from the ballot, from the debate, and from the voting booth.

As the election of 2000 slid into weeks of recounts, litigation, and protests, it must have come as something of a shock to many that partial responsibility for the situation was placed upon the shoulders of the Green Party candidate for president. The Green Party won almost 3 million votes and almost 3 percent of the total vote across the nation.[52] In Florida, the Green Party candidate received nearly 100,000 votes where only 536 votes separated the Republican and the Democratic candidates for president. The shock of the many would have been born of the fact that so few would have expected the Green Party to have any role at all in the election. Due to onerous rules of ballot access, the Green Party did not appear on the ballot in seven states of the Union (totaling fifty-seven Electoral College votes).[53] The laws were unsuccessfully challenged in court.[54]

One criterion that many states use to determine ballot access is the percentage of the vote received by a party in the previous election cycle. To increase associational experimentation and develop broader support, parties have attempted to use fusion balloting. Fusion voting permits one candidate to receive the nomination from multiple parties and is critical for the flourishing of smaller parties in an electoral arena that does not follow the rules of proportional representation. As an example, the Green Party could have the same candidate on the ballot as the Democratic Party. In this case, it would allow Green Party members to vote for the Green Party without worry that the right-wing party might win via a split vote. It also broadens the representational base of the victorious candidate. Nonetheless, the Supreme Court has held that states may outlaw the practice and most do. The effect of weakening and ultimately excluding multiple parties was cited by the Court as a principle in defense of these laws; exclusion as intent and effect became the guiding light of the law. Here is the Court's majority in the case of *Timmons v. Twin Cities Area New Party* (1997): "Minnesota fears that fusion would enable minor parties . . . [and] the Constitution permits the Minnesota Legislature to decide that political stability is best served through a healthy two party system."[55] An imagined stability secured via a practice of exclusion thus trumped democratic expansion and participation.

Of course, the Green Party did make it onto the ballot in the other forty-three states, including in Florida. And unlike previous election cycles, the Green Party candidate was a well-known individual prior to his candidacy for the presidency.[56] Despite this, or perhaps because of this, he was excluded from participating in any of the nationally televised debates. The decision of who is and is not included in the debate occurs outside of democratic channels in the United States. The presidential debate commission is a private nonprofit corporation funded by private wealth. Consequently, state power may be called upon to police the exclusion of the candidates under the laws of trespass.[57] But since it was not the state that made the decision to exclude, the protection and values of the First Amendment are ruled inapplicable. And even when it is a public entity organizing a debate and thus subject to First Amendment scrutiny, the Court has been forgiving of such exclusions so long as they are formally "neutral."[58]

Richard Pildes has argued that the Court's jurisprudence regarding third parties demonstrates a fear of "disorder" by the Court, a fear that helps explain the ruling in *Bush v. Gore*. Although Pildes describes the Court's jurisprudence as representing one view of the prerequisites for democracy, he acknowledges a key point: the fears that have been elevated to constitutional value in the jurisprudence of the Court have historically defined "arguments about the desirability of democracy itself."[59] It is within a theory of pragmatist "order" that the most coherent defenses of *Bush v. Gore* have been made.[60] Without the Court's intervention: anarchy and lawlessness. However, if order, rather than participation, was already the watchword of the law of democracy, then the production of an "order without law"[61] in the decision suggests an authoritarian logic transcending any boundary between the law and its imagined other. The only question then is, which lawlessness? And if it is a democratic lawlessness in open antagonism with an authoritarian lawlessness, then the return to the rule of law from which we have allegedly departed will in fact also be the trump card for the latter.

The exclusions of the law of democracy extended all the way down to the voting booth, and this exclusion preceded any legal controversy in the particular case or election. Again, the mantra of the effort to sustain the recount was this: count every legal vote. By counting every legal vote, it was imagined that democracy would be vindicated and affirmed. Speaking almost a decade after the case, Akhil Amar asserted that the provision of the Florida code authorizing recounts in this situation was in "harmony with the spirit and grand principles of the state constitution . . . which emphatically affirms the people's right to vote and the right to have every lawful vote reflecting a clearly discernable voter intent counted equally."[62] The imagined constitutional commitment to democracy was likewise presumed by Richard A. Epstein, who agreed with the ultimate decision in *Bush v. Gore* but did so on Article II grounds rather than upon equal protection. Epstein rejected an equal protection analysis by distinguishing the facts in Florida with earlier cases involving poll taxes or literacy tests and concluded that, by contrast, nobody in Florida was "excluded from the polls."[63]

To say nobody was excluded from the voting polls in the election of 2000 is in some sense perfectly true, but the truth of the statement makes false the pretense of democratic inclusion. The statement is true to this extent: *only* nobodies were excluded from the polls. Article VI, section 4 of the Florida Constitution, the same constitution that received such effusive praise from Professor Amar for its democratic principles, sets forth the following prohibition: "No person convicted of a felony, or adjudicated in this or any other state to be mentally incompetent, shall be qualified to vote or hold office until restoration of civil rights or removal of disability."[64] No person convicted of a felony shall vote, and the felony conviction thus transforms the individual into no person at all politically speaking. Their legal personhood is abolished, and they are politically disappeared. In the United States, more than 6 million people are excluded from voting by these legal banishments, and the numbers only grow.[65] In Florida, between 1995 and 2005, it is estimated that over 200,000 persons were disenfranchised in the state of Florida, and between 2010 and 2016, another 150,000 Floridians were purged from the voting rolls.[66] By 2017, 1.6 million people in Florida stood disenfranchised, and the racial breakdown suggests an apartheid-like electoral system as more than 20 percent of African Americans in Florida cannot cast a ballot.[67]

Every legal vote requires a legal person. When one is focused almost exclusively on counting *legal* votes, then the necessity of giving any account of the expanding illegality of persons in the community is lost. Martin Luther King Jr. described the cumulative effects of daily living with white supremacy under Jim Crow as "forever fighting a degenerating sense of nobodiness."[68] Article VI of the Florida Constitution produces this in a singular act and enshrines it as basic law. The constitutionalization of nobodiness first emerged in the white response to Reconstruction. Reactionary legislatures across the South enacted laws to disenfranchise newly emancipated black voters, and this included an expansion of felony exclusions.[69] And the legacy of this is to be found in the extraordinary number of African American citizens who are *today* denied the vote under these anti-Reconstruction provisions. Approximately 8 percent of black Americans are barred from the polls, forbidden to cast any legal vote at all.[70]

The U.S. Supreme Court has upheld laws that disenfranchise both those currently incarcerated as well as those convicted felons who have completed in full their prison and probationary terms. In *Richardson v. Ramirez*, the Court rebuffed a constitutional challenge to these laws. In his dissent, Justice Thurgood Marshall argued that the text of the Fourteenth Amendment should be read against a background commitment to democracy and that any restriction on casting a vote strikes "at the heart of representative government."[71] Further, any acceptance of this exclusion as being consistent with constitutional value sanctified and solidified a rule and order that had "its origins in the fogs and fictions of feudal jurisprudence."[72] The federal courts have also rejected more recent challenges to these feudalistic laws.[73]

In addition to the disparate impact upon historically subordinated racial classes (that is, those members of the racial class are more likely to be barred from voting, and the disbarment of increasing numbers of that class weakens politically the class *as a* class), we should perhaps begin to think of ex-felons as a class unto themselves. For the explosion of policing and criminal production in the United States has leaned heavily upon a campaign of turning acts of crimes committed by individuals into individuals defined solely by the fact that they have committed a crime.[74] Thus, they are not simply punished for this or that amount of time but are in fact politically banished even after the particular time of punishment. This fact should heighten the solicitude of equal protection analysis given that a central factor of that analysis is whether the class in question is able to defend itself in the democratic process. Here, the class as a class is born and bound by nothing less than the exclusion from the democratic process. That there exists today a swelling class of the excluded who are a class due to their exclusion only confirms Justice Marshall's observation in *Rodriguez*: the fogs and fictions of feudal jurisprudence have been brought forward from the past and find new vitality in the political life of the present.

Democracy is thus suffering from a proceduralist perspective: each and every individual is not respected by or included within the process. Democracy is suffering from a multicultural and antiracist perspective: African Americans are subordinated and the *Herrenvolk Republic* endures.[75] Democracy is suffering from a membership-centered perspective: the material feudal fact can only mock universal and communal pretensions. Democracy is also suffering from a consequentialist perspective: disenfranchisement has reached levels "sufficient to change election outcomes," and the 2000 election would "almost certainly have been reversed had voting rights been extended" to disenfranchised felons.[76] The quadrennial angst about which way some swing state might swing in the presidential race hinges on the exclusion of voters. *But for* systemic exclusionary practices, many swing states would not swing.

Contemporary political grammars and electoral strategies in the United States rest upon the exclusion of 6 million people from the voting booth. Counting "every legal vote" will in no way alter the fact that the "legal" is precisely that which has politically abolished and banished several million citizens from citizenship. No other country in the democratic world excludes those convicted of felonies to the extent that the United States does or produces such astronomical numbers of those convicted. This is another way of saying that, properly speaking, the United States is not rightly a member of the democratic world. Protesting for democracy's realization by expressing a desire for the "rule of law" shepherded by apolitical judges, rather than "political partisans,"[77] in fact secures rather than challenges the antidemocratic order. The danger is not that the law is overrun with political partisans. Democracy is not in need of neutral "umpires" in the law; democracy *is* in need of friends and partisans rooting for its success and facilitating the realization of its participatory promise.

### Conclusion

On the tenth anniversary of the decision in *Bush v. Gore*, a lawyer and journalist reported a curiosity about *Bush v. Gore*, a curiosity rendered visible both in retrospect and in contrast to another epoch defining case, *Brown v. Board of Education of Topeka*. Whereas the decision by the Court in 1956 to strike down state-mandated segregation in public education ushered in a new legal regime, *Bush v. Gore* could point to no such legacy. Consider: during the ten years following *Brown v. Board of Education of Topeka*, the

Court had cited the case over twenty-five times, but during the ten years after *Bush v. Gore*, it had cited the case not once: *zero*.[78] *Bush v. Gore* was not to be used as precedent in the law, and it was not. However, it was the logic of the constitutional zero itself that would escape the particular political struggle and establish itself as a precedent for the future to come. And it is the multiplication of that zero as a modality of governance and rule that would stand as a far greater consequence of the decision than the particular man the Supreme Court selected to lead the executive power. Although, given that he had assumed power via anti-constitutional means, one can at least understand how dense the attraction must have been to rule according to its non-rules when crisis came again.

*Chapter 2*

# The Executive Power: A Law That Is No Law

*Our interrogations in Guantanamo were conducted . . . in circumstances so prolonged that it was practice to have plastic chairs . . . that could be easily hosed off because prisoners would be forced to urinate during the course of them.*

*Another practice . . . was "short shackling" where we were forced to squat without a chair with our hands chained between our legs and chained to the floor. If we fell over, the chains would cut into our hands. We would be left in the position for hours before an interrogation, during the interrogation [which could last as long as twelve hours], and sometimes for hours while the interrogators left the room. The air conditioning was turned up so high that within minutes we would be freezing. There was strobe lighting and loud music that would be played that was itself a form of torture. Sometimes dogs were brought in to frighten us. . . . Sometimes detainees would be taken to the interrogation room day after day and kept "short shackled" without interrogation ever happening, sometimes for weeks on end.*

—Shafiq Rasul and Asif Iqbal, detainees at Guantanamo
(Human Rights Watch 2004)

*Perhaps the oddest thing about my fortieth-birthday trip to Guantanamo and the naval brigs was that the plane was full of lawyers. This was an apt metaphor for many of the Bush administration's terrorism policies: never in the history of the United States had lawyers had such extraordinary influence over war policy as they did after 9/11.*

—Jack Goldsmith, Assistant Attorney General,
Office of Legal Counsel (2007)

## The Torture Camps

The attacks upon the World Trade Center and Pentagon in 2001 simultaneously constituted a crime against humanity—as an intentional and systematic assault upon a civilian population with weaponry that would by
definition kill and maim innocent persons—and a crime against Empire in
the deepest sense imaginable as an assertion and enactment of equality.
Both crimes are linked in that this creation of terror via a technologically
advanced aerial assault upon densely populated metropolitan areas also signaled the end of great-power state monopoly over such forms of violence.
Since 1945, such actions had been the principal language of colonial
engagement in Cold War campaigns of proxy confrontation. For example,
the entire foreign policy establishment in the United States spoke constantly
about the campaigns of carpet bombing of Vietnam, Laos, and Cambodia
as an attempt to "communicate" to rivals who could speak the same language and as a sign of force to those who spoke none at all—an instruction
in behavioral training to animalized human herds across the globe. After
1989, that monopoly contracted further. Thus, the attacks of September
11, 2001, constituted a particularly shocking new fact arriving amid the
triumphalist discourse of sole superpowerdom and indispensable nation-
hood: the reemergence of multivocality in the grammars of modern mass
terror and this time from subaltern locales. The disorientation generated
by that combination in part explains why the incongruity between the box-
cutters used by the hijackers, on the one hand, and the transcontinental jet
planes at their disposal, on the other, so captured the U.S. public imagination immediately after the attacks. That anyone could now command such
powers signaled a new egalitarian moment.

This new equality challenged a variety of orthodoxies and could be
properly viewed as an "existential" threat when existence beyond them had
become unimaginable. Survivalist rhetorics that dominated after 9/11 continued a pattern of apocalyptic political thinking in American life that in
the twentieth century had produced the slogan "better dead than red" at
the level of folk talk and sustained the doctrines of mutually assured
destruction in the higher realms of theorization and policy. After the cessation of the Cold War, speculations about the "end of history" only affirmed
this trend as the global order became pictured not as a choice but as an
inexorable logic. Standing against it was viewed as akin to standing against
gravity or the sunrise. So, whatever historical claims or political visions

present in/presented by the attacks on the United States were immediately transformed into gibberish from some medieval point in time proffered by men with whom nothing could be negotiated. From this perspective, the oft-repeated mantra that the United States "does not negotiate with terrorists" stands as something other than cowboy-inspired stubbornness; it is in fact a hegemonic worldview immune to changes in style or party.[1]

In addition to a general background of systematic nonrecognition of equalitarian claims and a refusal to acknowledge rival systems presented by political equals (they are linked yet distinct), a constellation of more specific antagonisms and desires was inflamed by the 9/11 attacks. Organized by a religious cult with ties to Islam and carried out by members with nationalities of Middle Eastern origin, they were woven into preexisting efforts to maintain Anglo-American political economies of oil, viewed through the dynastic familial dramas of the nonelected and judicially installed executive power, seized upon by the imperial hypernationalist ideologues of the neo-conservative Right,[2] and narrated with theological urgency by powerful fundamentalist Protestant Christian sects and "theoconservative" Catholic intellectuals within the United States.[3] From this brew emerged a level of fanaticism and imprudence that would lead to a worldwide spasm of militarized violence by an American-led "coalition of the willing." A campaign to defeat religiously organized political forces in Afghanistan that it had previously helped create and maintain during the 1980s came first,[4] with massive bombardment and occupation commencing in October 2001. Planning turned almost immediately afterward to Iraq, a state and society that had already endured a decade-long state of siege and periodic bombing by the United States and a state and society with zero connections to the attacks that the United States claimed to be confronting and rebuffing. Denied anything resembling an imprimatur of UN legitimacy, the United States nonetheless launched "Operation Iraqi Freedom" in March 2003. Subsequently, UN secretary general Kofi Annan would judge the invasion and occupation to be an illegal breach of the UN charter.[5]

In each theater of war, the United States established detention centers to assist in coordinating the prosecution of the "global war on terror," a war that had explicitly established the entirety of the globe as its field of battle. Iraq and Afghanistan were but pressure points and open fronts. For perhaps the first time in the history of modern nation-states, a war without horizon was envisaged. Such a vision both abolishes all boundaries of political geography and erases the temporal prospects of an end to the action. As

Judith Butler has rightly observed, here "state power restructures temporality itself, since the problem of terrorism is no longer a historically or geographically limited problem: it is limitless and without end."[6]

This "without end" thus logically segued into something of a modality of rule, and that rule has been exposed as intimately and intentionally brutal. At Bagram Air Base in Afghanistan, at Abu Ghraib prison in Iraq, at Guantanamo Bay in Cuba, at the U.S. naval brig in Charleston, South Carolina, and at countless other CIA-run "black sites," the United States systematically inflicted mental and physical suffering upon detainees. Early efforts to portray the spectacular acts of state-orchestrated sadism that burst into public view with the photographs from Abu Ghraib as nothing more than the curious and isolated work of a few "bad apples" have failed. The Senate Intelligence Committee Report on Torture states that detainees were "tortured" as a matter of policy and that the techniques were "cruel, inhuman, and degrading."[7] Even the author of the Department of Defense's report on the conditions at Abu Ghraib, Major General Antonio Taguba, declared that the abuse was not aberrational; it represented instead "a regime of torture."[8]

In keeping with the production of a regime, the first stories emerging from the various prisons and camps were reliably consistent and patterned. The first established camp was in Afghanistan at Bagram Air Base. It was intended as a temporary detention center after the U.S. invasion began in 2001, with two primary functions: to gather intelligence for the war of occupation and to determine who would be sent on to detention at Guantanamo Bay. Interrogation practices included beatings, hanging detainees from ceilings for long durations of time, sexualized abuse, sleep deprivation, and interrogations during surgeries. Numerous prisoners died during the torture sessions, including a young Afghani man in 2002 who was beaten while shackled and stomped under foot with such ferocity that the tissue on his legs had been "pulpified" to the point of falling from the bone.[9]

But death is not the aim; establishing "facts" is. As a previous White House advisor helpfully explained, in a manner so candid as to shock those so embedded in the conditions of the practice that they had long ago forgotten its truth, "[W]e are an Empire now, and when we act, we create our own reality."[10] The unilateralism creating the camps and the uncertainty that permeates them are thus not impediments to the campaigns of "enduring freedom" but are rather the ineluctable core of their being: the radical certainty of making facts and the dreadful uncertainty of becoming one restore the asymmetries disrupted by the presumptuous attacks of 9/11. One Guantanamo prisoner provides a glimpse into the phenomenology of this from the other side: "I think the worst was not knowing . . . not knowing why you're there or when you will go home."[11]

Every aspect of Guantanamo aimed toward creating reality, teasing it out methodically. All structures and practices and norms and procedures of the camp were merged into the logics of interrogation. Psychiatrists were deployed, medical personnel treating the detainees worked in tandem with the interrogators, and the camp commanders for the "first time integrated military intelligence personnel with the military guard force, blurring a line that had previously been impermeable in the Army."[12] Like a mantra, it was repeated: the work done was to "set the conditions" for interrogation. Prior to arrival at Guantanamo, the detainees were subjected to the ordeals of Bagram and then chained for a cargo flight halfway around the world. Once there, the camp commanders placed them into metal cages outside in the Caribbean sun, multiply shackled and clad in orange jump suits; the imagery is now an iconic representation of the nation.

Conditions in the cages of Camp X-Ray, the name of the temporary camps initially established at Guantanamo, bordered on the exotic as scorpions, rats, and snakes wandered into the prisoners' open-air cages.[13] This too would help "set the conditions" and establish the "facts" of the wildness of the detainees. Who but the beasts would live among them? However, the cages left open, literally, the possibility of communication between detainees and thus undermined the attempt to fully break them. To counter this, American officials built a more modern and permanent camp at the base, Camp Delta. The new container structures were explicitly modeled upon supermax prisons in the United States. Now, prisoners could be fully isolated in individual cells and communication between the inmates ceased. Time alone in the cells ranged from twenty-two to twenty-four per day, and many prisoners slowly went mad: an attorney visiting Guantanamo reported that his client took advantage of the brief time out of his cell to discuss legal matters as an opportunity to find the tools necessary to attempt suicide via hanging.[14] This detainee survived; others have been luckier in finding success. And in a perfect loop of logic, the eruption of mass suicide attempts in response to the conditions at Guantanamo became the very basis and rationale for the conditions at Guantanamo. Camp commander Admiral Harry Harris summed it up precisely when he stated that the detainees "have no regard for life, either ours or their own. I believe this was not an act of desperation, but an act of asymmetrical warfare waged against us."[15]

If Guantanamo Bay was where the "worst of the worst" in the global struggle went to establish the facts of that claim, all of Iraq itself was transformed into a laboratory of investigation and truth making in the War on Terror. The pure fantasy of the public rationales for the American invasion—weapons of mass destruction, imminent nuclear assault, linkages between Al Qaeda and the regime, the hidden hand of Saddam Hussein in the attacks of 9/11, the liberationist urgings of the Bush administration—worked to heighten and intensify these conditions. Most notoriously, a much-hated symbol of Baathist power in Iraq, the prison at Abu Ghraib on the outskirts of Baghdad, quickly turned into an enormous torture chamber operated by occupying American forces. Repeating the breakdown of operational boundaries at Guantanamo, military intelligence "*actively requested* that MP guards set physical and mental conditions for favorable interrogation."[16] Sexualized humiliation ran rampant in the prison. American guards/soldiers/interrogators stripped the detainees, threatened them with rape, exposed their genitalia to packs of dogs, forced them to pile upon each other naked while threatening to shoot them if they did not comply, photographed them in scenes of forced masturbation, and raped them with inanimate objects. A detainee describes the actions of the most well-known guard of the Abu Ghraib prison, Army Private Charles Granier: "Granier and his helper they cuffed one prisoner in Room #1, named [redacted], he was an Iraqi citizen. They tied him to the bed and they were inserted [*sic*] the phosphoric light in his ass and he was yelling for God's help. . . . That was Ramadan, around 12 midnight approximately when I saw them putting the stick in his ass."[17]

### The Torture Memos and the Twin Specters

Much of the opposition to this regime of torture figures the practices and spaces of interrogation outside of the law and as the corruption of law. For many, the law is both the object of the first turn and the very last thing to cling to.[18] If only the law could be brought to these sites emptied of it; if only the law present could, at long last, extinguish its impurities and resist the temptations that perpetually corrupt and sully it. On the first account, we are confronted by a definitional injustice or impossibility of justice, the specter of lawlessness. Guantanamo Bay is thus witnessed as an "outlaw prison"[19] and stands as a troubling and exemplary totem of an emerging "lawless world."[20] Thus, the violence of the imperial camps and prisons becomes unmoored from the practices and histories of the law and floats in a netherworld off the shore of the law's domain. In this utter absence of law, in this spatial/temporal break from tradition and constituting value,[21] a reign of pure discretion is understood to endure: a rule without rules. This vision is partially captured in the rhetorically powerful description of Guantanamo as a "legal black hole."[22]

At this juncture, one must return to this chapter's opening assertion by Jack Goldsmith (Office of Legal Counsel [OLC] lawyer under Bush) that a plane full of lawyers en route to Guantanamo could serve as a metaphor for the nature of the battle; it should also be apprehended in all of its literalness so that the metaphor not feel strained. Against the expulsion of the camps into outlaw status runs the jarring fact that such exquisite legal attention and devotion have been showered upon these spaces of brutality. Indeed, it has been widely noted that lawyers have been central, even if not sole, architects of the torture regime. The camps and prisons at Guantanamo may be lacking in many amenities, but "law" is not exactly one of them. And although the law under consideration ultimately undoes itself and works against its own possibility while nonetheless realizing the full power of law (however unintentionally, if intentionality is even relevant), that auto-negation cannot obscure the presence of that which is being nullified. As such, the camps are decisively *not* beyond the law or strangers to it; they are not lawless.[23] And, importantly, this was true *prior* to the limited rulings extending jurisdiction to Guantanamo (but not Bagram[24]) in cases such as *Rasul v. Bush* (2004) and *Boumediene v. Bush* (2008). Stated simply, the law was never not present in the camps and prisons.

This inconvenient presence of law has not been entirely ignored; instead, the animating law has been denounced for being "political." Man's antique telos is now his original sin, insufferable in a "nation of law, not men." A series of confusions tear open the thin membrane between politics and law; politics as such infects it, and its spread is the sure ruin of law: the great malady is politicization. This diagnosis emerges from multiple locations and binds a type of consensus, a consensus that not incidentally serves as a principal violence of the law.[25] From the liberals comes a critique of the Bush justice department for its "pervasive politicization" of the law;[26] from the political Right comes the same accusation against the Obama administration; back and forth, ever tighter bound, the antipolitical consensus binds. Merely political: this is how one of the lawyers metaphorically "in the plane" brushes off his critics; the charge now serves as a perfect prophylactic from accountability, severing judgment from all its historical roots.[27] The disdain for politics shines even brighter in a slim denunciation of the lawyering responsible for the camps and prisons. Confronting protests against his school for allowing the ongoing tenure of a torture lawyer as professor, the dean of UC Berkeley's School of Law acknowledged that the professor in question had provided some "bad ideas and even worse advice during his government service." But the true vice for the dean of the law: "What troubles me *substantively* with the analysis in the [torture] memoranda is that they reduce the Rule of Law to the Reign of Politics."[28] This critique by the dean, in fact (shall we say, "substantively"?), insulates the legal architects of the camps by acceding to and affirming the proposition that the crisis is simply the appearance of politics per se. Settling the confusion over disputed reigns becomes paramount at the same instant that it becomes oddly empty: the rule of law now carries no substance other than it simply being in place, and the only route to combating the facts of the camps and the "law" that produced them is disgraced.

Emptiness here is filled by history or, rather, by memory. A nostalgia rules in law's stead for law's return. It is a movement for restoration that dares not pause to consider what has been lost because the "what" would invariably be a reopening of the wound it labels "politics." The nostalgia is for an intertwined ideological-temporal return to law as such, and as such, it is for a law that never was, devoid of the tumults exceeding it and bringing it into being as well as the politics always irrigating and sustaining it. Against this one must return to the old legal realist observation of Llewellyn that the law is what the law does but without reducing the law to a tool ready to be wielded by any or by all or to a positivist "fact" to be observed in grids of empirical measurements. Law works not as an instrument but instead as a relationship and a practice. One does not apply the rule; one "practices the law." As relationships and practices, they are thus open, in a sense, but they also carry the weight of the past in a manner that shatters all romance; it is, no doubt, an order of rule. Thus, the siren calls for the return and restoration of "the rule of law" against the camps (or in them?) must answer a historical question, a *political* question: the return of what?

Before turning to a past that is heralded as the hope for the future, proper attention must be given to the "law" that produced the imperial detention centers in question. For here, a genuine radicalism is at work. In using the term "radical," I do not intend it as a pejorative or polemic; nor do I intend it to function symbiotically with either Empire or with violence, independently or in relationship with the law per se. Rather, the radicalism of the law engendering the camps rests upon the fact that the interpretations of the law break the bonds of the practice of law while nonetheless relying upon the aesthetics, institutions, and powers of legitimization of the law. And in this there rests some other movement besides an outside-to-the-inside turn of exception and a concomitant "force of law" without it.[29]

Interrogations: Were there to be limits? If so, where were they? How were they to be found? The commander-in-chief did not establish the answers without the help of counsel. Even the installed executive, with all of his bluff and bluster, could not do without it. And so in the late summer and early fall of 2002, lawyers within the OLC in the Department of Justice and Judge Advocate General (JAG) lawyers within the Department of Defense began to tackle the questions. Collectively, the responses would come to be known publicly as "the torture memos." Multiple legal texts are in play: treaties, federal statutes, legislative histories, the Constitution. On August 1, 2002, the OLC sent a memo to the attorney general interpreting the federal statute implementing the Convention Against Torture and Other Cruel, Inhuman and Degrading Treatment or Punishment. The law criminalizes any "act committed by a person acting under the color of law specifically intended to inflict severe physical or mental pain or suffering (other than pain and suffering incidental to lawful sanctions) upon another person within his custody or physical control."[30] The memo zeros in on two elements of the statute: the intent requirement and the definition of pain/suffering. First, a high barrier to establishing intent is erected. An infliction of the forbidden pain "must be the defendant's precise objective." Ruminating between theory and precedent, the authors of the memo argue that "even if a defendant knows that severe pain will result from his actions, if causing such harm is not his objective, he lacks the requisite specific intent." The door thus cracks open for all types of force against detainees, although the closet door for the sadist remains temporarily closed; the sin of the guards at Abu Ghraib was not that they pushed too far but that they enjoyed it too much. Continuing with the analysis of intent, counsel tells us that specific intent will also fail to be established with a "showing that an individual acted with a good faith belief that his conduct would not produce the result that the law prohibits."[31] Now, the opinion begins to establish the conditions by which its own analysis will work to "take the gloves off" since the legal opinions themselves can establish the required "good faith" that will prevent conviction. Officials in the field thus wait for word from the lawyers because the word will potentially immunize them from legal sanction; once that word arrives, the primary limits will be the efficiency of technique, on the one hand, and the fears of publicity, on the other (suspending for the moment the Nuremberg principle of refusing orders). As illustration, one CIA interrogator informed a tortured detainee that the detainee "would never go to court, because 'we can never let the world know what I have done to you.' "[32] The interrogator's worry is not legal accountability but that the world at large might come to "know."

Understanding what the law prohibits requires turning next to the definition of "severe pain or suffering." Immediately, an invocation of the canons of statutory interpretation: one begins with the text and its ordinary/natural meaning. The meanings become elusive; what exactly is "severe"? Indeterminacy drives the line of transgression to an extreme, thereby transforming a statute designed to forbid the abuse of detainees into one enabling a multitude of techniques. Jeremy Waldron has critiqued this interpretative line pushing in the following manner: "One way of thinking about the need for precise definition involves asking whether the person constrained by the norm in question—state or individual—has a legitimate interest in pressing up as close as possible to the norm, and thus a legitimate interest in having a bright line rule stipulating exactly what is permitted and what is forbidden by the norm."[33] Choosing between these two approaches, between the line pushing for interrogation advocated by the lawyers in the OLC and the anticruelty normative order for rule making advocated by Waldron, is an inescapable jurisprudential moment and one ultimately undecidable on grounds other than political vision. True, other interpretative moves that look more rightly "legal" to the outsider will sustain the elaboration and defense, but they will be just that: supplements. Such an observation is not remotely fatal to the practice of law; political vision is the very opening of law and that to which law must ever return *in practice*. Often the practice will return in a subterranean manner, beneath not just veneers of ideology but secretly embedded in the steady hum of a million quotidian engagements and transactions. In other moments, the move is from assumption to question, and political thinking bursts forth as the pivotal (that on which the law turns) calculation. Briefly, then, the fact is that the law cannot escape politics, and politicization brings to the fore the politics always already present in the law.

The lawyers of the torture regime believe the "key" to unlocking the secrets the detainees carry inside of Guantanamo, Abu Ghraib, Bagram, and other "black sites" is to be found in that line demarcating severe/not severe. It is now high tide for imperial consequentialism: the "dictionary defines 'severe' as 'unsparing in exaction, punishment, or censure' or 'inflicting discomfort or pain hard to endure; sharp; afflictive; distressing; violent; extreme; as *severe* pain, anguish, torture.' "[34] That severe is severe begs the question, but from the plain language, they conclude that the "pain or suffering must be to such a high level of intensity that the pain is difficult for the subject to endure."[35] Unsure now as to the limits of the endurable (pulpification of the flesh? Shackled beatings? Sensory deprivation? Anal rape? Some combination? Something else?), the memo looks to other sections of the federal code "to shine more light on its meaning."

What do they find in enlightenment? They discover that the "phrase 'severe pain' appears in statutes defining an emergency medical condition for the purpose of providing health benefits."[36] Determining an emergency medical condition is admittedly far afield from establishing a limit on the forces of interrogation, but they have found what they are looking for: an extremity. A provision entitling care somehow serves as the basis for inflicting pain upon detainees until they need it. The conclusion from the lawyers: to meet the statutory requirement of "severe pain," the subject of interrogation must suffer a "sufficiently serious physical condition or injury such as death, organ failure, or serious impairment of body functions."[37]

One can sense the mental gears churning even at this undeniable outer limit, wondering what constitutes "failure" with regards to organs, what bodily functions might be impaired without being serious, and what does "serious" modify, the impairment or the function—at one moment it is "permanent impairment of a significant body function," but in the next sentence, it is "serious impairment of body functions." If they die, you are doing it wrong, but what short of death impairs "doing it"? The lawyers press onward but now unmoored from statutory text. Classic legal reasoning: in the alternative, "even if an interrogation method arguably were to violate Section 2340A [the torture criminalization statute], the statute would be unconstitutional if it impermissibly encroached upon the President's constitutional power to conduct a military campaign." The president has the power to order interrogations as part of a military campaign; his powers are at a zenith in a time of war; we are in a state of permanent war; thus, "*any effort* to apply Section 2340A in a manner that interferes with the President's direction of such core war matters as the detention and interrogation of enemy combatants" must be constitutionally impermissible.[38] To arrive at this maximalist conclusion on the depths of executive power, the memo looks primarily to the "text, history, and structure" of the Constitution and conveniently fails to consider the central presidential powers' case in modern times, *Youngstown*.[39]

*Youngstown* stands as a rebuke to unchecked inherent executive power in times of war. In 1952, President Truman issued an executive order seizing the majority of privately owned steel mills in the United States. Escalating conflicts between labor and capital threatened to disrupt the level of steel production to a degree that the president deemed a threat to continued war in Korea. The Supreme Court held the seizure to be an unconstitutional exercise of executive power notwithstanding the situation in Asia and the explicit declaration of necessity for "national defense." Justice Black's opinion for the Court held, "We cannot with faithfulness to our constitutional system hold that the Commander in Chief of the Armed Forces has the ultimate power as such to take possession of private property in order to keep labor disputes from stopping production. This is a job for the Nation's lawmakers, not for its military authorities."[40] In an influential concurrence, Justice Jackson put presidential power into motion as interdependent with and contextually related to the powers of the legislative branch. He writes, "Presidential powers are not fixed but fluctuate, depending upon their disjunction or conjunction with Congress."[41] Significantly, Justice Jackson placed executive power at "its lowest ebb" when the president "takes measures incompatible with the expressed or implied will of Congress."[42]

Does *Youngstown* block the desire to refuse the limits placed upon interrogations and confinement in Section 2340A? Whatever answer one might give to this question, it is unavoidable as a question when interpreting the powers of the president in times of war and especially when those powers purportedly render applicable congressional statutes as constitutionally moot. Several experts in this area have noted this omission in the memo.[43] Douglass Cassel of Northwestern Law School describes the refusal to consider and engage binding case law as "not just poor judgment, that's incompetence."[44] One must go further: it is not law at all. And to be perfectly clear, it is *not* because it is "political" as opposed to "legal." Let's consider another case to see how critical it is to enter into the orbit of precedent (even to break from it), in practice. After the attacks of September 11, 2001, the spokesperson for the regime warned all residents in the United States that they should "watch what they say, watch what they do." Imagine if the president had subsequently turned to his counsel and inquired whether the federal government possessed the power to criminally prosecute those who failed to heed these grim warnings. More exactly, imagine that he wanted to pass a law making it illegal to make *any* false statements about the commander-in-chief. Would that be constitutional?

All routes of consideration would inevitably lead to the landmark case of *New York Times v. Sullivan* (1964) in order to answer that question. This case held that public officials could not recover civil damages for defamatory statements relating to their official conduct absent a showing of "actual malice." My hypothetical involves criminal libel, but this would not alter the centrality of this ruling in any analysis. One simply could not form a *legal* opinion regarding libel against a public official without working very closely with the facts of the case, the holding by the Court, and the reasoning justifying it. Again, producing a legal opinion on this question would cease to be a legal opinion in any meaningful sense if this case was simply ignored. If that gap occurred on a law student's examination, the grade would be failure; if it were found in the work product of a practicing attorney, the penalty would be disbarment for negligent practice.[45]

So, we have in the August 1, 2002, "torture memo" a legal opinion effecting the force of law without being "law" at all. It constitutes not a novel turn in the law but a turn *against* it. Thus, the spaces opened up and the practices set into motion by the memo tear asunder the constitutive bonds holding together the practice of law, but they are by no means "outlaw": they rule as law and draw their force through the institutions from which they emerge (the OLC), the professional credentials of the authors (the elite sector of the profession), the form through which they communicate (the genre of the legal memorandum), and the power that they confer (the immunity they bestow upon the interrogators). It is a thoroughly legal regime that completely undermines the rule of law even as it extends it. We have returned again to Magritte's "double cipher" where annulment is simultaneous with accomplishment.

Crucially, rejection of the law that is not law, this rule of a juridically spectralized anti-constitutionalism, does not adhere necessarily/definitionally to a specific political position in the legal community even as this rule takes definite ideological form as a modality of right-wing governance. So off the mark was the reasoning that the memo was withdrawn when a new head of the OLC (Jack Goldsmith) took the position in 2003. A self-described movement conservative and a Bush appointee, Goldsmith felt compelled to repudiate the work. Defending this move, he explained, "On the surface the interrogation opinions seemed like typically thorough and scholarly OLC work. But not far below the surface there were problems . . . the health benefits statute's use of 'severe pain' had no relationship whatsoever to the torture statute . . . the clumsy definitional arbitrage didn't even seem in the ballpark."[46] That is, both the statutory interpretation substituting the trigger for a health right as the threshold limit of violence before torture *and* the constitutional explication asserting absolute power in the executive to apply/not apply techniques constituting torture had absolutely "no foundation in law."[47]

We must not confuse this critique of new modalities with a moral-ethical claim on behalf of the detainees in a project of universal human rights. That is not the point here. It does not hold that this rule must lead to the camps any more than the inverse proposition that defeating this rule must close them. The radicalism of the memos and the asymmetries that they extend clearly helped produce the facts of the camps and prisons of empire. But those facts do not speak in and of themselves to a negation of the law in the practice of the law. One could make that move, and many do, through either the trumping language of international humanitarianism or the theologies that divinize man and/or subject him to sacred and inviolable rule. Quite different (even if potentially convergent politically in labors of coalition) is (1) the argument that the law of the camps cannot be law since it fails to meet the universal laws of man or the unyielding orders of Nature (divine or not) from (2) the argument that the interpretative norms constituting the practice and the rule of law are coming unhinged. That unhinged rule threatens many values (even as it opens the possibility of realizing others if properly conceived) and despite appearing most brutally in the camps, we must see in that something other than its exclusive signature.

Anti-constitutionalism breaks faith in and with the law, but that should not lead to a misplaced faith in that which is broken. Jeremy Waldron is correct to claim that the torture memos are "shocking as a jurisprudential matter," but he goes further to state that they rattle his "faith in the integrity of the community of American jurists."[48] For Waldron, torture is normatively antithetical to the values supposedly embedded in a community that has devoted its very existence "to the study of the Rule of Law and the education of future generations of lawyers."[49] This could be read as a political standard by which to judge the law, and it is certainly that. However, it works as something more than a paradigmatic mooring: his confession of shock and a loss of faith suggests a historical understanding undergirding the constitutional vision. That is, it is a narrative of loss. Ironically, the violence of the camp again becomes figured as aberrational, new in time.

## The Prison-Industrial Complex and the Rule of Law

Upon closer inspection, or from "experience" in the case of groups historically subordinated by and through American law, there is no break at all in terms of the togetherness of violence and law. More specifically and on point, the operation of governance via the mechanisms of policing and detention is well established within the "homeland" and has been for some time.[50] Preventive detention, policing discretion, life internment, expanded surveillance, systematic yet randomized violence (the very definition of "terror") by state and state-contracted officials inside and outside the prisons, proliferating executions: these have all become what the law is. Why should it come as any surprise that the only thing that President Bush could imagine giving the newly liberated Iraqis as penance for Abu Ghraib was a newly modernized maximum-security Abu Ghraib?

Recall again that when the detainees at Guantanamo continued to show resistance, the camp commanders turned their eyes homeward and imported the architecture of the supermax prisons to the island base. Bush's successor, President Obama, demanded that we close the Guantanamo camps as they had become a source of shame for the nation, somehow believing that the supermax prisons at home could be a source of its pride. Consider also the following *rebuttal* to right-wing criticisms of moving the detainees to American "soil":

> As military and national security officials who have spent our entire careers fighting to protect the American people and defend the country from attack, we all agree that the prison facility at Guantanamo Bay needs to be closed—as do five former Secretaries of State, Gen. David Petraeus, Joint Chiefs of Staff Chairman Adm. Mike Mullen, and Defense Secretary Robert Gates. We also agree with you that the discussion over closing Guantanamo and moving the detainees to a new facility needs to occur, as you have said, in a "civil and rational way." That is why we were disappointed last

week—during a town hall meeting in Standish, MI, whose prison is a possible site to detain terror suspects—to hear you politicize such a critical national security [issue]. . . . The former warden of the Supermax facility said prisoners "spend up to 23 hours a day in their cells, every minute, every meal. The window in their cell is blocked so they can't see the mountains." Yet you stated that detainees housed in America "would have greater opportunities to command and control their networks through outsiders and to spread radical jihadist ideology." The Supermax warden also stated that Ramzi Yousef has never left his cell. If the same—if not stricter—standards are applied to Guantanamo detainees held domestically, then how exactly would they command terrorist networks overseas? . . . Whether it's in Standish, Michigan or the halls of Congress, politicizing national security is always dangerous. We ask you to return the debate to the "civil and rational" in order to stop the spreading of fear that plays into the very hands of the enemies we are trying to defeat.[51]

What could be more apolitical and rational than a prison that holds people in cells for twenty-three hours per day with no view of the outside? And some prisoners *never* leave their cell, the warden reports, with the pride of a craftsman. Such conditions, as at Guantanamo, drive prisoners insane; they lose the capacity of language, they begin to hallucinate, and they mutilate their bodies in the hope of death, but even that hope is extinguished, taken from them by the warden. Prisoners have compared the experience to "living inside of a tomb."

These institutions are not improvisations by rogue soldiers armed with dubious legal memoranda; rather, they are run by officials and backed by jurisprudence. The Thirteenth Amendment to the Constitution abolished slavery in 1865, but its text contains a key exception: "Neither slavery nor involuntary servitude, except as punishment for crime whereof the party shall have been duly convicted, shall exist within the Unites States, or any place subject to its jurisdiction" (1865). Prisoners' rights will always be on the verge of turning into something of a conceptual and practical oxymoron if the concept of slavery is permitted to invade the category. Before *and* after 1865, American courts frequently "spoke of prisoners as slaves of the State."[52] After halting reforms in the early 1960s, prisoners have been

reduced again to that condition in practice, in culture, and in jurisprudence. During the past forty years, an unrelenting counterassault has been
waged on those social movements inside and outside the prison that have
sought to abolish slavery without exception. The law defeated them: in
"virtually every major segment of prisoners' rights jurisprudence, the
[Supreme] Court's impact has been devastating."[53] The tombs of supermax
are thus a realization and enactment of "law," and if the imagined path
ahead is for the return of the rule of law without and against politicization,
it will lead us inevitably back into them, sealed inside the "civility and
rationality" of the age.

"Circulation" has defined the relationship between the prison-industrial
complex of the mythical homeland and the far-flung imperial camps and
prisons of the enduring freedom beyond it.[54] So much movement and
cross-fertilization are happening. A lone figure nonetheless stands out, as a
sign: the American guard Granier of Abu Ghraib. Flowering as a true sadist
in the Baghdad prison and thus running amok of a cardinal virtue of the
regime by finding genuine enjoyment in the pain he inflicted, his "work"
in the prison was a familiar work. He was a reserve member of the Army,
not a career military officer, and thus maintained a civilian job before being
called up and sent to Iraq. The Taguba report notes somewhat dryly his
occupation, in an addendum authored by a psychiatrist from the Air Force
providing a "psychological assessment" of the abuse at Abu Ghraib: "CPL
Granier had a civilian prison job."[55] Granier himself saw the connection
between his prison job and the torture regime when he told an official that
"the Christian in me knows it's wrong [the torture], but the corrections
officer in me says, 'I love to make a grown man piss himself.' "[56] Unsurprisingly, the Associated Press reports that an abuse "scandal" erupted in the
prison where Granier worked as a guard in rural Pennsylvania prior to his
deployment. Dozens of prison officials were implicated in it, although Granier apparently was not. From the report: "Prisoners in the Pennsylvania
scandal claimed in dozens of lawsuits that abuse was widespread at the
maximum-security state prison and included beatings, sexual assault and
body cavity searches in full view of other guards and inmates."[57] Again, the
law is first and foremost *a practice*.

As a practice, the violence of American law works asymmetrically,
unequally. This legal tradition came into being, one might say, in the policing and production of difference. It is the proliferation of distinction, the

practice of governance through it, that makes nonsensical Giorgio Agamben's claim that "our age is nothing but the implacable and methodical attempt to overcome the division dividing the people . . . in a biopolitical project."[58] The political and constitutional history of the United States is rife with a fanaticism of distinction and division. Even at the historical moment of greatest intensity in the attempted fusion of blood and citizenship, in tracing citizenship through the performances of lineage, one finds a legal doctrine of "separate but equal." The lie of the latter half of the doctrine affirmed and produced the truth of the first. And the white supremacists of the country, especially those in the American South, could entertain neither the liquidation of subordinated races nor their exile in schemes of Garveyite emancipation, if for no other reason than their sense of self as people (one cannot be superior unless there is something to be superior to) and their base of economic wealth would have literally disappeared.

Thus, it is of no surprise that the prison systems in the American South after Reconstruction reintegrated the private law of contract with the public law of peonage, thereby producing a racialized system of prison labor that worked both as profitable labor and also as a means of disciplining and racializing labor on the other side of its walls.[59] The laws of Mississippi, for example, made it "illegal for a tenant farmer to break his contract after taking an advance, no matter how small."[60] The largest prison in Mississippi at the time, Parchman Farm, had an African American population of 90 percent and "functioned as a working plantation," including whippings as punishment for violations of prison rules.[61] Producing caste and accumulating racialized capital required the law but was in no way exclusive to it. As is well known, the same period and place also witnessed a record number of lynchings of African Americans.[62] Consequently, the violence of the regime unraveled the dyadic schema of an inside/outside the law, inside/outside the state, or inside/outside the norm and its exception. It was the very production of difference, of bodies, of law, and of violence that made it such an enduring order. As Kendall Thomas has written, such governance is neither the opposition of law-violence nor the collapse of all violence inside or outside the law; rather, the relationship between the violence of the law and the violence outside the formal institutions of the law is "not merely coincident, but coordinate."[63] Thus, white plantation owners would develop a theory of "law in action" decades before the progressive legal scholars at Yale and Columbia and Wisconsin: "there are four kinds of law in Mississippi, whites liked to say: statute law, plantation law, lynch law, and Negro law."[64]

This is governance with both the "contract and the whip" working as coordinate powers in a racialized capitalist economy rooted in and transforming a society no longer feudal yet not quite "modern."[65] These practices produced and were produced by laws written and unwritten and are irreducible to a singular decision, order, or locale of sovereignty. One does not find in them the secret and unfolding paradigm of modernity, or the West, or the Law; one finds only the particular convergences and departures of a variety of constitutional stories, political histories, material relations, and institutionalized epistemologies. Other peoples in other times have taken other turns, even if and when they have cross-pollinated ways of thinking and coproduced the sociopolitical contours of contemporary being. Parchman Farm is not Auschwitz, Granier is not Eichmann, the tortured Yemeni prisoners of Guantanamo are not the exterminated Jews and Gypsies of the Reich, the decrees of the French Constituent Assembly are not the amendments of the U.S. Constitution, the union of Madison's states is not the unity of Rousseau's nation, and the undoing of a tradition is not the decisive suspension of an order.

Granier's prison—the one in Pennsylvania, with its "scandal" of routinized violence—was every bit as racialized as the plantation factory of Parchman Farm in the regime of the Old South. An article from the *Los Angeles Times* gives an account of the prison: "It was built for 1,500 of Pennsylvania's hardest-core prisoners, including about 110 on death row, and had the perks of modern corrections, such as central air conditioning and cable TV. But it was not immune from the age-old tensions of such institutions. While almost 70% of the inmates were black, many from big cities, SCI-Greene was in a rural part of the state near the West Virginia border, and more than 90% of the guards were white."[66] Space here will not allow a proper and full accounting of the multitude of forces that produce the 70/90 divide within that prison or a mapping of the differences between the policing of the present and the Jim Crow of the past. Those differences cannot be collapsed, but the continuities with or reconfigurations of that past cannot be denied.[67]

Despite existing in a post–*Brown v. Board of Education of Topeka* jurisprudential world, the racism of the prisons enjoys the prestige and confirmation of the judicial word. As Michelle Alexander discusses in her book

*The New Jim Crow*, two cases are emblematic: *McKleskey v. Kemp* and *United States v. Armstrong*.[68] The first, *McKleskey v. Kemp*,[69] provided constitutional safe harbor for a racially discriminatory *practice* of administering the death penalty. The condemned in this case (a case originating from a Georgia state court) was an African American man convicted of murdering a white police officer. On appeal, the lawyers for McCleskey submitted a statistical study demonstrating that defendants in Georgia "charged with killing white victims were 4.3 times as likely to receive a death sentence as those charged with killing blacks" and that black defendants "who kill whites have the greatest likelihood of being sentenced to death."[70] The Supreme Court accepted the validity of the study but held that the statistics do not "*prove* that race enters into any capital sentencing decisions or that race was a factor in McCleskey's particular case."[71] Thus, he was killed by the state. The Court worried that a holding in the alternative would open up constitutional challenges to inequality in all areas of criminal punishment. Michelle Alexander correctly identifies the Court's mission: "[T]he Court's opinion was driven by a desire to immunize the entire criminal justice system from claims of racial bias."[72] That fear of a "slippery slope" to equality was given as *a reason for* sustaining the application of the death penalty in the *McCleskey* case. This is a piece of one juridical cloth with the torture memos' devotion to proving specific intent in the particular case; the regime as a regime recedes into the background of the law and becomes its very condition of enactment.

Another critical case in this vein, deepening the tradition that informs the present, came from the Supreme Court a decade later in *United States v. Armstrong*.[73] There, a black defendant asserted a violation of equal protection (under the Fifth Amendment's Due Process Clause) after being prosecuted by the federal state for a violation of the laws prohibiting the sale of crack cocaine. An affidavit presented by the defense at trial showed that of the twenty-four cases prosecuted in that federal district for dealing crack cocaine, every single defendant was black.[74] Chief Justice Rehnquist, writing for the Court, held, "In the case before us, respondents' 'study' did not constitute 'some evidence tending to show the existence of the essential elements of' a selective prosecution claim. *Berrios, supra*, at 1211. The study failed to identify individuals who were not black, could have been prosecuted for the offenses for which respondents were charged, but were not so prosecuted."[75] The Court explained the reasoning for not permitting further discovery to proceed in this case:

Having reviewed the requirements to prove a selective prosecution claim, we turn to the showing necessary to obtain discovery in support of such a claim. If discovery is ordered, the Government must assemble from its own files and documents which might corroborate or refute the defendant's claim. Discovery thus imposes many of the costs present when the Government must respond to a *prima facie* case of selective prosecution. It will divert prosecutors' resources and may disclose the Government's prosecutorial strategy. The justifications for a rigorous standard for the elements of a selective prosecution claim thus require a correspondingly rigorous standard for discovery in aid of such a claim.[76]

This second line of reasoning must be understood to theoretically subsume the first even as they are presented separately: the constitutional transgression of equality must be shown in each and every case to be specific and intentional in that particular case in part to not slow down or diminish the prosecutorial powers and practices of the state. Attempting to show discrimination in each and every particular case would bog down the racialized prosecutorial state, divert its resources, and reveal its aims, and therefore the policies must continue uninterrupted, at once prima facie and yet "undiscoverable."[77]

We can call this, for short, at present "the rule of law."

So, the concern that the imperial camps and prisons are raging, unchecked wildfires of arbitrary lawlessness, that they, as Judith Butler has argued, lay waste to "the Constitution and the rule-of-law,"[78] must open up to another danger on the horizon: the smooth calculation and operation of the law, its extension to these sites and these peoples, not its suspension but its presence in a nonparadoxical and nonnegating form. One might say that it is the very potential of its nonsuspension that poses a conundrum. Even now, with the slow extension of the ancient writ of habeas corpus and the attempt to "fix" (shall we doubt its double meaning after *United States v. Armstrong*? After *McCleskey v. Kemp*?) the military tribunals at Guantanamo, one can sense not the arrival of justice but the routinization of its other. Once political vision slips into the politics of the particular case and the intent specific to it, one has ceded the world before making the first claim upon it. Many scholars and activists have criticized the turn of the law or the rule of the law in producing the inequalities mapped in the cases

above. Some have compared the infamy of these cases to the paradigmatic and (ultimately) union-dissolving decision of *Dred Scott*.[79] But there is
something off in the analogy despite the sure-footedness of the impulse
behind it. For a result of the infamy of *Dred Scott* was the perfect clarity that
it provided, illuminating in the public mind what was at stake politically in
the formulation of the constitutional decision. Inescapable was the "what"
of the law as it ruled upon classes and on behalf of them; now, the "what"
so easily eludes our thinking precisely because we are invited to think as
the law now thinks: one defendant at a time.

The possibility of American jurisprudence as a "guide," the turn to it as
something that could "shed light on the question," is never far from the
minds of the architects of the camps. Again, all the thinking of the torture
memos was "legally framed."[80] In a memorandum from October 11, 2002
(this time from a JAG lawyer inside the Department of Defense rather than
an OLC lawyer inside the Department of Justice), entitled "Legal Brief on
Proposed Counter-Resistance Strategies," the author begins with the facts:
the detainees have developed "resistance strategies to interrogation," and
many interrogators feel constrained by the ambiguity of the rules; they do
not want to do "anything that could be considered 'controversial.' "[81] The
memo quickly dispenses with international law by determining that only
the limits of domestic law will govern: "[T]he United States is only prohibited from committing those acts that would otherwise be prohibited under
the 8th Amendment of the United States Constitution."[82] According to the
memo, the question determining the law of the Eighth Amendment is not
the injury suffered or the precise quantum of force brought to bear
(although an elaborate set of categories is developed, like steps on an infinite ladder) but whether the force was "applied in a good faith effort to
maintain or restore discipline, or maliciously and sadistically applied for
the *very* purpose of causing harm."[83]

Here is the text of the Eighth Amendment: "Excessive bail shall not be
required, nor excessive fines imposed, nor cruel and unusual punishment
inflicted" (1791). Constitutional limitations upon punishment must be
read in relationship to the rights articulated in the Fifth Amendment (the
right to due process and the right to not be a witness against oneself), the
Sixth Amendment (the right to a speedy and public trial), the suspension
clause regarding the writ of habeas corpus,[84] and the Fourteenth Amendment (incorporating the Eighth Amendment via the Due Process Clause).[85]
Thus, the jurisprudential history of the "cruel and unusual clause" deals

exhaustively with punishment inflicted after a conviction; that is, punishment arrived at via the mechanisms of the process due to the accused. Some punishments are forbidden by the very fact of their spectacular and prolonged display of pain—the predisciplinary exercise of sovereign power in the opening scenes of Foucault's *Discipline & Punish* would be an example; other punishments are limited according to the age and mental capacity of the condemned,[86] and still other constitutional limits seek to forge a theoretical bond between the severity of the crime and the extent of the punishment.[87]

The move to center the Eighth Amendment comes from all sides. One group of activists from the political Left (primarily, not exclusively) that has campaigned to have the lawyers and leaders of the torture regime held to account and brought to justice frame their call to action thusly: "Torture is illegal under both United States and international law. The Constitution prohibits cruel and unusual punishment under the Eighth Amendment, and it states that treaties signed by the U.S. are the 'supreme Law of the Land' under Article Six."[88] Further, they argue,

> Despite this well-established law, under the Bush administration, torture was authorized by George Bush and kept secret using classified designations. The White House requested legal memoranda to support its use of torture and it received those authored by a host of attorneys, including John Yoo, Jay Bybee, and Stephen Bradbury. Attorneys who advised, counseled, consulted and supported those memoranda included Alberto Gonzales, John Ashcroft, Michael Chertoff, Alice Fisher, William Haynes II, Douglas Feith, Michael Mukasey, Timothy Flanigan, and David Addington. . . . We have asked the respective state bars to revoke the licenses of the foregoing attorneys for moral turpitude. They failed to show "respect for and obedience to the law, and respect for the rights of others." . . . They failed to support or uphold the U.S. Constitution, and the laws of the United States, and to maintain the respect due to the courts of justice and judicial officers, all in violation of state bar rules.[89]

This criticism has been carried forth more broadly, displaying the sociocultural presence and prominence of legal discourse in shaping political questioning and the ongoing reduction of political questioning to the issue of "legality." On the television show *60 Minutes*, the host Leslie Stahl pushed the issue to the fore in an interview with Supreme Court Justice Antonin Scalia. And as was so often the case, Justice Scalia helped us to see all of the right things for all of the wrong reasons. Here is the exchange between the journalist and the jurist:

> STAHL: If someone's in custody, as in Abu Ghraib, and they are brutalized, by a law enforcement person—if you listen to the expression "cruel and unusual punishment," doesn't that apply?
>
> SCALIA: No. To the contrary. You think—Has anybody ever referred to torture as punishment? I don't think so.
>
> STAHL: Well I think if you're in custody, and you have a policeman who's taken you into custody. . . .
>
> SCALIA: And you say he's punishing you? What's he punishing you for? . . . When he's hurting you in order to get information from you, you wouldn't say he's punishing you. What is he punishing you for? You punish somebody. . . .
>
> STAHL: Well, because he assumes you, one, either committed a crime . . . or that you know something that he wants to know.
>
> SCALIA: It's the latter. And when he's hurting you in order to get information from you, you don't say he's punishing you.[90]

On the one hand, Scalia's assertion that torture is never used for punishment is patently false. On the other hand, the converse—that torture is therefore always punishment—does not really hold either. So, the curious legal proposition takes root: whatever one's position on torture at Guantanamo or Abu Ghraib (and it is telling that in American life we have such a diversity of positions on this), it is not "punishment" at all. Constitutionally, the deprivation of life/liberty must follow along familiar procedural routes—namely, the trial. And this is at the heart of the radical reversal of the juridical schema at those sites: the punishment precedes the procedure, which makes it not punishment and thus makes superfluous the procedure that is yet to come.[91] A key fact of the reversal of procedure and punishment is that the law is not abandoned; it is misplaced. That misplacement does indeed undo the law, but it also oddly pays a steep tribute to the law: all of the strange reversals and interpretations affirm rather than suspend. The flood of the law washes into these allegedly "outlaw" spaces situating each and every relationship within them. If one was forced into using the theoretical language of norm/exception, one would have to press Alexis de Tocqueville's observation about the place of law in America against Giorgio

Agamben's view of sovereign indistinctions: the norm haunts the exception, not vice versa.[92]

In saying this, I do not affirm the existence of these spaces as constituting a "no man's land between public law and political fact."[93] The very distinction between "public law" and "political fact" can only be interpreted and understood through the grid of a particular political ordering; public law is always already an element of political fact, and only through the organization and making of political/not political fact does the public law operate. Here we can lean upon and relearn from Carl Schmitt—as well as the Marxist tradition and most feminist critique—in his writings on the "highly political" nature of even the seemingly tranquil vocabularies of civil law (tort, contract, etc.): "A word or expression can simultaneously be reflex, signal, password, and weapon in a hostile confrontation. For example, Karl Renner, a socialist of the Second International, in a very significant scholarly publication . . . calls rent which the tenant pays the landlord 'tribute.' Most German professors of jurisprudence, judges and lawyers would consider such a designation an inadmissible politicization of civil law relationships. . . . For them the question has been decided in a legal positivist manner, and the therein residing political design of the state is thus recognized."[94] It is the very "political design" of the Constitution that recedes from view when the imagined "limit" between law and politics is located in the "abolition of the legislative, executive, and judicial powers."[95] First, the separation of powers was explicitly designed to thwart democracy in protection of the interests of private property, an interest conceived as the precondition of constitutional order.[96] The newfound romance with this separation has yet to grapple with the powers solidified and made victorious by it. Second, sovereignty has never been established as a constitutional fact; it is always a constitutional question or future and remains one.[97]

## Conclusion

A political movement that envisions the defeat of the camps by the return or restoration of the "rule of law" misses several critical points at its own risk: (1) the precondition and condition of law is politics, as practice and pivot, and depoliticization as a telos will always work as a political fact in relationship to it; (2) the practices of the law (and by this we mean the law in question since it is only to be in motion as a practice) stand soaked in violence, a violence delivered through an enactment and policing of differences, differences colonially informed and juridically prescribed as a "tradition"; and (3) these new zones of violence are not "lawless" or rogue in their configurations—they are not strangers to the law even as they are "not law."

Some will point to calls by President Obama to close Guantanamo before he left office as a sign of hope. But on what ground does this hope rest? If the ideal being posited is the simple integration of so-called enemy combatants into the prison-industrial complex, then violence will become coherent in a juridical sense but entrenched as a political fact. Nonetheless, one might still hope that the violence done *to* the law, even if not the violence done *by* the law, will be ended by the closure of the offshore camps and prisons. At the most concrete level, it must be noted that the Obama administration advocated for closing Guantanamo but opposed even extending habeas protection to those held in Bagram.

But more fundamentally and importantly, none of the legal architects of the torture regime have been held to account for their craftwork. In fact, they have mostly failed upward in a spectacular fashion: Bybee now occupies a seat on the prestigious Ninth Circuit Court of Appeals, and Yoo holds the Emanuel S. Heller Chair of Law at the University of California, Berkeley. President Obama, in a decision many judged wise and prudent, elected bipartisan goodwill over justice when he decided very early in his first term that no prosecutions would be pursued against the torture regime's masterminds. As a theoretical matter, both amity and justice might (and here, following the analysis in the preface, we can only say "might") have held together had he issued pardons to those implicated individuals for the pardons could have stood as a clear sign of the criminality it forgave. But even this minimalist gesture was seen as a threat to harmony. Instead, the president issued an executive order to halt the most excessive forms of abuse and torture and reintegrate the violence into the previously existing standards.[98]

In making these two decisions, the decision to forego prosecutions and the decision to return to early forms of legality, the president believed they together would enable the polity to look "to the future, not the past."[99] The irony is that the future is in fact contoured by the past of the torture regime as the future lacks the capacity of becoming distinct from that past it seeks to supersede. As the Senate Select Committee Report on Torture noted, the limitations of the executive order "are not part of U.S. law and could be overturned by a future President with the stroke of a pen."[100] The Senate report also stated its aim to "shape detention and interrogation policies in the future."[101] The report began with the observation that waterboarding, near-drowning, sleep deprivation, unnecessary rectal feeding, prolonged ice baths, and isolation in dungeons were "in violation of U.S. law" and that "existing U.S. law and treaty obligations should have prevented many of the abuses."[102] Further, the central purpose of the Senate's report is to ensure that "U.S. policy will never again allow for secret indefinite detention and the use of coercive interrogations."[103]

However, the failure to prosecute the violations of existing law is the effective negation of those laws. Only a presidential decision stands against the full return of the entire medieval carnival of cruelty, and Obama's successor is nothing if not a carnival barker. Indeed, President Trump has expressed great enthusiasm for both keeping Guantanamo Bay open and sending more people there for "interrogation."

A law that is no law: this is now the law of torture in the United States. We are thus left with nothing more than increasingly empty incantations of "hope" and rapidly diminishing grounds for it.

## Chapter 3

# The Legislative Power: This Death
# That Leads to Life

*Living well, the search for the good life, means living not only in the here
and now but in the past, not only in the past, but for the future.*
—J. Broek, N. Jacobson, and S. Wolin, "Academic Freedom
and Student Political Activity"

*The District Court shall determine de novo* any claim of a violation of
any right. . . . Nothing in this Act shall constitute a precedent with
respect to future legislation.
—"Terri's Law," An Act for the Relief of the
Parents of Theresa Marie Schiavo

## Terri Schiavo and Constitutional Rights

On Sunday, March 20, 2005, both chambers of the U.S. Congress voted
overwhelmingly to pass "An Act for the Relief of the Parents of Theresa
Marie Schiavo."[1] The one-page law provided the following:

*Sec. 1. Relief of the Parents of Theresa Marie Schiavo.*
The United States District Court for the Middle District of Florida
shall have jurisdiction to hear, determine, and render judgment on
a suit or claim by or on behalf of Theresa Marie Schiavo for the
alleged violation of any right of Theresa Marie Schiavo under the
Constitution or laws of the United States relating to the withholding

or withdrawal of food, fluids, or medical treatment necessary to sustain her life.

*Sec. 2. Procedure.*
Any parent of Theresa Marie Schiavo shall have standing to bring a suit under this Act. The suit may be brought against any other person who was a party to State court proceedings relating to the withholding or withdrawal of food, fluids, or medical treatment necessary to sustain the life of Theresa Marie Schiavo, or who may act pursuant to a State court order authorizing or directing the withholding or withdrawal of food, fluids, or medical treatment necessary to sustain her life. In such a suit, the District Court shall determine de novo any claim of a violation of any right of Theresa Marie Schiavo within the scope of this Act, notwithstanding any prior State court determination and regardless of whether such a claim has previously been raised, considered, or decided in State court proceedings. The District Court shall entertain and determine the suit without any delay or abstention in favor of State court proceedings, and regardless of whether remedies available in the State courts have been exhausted.

*Sec. 3. Relief.*
After a determination of the merits of a suit brought under this Act, the District Court shall issue such declaratory and injunctive relief as may be necessary to protect the rights of Theresa Marie Schiavo under the Constitution and laws of the United States relating to the withholding or withdrawal of food, fluids, or medical treatment necessary to sustain her life.

*Sec. 4. Time for Filing.*
Notwithstanding any other time limitation, any suit or claim under this Act shall be timely if filed within 30 days after the date of enactment of this Act.

*Sec. 5. No Change of Substantive Rights.*
Nothing in this Act shall be construed to create substantive rights not otherwise secured by the Constitution and laws of the United States or of the several States.

*Sec. 6. No Effect on Assisting Suicide.*
Nothing in this Act shall be construed to confer additional jurisdiction on any court to consider any claim related—

(1) to assisting suicide, or
(2) a State law regarding assisting suicide.

*Sec. 7. No Precedent for Future Legislation.*
Nothing in this Act shall constitute a precedent with respect to future legislation, including the provision of private relief bills.

*Sec. 8. No Affect on the Patient Self-Determination Act of 1990.*
Nothing in this Act shall affect the rights of any person under the Patient Self-Determination Act of 1990.

*Sec. 9. Sense of the Congress.*
It is the Sense of Congress that the 109th Congress should consider policies regarding the status and legal rights of incapacitated individuals who are incapable of making decisions concerning the provision, withholding, or withdrawal of foods, fluid, or medical care.

A president well known for a propensity to retire early in the evening roused himself in the wee hours of the night (1:11 a.m.) to sign the bill into law. Almost all observers agreed, then and now, that "Terri's Law," as it came to be known, was an extraordinary piece of legislation.[2] Here, an atrophied and dysfunctional constitutional system, purposely designed to operate in antidemocratic rhythms (and so from another perspective *perfectly* functional), suddenly moved at electric speed. The spectacle suggested the gravest of public emergencies, a collective political crisis of first-rank constitutional import. And the rhetoric ratcheted upward as if to confirm this: it was a matter of "life and death."

Yet, one facet of the genuinely extraordinary nature of this statute surely rests in how achingly ordinary the facts generative of the case were. The end-of-life decision in the Schiavo case is commonplace as familial-medical practice, thoroughly regulated at the level of state law,[3] and hardly sui generis in the realm of federal constitutional jurisprudence.[4] Even a fierce critic of the decision (of the state order to remove the feeding tube from Schiavo and the federal courts' refusal to enjoin that order) acknowledged as much:

"This sort of thing, of course, happens all the time. The exceptional feature of the Terri Schiavo case is not the situation it presented or the result it produced, but the extraordinary attention it received, out of all proportion to anything genuinely unique about its facts."[5] One should not treat "life and death" cheaply, but one should not quickly overthrow legal thought with deceptively simple existential slogans either.[6] After all, "life and death" might also be rightly called the "day-to-day" or the already proper objects of that which we call "law."

The issue of proportionality then becomes a central one. What precisely is at stake in the matter? How would one measure proportion, in regards to time and object? What stands to be vindicated or brought forth? A new set of values in which proportion becomes moot? If so, then what dies when time and object escape the contours of proportionality, when the present is the only thing present?

The federal legislation passed in relief of the parents of Theresa Marie Schiavo followed years of dispute and litigation in the state court system. Terri Schiavo went into a "persistent vegetative state" in 1990 after suffering a heart attack. In such a condition, Schiavo "had little or no cognitive capacity."[7] To keep her alive, doctors placed a feeding tube inside her to provide nourishment. Not until 1998 did her husband seek to have the feeding tubes removed. The litigation developed from a disagreement between Terri Schiavo's husband and her parents as to whether Schiavo would want (or, more precisely, would have wanted) to cease this kind of treatment in such a permanent vegetative condition.

As noted, that litigation transpired within fairly settled legislative and constitutional arrangements. The radicalism of Terri's Law may be best approached from the shores of these broad jurisprudential settlements, settlements singularly suspended in the passage of Terri's Law. As method, this starting move moves closely with traditional conservatism. And as settlement stands starkly against suspension as value and practice, we can see that an issue presented by this matter is the opening of fissures on the Right regarding the place of constitutionalism in the constellation of their thinking.

The modern landmark case in the United States that first addressed the profound advancements of technology in the domains of medicine and directly confronted technology's ability to reroute the path from, and redraw the line between, life and death was the 1976 New Jersey Supreme Court case of *In Re Quinlan*.[8] Karen Quinlan collapsed at the age of twenty-two for unknown reasons and suffered severe brain damage due to a lack of oxygen. She never regained consciousness and entered into a "chronic vegetative state" whereby she lost the ability "to talk, to see, to feel, to think."[9] The hospital provided her with nourishment through a "nasal-gastro tube," yet she became "emaciated, having suffered a weight loss of at least 40 pounds," and her posture was described to the court as "fetal-like and grotesque."[10] Quinlan also required the assistance of a respirator to breathe. Doctors treating Quinlan presented no hope of recovery for her. The case arose when her father, Joseph Quinlan, sought declaration of guardianship and power to discontinue "extraordinary medical procedures allegedly sustaining Karen's vital processes and hence her life."[11]

The New Jersey Supreme Court ruled for Joseph Quinlan, but critically and explicitly, it was Karen Quinlan's rights that the court understood as being vindicated. The court held that if Karen "were miraculously lucid for an interval . . . she could effectively decide upon discontinuance of the life-supporting apparatus." Further, the court stated that "we have no hesitancy in deciding . . . that no compelling interest of the State could compel Karen to endure the unendurable" and that there "comes a point at which individual's rights overcome" any state interest in the "preservation and sanctity of human life."[12] Confronting the reality of Karen's condition and not willing to defer temporally to some miraculous interlude of lucidity and right-bearing assertion by Karen, the court rescued the right from practical oblivion by allowing the family guardianship to assert it upon Karen's behalf. At the same time, the court discovered absolutely "no parental constitutional right that would entitle [Joseph Quinlan] to a grant of relief *in propria persona*."[13] The right being preserved was one of privacy, a right developed and defined in a series of U.S. Supreme Court cases that the New Jersey Supreme Court drew upon: *Griswold*, *Eisenstadt*, *Stanley*, and *Roe*.[14]

In the U.S. Supreme Court, the constitutional right to refuse medical treatment was assumed in *Cruzan* and affirmed in *Glucksberg*. In *Cruzan*, the Court considered a constitutional challenge to a Missouri law requiring "clear and convincing evidence" that a person in a "permanent vegetative state" would have wanted the life-sustaining medical procedures halted. There, the parents of Nancy Cruzan sought to have a feeding tube removed from their daughter after she suffered permanent brain damage in an automobile accident. Nancy Cruzan did not have a living will. Her parents claimed that Nancy had expressed several times before the accident that she would not want such medical measures deployed to extend her "life."

The Supreme Court held in a 5 to 4 vote that the Missouri law did not violate the Constitution's Fourteenth Amendment's Due Process Clause. Specifically, the majority ruled that the standard of evidence did not violate Cruzan's substantive liberty interest. However, the Court did *not* deny the existence of a right that must be accorded significant constitutional value. Indeed, eight members of the Court agreed that a significant constitutional right was implicated in the *Cruzan* case. The dissenting justices argued that the evidentiary standard demanded by Missouri set the bar too high and created an unconstitutional burden on the freedom in question. The crux of the disagreement centered on what countervailing weight (if any) the state's general interest in "preserving life" might receive. With the exception of Justice Scalia (who concurred in the judgment but not the majority's reasoning), an overwhelming consensus emerged on the Court in *Cruzan* that a person has "a constitutionally protected liberty interest in refusing unwanted medical treatment."[15]

In the case of *Washington v. Glucksberg*, the Court did not extend this right to protect a general "right to suicide."[16] Writing for the majority, Chief Justice Rehnquist acknowledged that the Due Process Clause is not exhausted by formal process concerns and that it "provides heightened protection against government interference with certain fundamental rights and liberty interests." Following a very conservative path of interpretation, the Court reiterated that only those fundamental rights "deeply rooted in our legal tradition" would trigger heightened scrutiny under substantive due process analysis. This was clearly no avant-garde majority writing the opinion. However, in mapping the liberty interest in question as outside the parameters of "tradition," the Court distinguished this holding from the one reached in *Cruzan* and, in so doing, reaffirmed the basic thrust of that holding:

> We began with the observation [in *Cruzan*] that "at common law, even the touching of one person by another without consent and without legal justification was a battery." We then discussed the related rule that "informed consent is generally required for medical treatment." After reviewing a long line of relevant state cases, we concluded that "the common law doctrine of informed consent is viewed as generally encompassing the right of a competent individual to refuse medical treatment." Therefore "for purposes of that case, we assumed that the United States Constitution would grant a

competent person a constitutionally protected right to refuse life-saving hydration and nutrition." . . . The right assumed in *Cruzan*, however, was not simply deduced from abstract concepts of personal autonomy. Given the common-law rule that forced medication was a battery, and the long legal tradition protecting the decision to refuse unwanted medical treatment, our assumption was entirely consistent with this Nation's history and constitutional traditions.[17]

This opinion flows from the pen of one of the most conservative and authoritarian justices in Court history; even he here could locate a "right" and, importantly, do so with zero violence to his political and interpretative constitutional commitments.

So, a zone of movement for nonamending electoral politics remained open with respect to end-of-life decisions: states could distinguish the refusal to accept medical care (including feeding tubes) from assisted suicide,[18] and states could employ a range of evidentiary standards in assessing the "decision" of the individual (e.g., "best interests," "clear and convincing," etc.), but they could not prohibit the exercise of the fundamental right (i.e., could not override a living will with a generalized state interest in the "sacredness" of life). At this juncture, all states have responded by passing laws to regulate end-of-life decision making, and at the time of Terri's Law's passage, "virtually every state had legislatively provided that individuals are entitled to specific advance directives and/or to appoint health care proxies to direct their medical treatment if they should become incompetent."[19] As in Nancy Cruzan's case, Schiavo did not have a living will either expressly stating her desires regarding medical treatment or establishing a health care proxy empowered to make end-of-life decisions. And as in Nancy Cruzan's case, the state of Florida set forth a "clear and convincing" evidentiary standard. Thus, any conflict during the resolution of this particular case would be factual absent a direct constitutional challenge to the established law.

Predictably, the initial litigation in the Schiavo case centered on fact, not law. The parties in conflict were the parents of Terri Schiavo and the husband of Terri Schiavo. Normally, statutory schemes governing in the absence of a living will designate a presumptive order of caretaking responsibility. For example: the partner/spouse first, the parents second, the court's guardianship third. The Florida statute went further and allowed family members who disputed the default proxy's decision to challenge it in court.[20] This is the legal crevice in which the familial dispute took root. As such, O. Carter Snead's point is well founded: "[B]oth the Schindlers [Terri Schiavo's parents] and Mr. Schiavo [Terri Schiavo's husband] agreed from the outset that the relevant good to be defended was Ms. Schiavo's right to autonomy and self-determination . . . all parties to the conflict agreed that self-determination was the paramount value."[21]

Based upon evidence presented at trial in 2000, a Florida judge held that Terri Schiavo would have elected to have the feeding tube removed in such a permanent vegetative condition. In early 2001, a Florida appellate court upheld the trial decision. In April 2001, the Florida Supreme Court refused to stay the order to remove the feeding tube and thus let stand the appellate court decision. After a motion was filed alleging new evidence, the case was remanded back to the trial court by the Florida appellate court. In June 2003, the trial court again ruled that the feeding tube should be removed. Again, the state appellate court upheld the decision, and again the Florida Supreme Court declined to disturb the ruling. In October 2003, the Florida legislature passed its own version of "Terri's Law" (a year and a half prior to the federal version). This law authorized Governor Jeb Bush to issue a "one-time" stay and also called for the appointment by the courts of a special guardian to issue a report on Schiavo to the governor and judiciary. The special guardian issued the following judgment: "[T]he trier of fact and the evidence that served as the basis for the decisions regarding Theresa Schiavo were firmly grounded within Florida statutory and case law, which clearly and unequivocally provide for the removal of artificial nutrition in cases of persistent vegetative states, where there is no advance directive, through substituted/proxy judgment of the guardian and/or the court as guardian, and with the use of evidence regarding the medical condition and the intent of the parties that was deemed, by the trier of fact to be clear and convincing."[22] The Florida courts again ordered the feeding tube removed and also ruled that "Terri's Law" violated the Florida Constitution.[23] After a series of stays pending further appeals, the feeding tube was removed from the body of Terri Schiavo on March 18, 2005.[24] By then, Terri Schiavo had been in a permanent vegetative state for almost fifteen years.

By this point in time, however, the factual question had begun to slip. Schiavo's parents introduced a religious dimension into the case late in the proceedings, arguing that Terri Schiavo's "soul" was in peril given recent statements by Pope John Paul II. Further, the Vatican spoke out explicitly against removing the feeding tube from Schiavo's body. Randall Terry of the antiabortion group "Operation Rescue" traveled to Florida and orchestrated vigils and demonstrations. Serious threats of assassination against court officials soon followed. These political interventions and movements quickly situated the case as a flashpoint in the contests over defining a "Right to Life." Consequently, the "public understanding of Terri Schiavo's death was refracted through the polarized politics of the abortion wars."[25] Social theorists allied with the campaigns to criminalize women who have abortions and doctors who perform them likewise linked the issues rhetorically, conceptually, and politically. Robert George of Princeton University's James Madison Program in American Ideals and Institutions argued that "those who oppose abortion, infanticide, assisted suicide, euthanasia, etc., as I do . . . view human life, even in developing or severely mentally disabled conditions, as inherently and unconditionally valuable."[26]

The religious forces on behalf of "life" were emboldened too by the calendar. The final state court order in Florida directing the removal of Schiavo's feeding tube occurred days before Palm Sunday in 2005. And like the glory of Christ entering into Jerusalem, the Congress of the United States fully entered into the Schiavo affair. From the "Palm Sunday Compromise" between the two chambers emerged the federal version of "Terri's Law." However, the divine flash seems to have blinded Congress to the fact that, properly speaking, it was no law at all. The law slices wide and deep through a variety of constitutional provisions and undoes the basic premises of the constitutional tradition while at the same time resting within some quintessential modes of "legality": the political-theological frenzy produced nothing more than a law granting federal courts "jurisdiction" in the case. The Congress simply refused to consider the Constitution as relevant,[27] yet it was not extrajudicial in its orientation: it was hyperjudicial.

Terri's Law granted the U.S. District Court jurisdiction to "hear, determine, and render judgment on a suit or claim by or on behalf of Theresa Marie Schiavo" for the violation of any right "relating to the withholding or withdrawal of food, fluids, or medical treatment." Only the parents of Terri Schiavo were granted standing in the case to file suit. Further, the law commanded that "the District Court shall determine de novo any claim of any violation of any right of Theresa Marie Schiavo . . . notwithstanding any prior State court determination and regardless of whether such a claim has previously been raised . . . the District Court shall entertain and determine the suit without delay or abstention in favor of state court proceedings." As for remedy, the law allowed for the district court to "issue such declaratory and injunctive relief as may be necessary to protect the rights of Theresa Marie Schiavo under the Constitution and the laws of the United States." The law suddenly shifts gears at this point and seeks to limit the intervention by declaring that "nothing in this act shall be construed to create substantive rights not otherwise secured by the Constitution and the laws of the United States." The singularity of the law is more deeply entrenched in the subsequent section of the act regarding time: "nothing in this act shall constitute a precedent with respect to future legislation."[28]

The Constitution of the United States contains an explicit prohibition to Congress: "No Bill of Attainder or *ex post facto* law shall be passed."[29] This limit is so central to the constitution of the Constitution that it is applied to the states as well.[30] A bill of attainder is legislation that singles out individuals or specifically named groups for forms of punishment. Tethered to the ex post facto clause, the text generates a value of generality in law and situates law within a particular conception of time. Both ideas are intertwined. Without dispute, Terri's Law singles out an individual. The constitutional question then hinges on whether the law falls within the category of being punitive. And this question leads us back to the analysis of the political values at stake.

If the "sacredness" of life trumps other values, including autonomy, then the legislation looks potentially more like relief and less like punishment: it was to "save" Schiavo.[31] But this is surely not so. Even the judicial defenders of abortion rights now use the language of "undue burden," suggesting that some burdens will be due.[32] The "culture of life" may ultimately succeed in exacting a terrible punitive price from women with unwanted pregnancies in the sacralization of the fetus, but only the depraved would call such suffering and sacrifice nonpunitive. Indeed, the punitive is integral to a broader campaign of sexual policing: in that world, burdens are *always* due. Analogously, insisting that Terri Schiavo endure decades more time on earth in a permanent vegetative state *regardless of what her wishes would have been* can be seen as punishment in the singular (a burden due), and in fact, the singularity may itself be conceived as an element of the punitive.

More damning for this legislation is the inconvenient fact that no body of U.S. law has *ever* held that a generalized "culture of life" may trump the right of the individual to refuse unwanted medical treatment. As we saw, this was at the heart of both *Cruzan* and *Glucksberg*, but it was not invented there: a conservative Court steeped in a conservative reading of due process found the right to be "deeply embedded" in the nation's law and traditions.

And it is worth recalling that the author of that opinion was Rehnquist, one of the two dissenting votes in *Roe v. Wade* and a dedicated opponent of constitutional protection for reproductive freedoms. Thus, the slippage from a question of fact to one of value (a formulation that in no way denies the value already present in fact) is of monumental importance: its real logic is a constitutional coup. Some academic defenders of the law hint at such. Robert George, for instance, states that "though we regard individual autonomy as an important value, we understand it to be an instrumental and conditional one . . . many of our opponents take precisely the opposite view: autonomy has intrinsic worth; so-called biological life is of instrumental or conditional value."[33] Michael Paulsen likewise hovers between fact and countervalue and expresses "very serious doubts about the moral propriety of the state" honoring the request "*even* where . . . the desire is expressed with unmistakable clarity."[34]

The "culture of life" perhaps signals some rival constitutional value. But a constitutional value such as this, almost by definition, must yearn for futurity and generalized applicability. A one-time law for a single individual is conceptually the antithesis of this. And such an anti-constitutional move as this clearly transgresses the guarantee of equal protection under the law. It consigns Terri Schiavo singularly to a bizarre legal universe where *Cruzan* governs the republic, but the "culture of life" governs her. Even assuming that it was designed for her "benefit," the dignity of equality is tarnished. Moreover, it assumes that the benefit of the privilege is a benefit rightly and universally desired. However, one must acknowledge a position stretching from Aristotle to Arendt that would shudder at the ease of the imagined trumping benefit of "life" extended in singular exception to the shared orders of the polity. That is, equality can be a good of such worth that the loss of it makes whatever individual gain won at its expense always a lesser value.

Terri's Law suffers from another infirmity. In placing religiosity in the governing fore, it potentially violates the principles of the First Amendment's Establishment Clause. The proliferating references to the "sacred," the evidentiary elevation of the clergy, and the open embrace of the Christian holiday by the authors of the legislation should all ring alarm bells. It seems clear that a new discursive order is attempting to congeal itself when a leading law professor on the Right writes in a prominent law review that "[r]espect for God's creatures suggests that inflicting pain or denying relief in situations where one has a duty to care is morally wrong. I believe

Michael Schiavo had an obligation to love his wife as Christ loved the Church."[35] And that regime thinks nothing of cheering the Congress on in this case for siding with Pope John Paul II in a "culture of life issue." In some sense, the case and the legislation are reduced to pure religious iconography, an expression of religious devotion. But more than that, the singularity of the case (in both time and object) oddly turns that constitutional vice into an anti-constitutional virtue: the one-time-only, the specific, the unrepeatable, and unpredictable: we have abandoned the order of the law for the structure of the miracle. And most disconcertingly: in a statute that does nothing more than grant federal courts "jurisdiction."[36]

### Rival Conceptions of "Life"

If we agree with Oliver Wendell Holmes's observation that the "life of the law has not been logic; it has been experience," what are we to make of this one? We can say that this experience exhibits a logic whereby the "culture of life" attempts to trump the "life of the law." One might say it is a fight to the death. To further explore this antagonism, to even begin to really understand the life and death of what, it will be useful to turn to another important case in constitutional law that establishes the obligations of the state (or lack thereof) in the protection of life, *DeShaney v. Winnebago County Department of Social Services*.[37] The case is perhaps best known for the brief dissent authored by Justice Harry Blackmun, a dissent that embarrassed many in the legal community for being too "emotional." That Justice Blackmun also authored the landmark case inaugurating the "culture of death," *Roe v. Wade*,[38] should not slide from our thought. Blackmun's dissent in *DeShaney* began with a lament: "poor Joshua!"

Joshua DeShaney, at the age of four, suffered a savage beating from his father that left him permanently brain-damaged and in a coma. Joshua's father abused Joshua for the duration of his young life. A year prior to the near-fatal beating, Joshua had entered the hospital covered in bruises, and the doctors reported the suspected abuse to the state's social services department. The department concluded that there was not enough evidence to remove Joshua from his father's custody, but they did offer counseling to the father. Soon after this first intervention by the state, Joshua returned to the hospital with further injuries. The state took no action. Social workers subsequently visited the DeShaney home each month and observed wounds on Joshua's head. The caseworker assigned to the case "dutifully recorded these incidents in her files, along with her continuing suspicions that someone in the DeShaney household was physically abusing Joshua, but she did nothing more."[39] A few months after this report, Joshua was again admitted to the emergency room with injuries consistent with physical abuse. The hospital communicated this information to social services, and social services visited the DeShaney home; however, the caseworker was unable to see Joshua during the visits as the father told her that Joshua "was too ill to see her."[40] Again, the state took no other action. The next recorded act of abuse left Joshua in the coma. The damage to Joshua was catastrophic: he will "spend the rest of his life confined to an institution for the profoundly retarded."[41]

Joshua's mother, who did not live in the DeShaney home, filed a lawsuit against the state of Wisconsin alleging a violation of Joshua's substantive due process rights (due process also secures the right to abortion and the right to refuse medical treatment). The Supreme Court held that the state did not violate Joshua's rights because no rights existed vis-à-vis the state in this case. Writing for a conservative-to-hard-right majority,[42] Chief Justice Rehnquist argued, "[N]othing in the language of the Due Process Clause itself requires the State to protect the life, liberty, and property of its citizens against invasion by private actors."[43] Moreover, a potential constitutional violation emerged from the opposite direction: "[H]ad [the state] moved too soon to take custody away from the father, they would likely have been met with charges of improperly intruding into the parent-child relationship, charges based on the same Due Process Clause that forms the basis for the present charge of failure to provide adequate protection."[44] Presumably, this majority would lend a more sympathetic ear to the right of the father than they did to the right of the child.

Bringing the *DeShaney* case to the fore helps illuminate critical issues in the politics of Terri's Law. The "culture of life" campaign in defense of Terri's Law advocated state action to violate the constitutional liberty interests of Terri Schiavo. Indeed, any limits imposed by the law on state interference would be trumped by "life." In much the same manner, opponents of *Roe v. Wade* feel little need to place breaks upon criminal sanction against women who elect to have an abortion. Women's liberty and women's equality are bested by the imagined state interest in the sanctity of life of the fetus.[45] So, on the matter of "state action" and private liberty, the gendered order of the power and the claimant of right inform the adjudication within a "prolife" framework. The subject of the specific right to abortion is gendered: the right to abortion is a bedrock of any possibility of women's rights as such.[46] And in the case of Terri Schiavo, like the earlier case of Karen Quinlan, it seems that the white feminine had to be rescued. Her helplessness and need for protection (*from herself*) were legible in explicitly gendered terms. As example, one legal scholar *sympathetic to* divining Terri Schiavo's intent and wishes in crisis medical situations could do so only by imagining how Schiavo would have viewed the decision: would she "have preferred to be seen as a 'loving wife' or a 'loving daughter'?"[47] A patrijuristic element is indispensable to the "culture of life."

While similarities run between these positions on liberty, a divide cuts deep on the life interest at stake. At first glance, it appears to be a simple contradiction, one captured by Justice Scalia's insistence that the sacredness of life "accorded the State the power to prevent, by force if necessary," Nancy Cruzan from refusing extraordinary medical intervention in contrast to Scalia's absolution of state indifference to the plight of Joshua DeShaney,[48] a contradiction captured by the current Republican Party's maximalist position against abortion, on the one hand, and its effort to discredit the nomination of (now-Justice) Elena Kagan to the Supreme Court for her views about *DeShaney* on the other,[49] a contradiction between the rhetoric of sacredness and the coordinated acts of fundamentalist-inspired blockades, bombings, and assassinations against abortion providers. This litany of seeming inconsistencies is sometimes produced to support an accusation of hypocrisy or "bad faith" politics by the partisans of "life," but what if instead of hypocrisy, there was a logic and a faith all too true?

That disquieting possibility is what liberal legal theorists have long sought to elide. In *Life's Dominion*, Ronald Dworkin acknowledges that a fundamentalist worldview has become more prominent in the United States and that this has contributed to an increasing polarization in politics generally and over abortion and euthanasia specifically.[50] He also recognizes the potential stakes: "[I]f the disagreement really is that stark, there can be no principled compromise but at best only a sullen and fragile standoff, defined by brute political power."[51] Spurred by a hope to avoid the "then" in that formulation, Dworkin attempts to undo the "if." Dworkin argues that, in fact, there is no radical disagreement in the constitutional and political turmoil surrounding the dominion of life. Rather, there exists a simple misunderstanding, "widespread intellectual confusion" over what the debates are really about.[52] The actual disagreement is "about how to best respect a fundamental idea we almost all share in some form: that individual human life is sacred."[53]

What Dworkin fails to engage is a sacred attachment that moves steadily against human life. Two historical events opened the door for this movement: the naturalization of end-of-life atomic rationality during the Cold War and the historicization of end-of-times Christianity with the founding of the State of Israel. Martin Jay succinctly captures this post–World War II political development: "Reinvigorated by the creation of the state of Israel in 1948, which emerged from the ashes of a penultimate holocaust, strengthened by the spread of Christian fundamentalism from the Bible Belt to new, often urban, settings, emboldened by its successful entry into the political mainstream with the rise of the New Right, religious apocalypticism has continued to grow in importance."[54]

How does one reconcile or situate an apocalyptic desire for revenge against this world with/in a discourse of "pro-life" passion? Only with the rise of this New Right do we see a "growing preoccupation, indeed obsession, with fetal life."[55] And this obsession has spread to the other end of life, to those who are here but not. Dworkin addresses these two instances as limits. The connection between abortion and euthanasia is one "between mortal questions at the two edges of normal life."[56] Apocalyptic thinking turns this formulation upside down. In his study of eschatological thinking, Jacob Taubes describes life as being "exiled in the world . . . the homeland of life is beyond the world."[57] But more, the beyond is rendered oppositionally: "Apocalypticism negates this world in its fullness. It brackets the entire world negatively."[58]

So, we can now understand the fetus and the patient in a permanent vegetative condition as negative figures vis-à-vis the life of time and history (and thus law). The fetus represents a life never-to-come, and the vegetative patient represents a death that never ends. They are the paradigmatic Edenic subjects of the culture of life and the first and last signatories to an anti-constitutional (non)order.[59] This pairing realizes in political mobilization and constitutional theory the theological reversal of Augustine in his *Confessions*: "For all I want to tell you, Lord, is that I do not know where I came from when I was born into this life which leads to death—or should I say, this death which leads to life?"[60] Shared ground thus splits open into the most elemental antagonism imaginable. Dworkin's liberalism cannot accommodate this split because it is a split with Dworkin's liberalism. William Connolly maps this antagonism as end points upon a "line of possibility," with one pole representing an "ethos of existential revenge" and the other pole signifying a "care for the future."[61]

That care for the future should become a faction in, rather than a presumption of, political life is troubling enough (and here one must note that some queer theorists on the Left have turned against futurity as well); more unsettling is the fact that the question of the "future" has become a pressing and perplexing one even for those inclined to labor on its behalf.[62] Long the ordering of the present *toward* something better than the present, the vector of futurity gathered thought and inspired political action across the spectrum of modern politics. Three thinkers in particular defined important dimensions of this increasingly eclipsed political temporality: John Stuart Mill, Karl Marx, and the Rev. Martin Luther King Jr.

Mill imagined a successful march of "Truth" through time tethered to civilizational progress differently configured in the political present: time was fractured spatially, geographically, racially. Marx discovered the path to the emancipation of laboring humanity from alienation in the unfolding world-historical logics and processes of material production: the future beckoned in the present undoing of the present as the seeds of the communist tomorrow were planted in the soil of capitalism's today. One simply had to wait for the bloom. King banked on labor in a different sense than Marx, believing that the hard work for social justice on earth occurred within a Christian metaphysics of time and that the divine arc of time nurtured and sustained the necessary labors required to bring the future about: "[T]ruth is not to be found either in traditional capitalism or in Marxism. Each represents a partial truth," and the future realizes a "synthesis which reconciles the truth of both."[63] Despite this shared progressive orientation, neither the liberal, the communist, nor the Christian socialist was blindly optimistic (or materially certain) with regard to the arrival of the future. Mill knew too well that truths could be lost and that progress could be overwhelmed by democratic absurdities and mediocrity. Marx foresaw the potential for "common ruin" in the place of universalized leisure and philosophy. And King perhaps despaired most of all that there was a possibility of being "too late" in politics and that we were in fact teetering on the brink of being there. We might even look back and think of King as the very last voice of the future, sounding when optimism and pessimism were in equipoise, when past/present/future still could hold as a coherent and viable slicing of time.

The contemporary political and theoretical consequences of the unraveling and repudiation of these progressive orientations and traditions are addressed directly by political philosopher Wendy Brown in *Politics Out of History.*[64] Brown begins the inquiry thusly: "[W]hat effects attend the emancipation of history (and the present) from a progressive narrative"?[65] More precisely: what is the condition of contemporary political life "out of these histories, indeed out of history as we have known it, which is to say, out of a history marked by the periodicity of this particular past/present/future and by the temporality of progressivism"?[66] With truth rendered infinitely plural and reduced to questions of strategy and with the proliferation of capitalist relations, ideologies, and rationalities across all of the land, Brown situates our time as being both postliberal and postmarxist. The dissolution of those twentieth-century rivals, liberalism and Marxism, leaves us utterly unmoored at best and relentlessly attached to past wounds and backward accounting at worst.[67] We can now grasp the predicament of being "out of history." Without registering agreement or disagreement on these observations and arguments at this juncture, my aim here is instead to query in response: what political projects and temporal identifications were always discordant with and discounted (or miscounted) by modernist enterprises? Brown's inquiry provokes us into asking what politics and politics of history are/have been outside of the history that we are allegedly out of; that is, what politics never were "in" it and, in fact, were arrayed against it? And to what extent do they circulate through the Schiavo affair?

A window into that outside opens in Brown's discussion of Marx and Engel's *Communist Manifesto.* Commenting upon the epoch-making influence of the text, Brown observes that "as a written text it is rivaled only by the Bible as a force in history."[68] But as Brown has helped us to see in her diagnosis of the present malaise we inhabit, forces do not simply work in history; rather, forces conjure and contour history as such. Thus, we must consider what forces kept at bay by the political forces of modernity have been unleashed upon the present by the disintegration of the latter, and what kinds of historical bearings do they inaugurate, from what counterhistories do they emerge, and to what relation do they stand to the constitutional or legal tradition under consideration?

The two primary aims of Enlightenment political projects, Truth and Emancipation, stood as the aim and end of a linear history. However "utopian" they may have been, they were resolutely conceived as earthly and realizable in human terms, even if they were shadowed conceptually by earlier theological forms and visions.[69] "Whoever takes on the apocalyptic tone comes to signify to, if not tell, you something. What? The truth, of course . . . and that is why there would not be any truth of the apocalypse that is not the truth of the truth."[70] But if the apocalyptic tone says "the end is beginning,"[71] then one must ask what is coming to an end and not just "to what ends"? For the thinkers of progress, the truth of truth would be the end of politics in the realization of life during the time of the world. For Marx, class antagonisms and the state "wither" after politics; for Mill, an eerie near-religious but not religious political silence prevails, where paradoxically the enemy of truth simultaneously heralds it; and for King, we inhabit a "beloved community" tied together in religiously informed brotherhood.[72] While Brown describes this linearity as being crippled by being "exposed epistemologically as theological," it is incumbent to recall that, however true that might be, it in no way negates the radical shift such linearity tied to reason and materialism effected.[73] Thus, what is important here is the negation of the biblical order of time for that of the *Manifesto*, to state matters loosely and crudely.

Hannah Arendt argued that Christianity broke from ancient cyclical historical orderings: "[A]ccording to Christian teachings, the relationship between life and world is the exact opposite of that in Greek and Latin antiquity: in Christianity neither the world nor the ever recurring cycle of life is immortal, only the single living individual. It is the world that will pass away; men will live forever."[74] Arendt further argued that the breaking of cyclical time by the early Christians did not in fact usher in the linear time familiar to modern accounts of history, for in "all truly Christian philosophy man is a 'pilgrim on earth' and this fact alone separates it from our own historical consciousness."[75] Our historical consciousness, by contrast, the one that Brown rightly diagnoses as being in disarray, is marked by perpetual temporal unfoldings at each end of the "present" according to Arendt: "[T]his twofold infinity of past and future eliminates all notions of beginning and end, establishing mankind in a potential earthly immortality. What at first glance looks like a Christianization of world history in fact eliminates all religious time speculations from secular history . . . thus [secular history] does not permit us to entertain eschatological expectations."[76]

A critical feature of the proliferating cracks in secular history is the reemergence of eschatological expectations in political life. These expectations are not simply entertained: they are feted. And more than a celebration of mere revelation, this orientation toward life and world does not wait faithfully or stand in anticipation: it is a movement *toward* a place out of time, the end of time. This is more than the disorganization of progress; it is the reorganization of progress in its negative form.

It may appear that this force in and of history simply materialized from the collapse of the old historical order, that it attempted to make sense when sense had evaporated. However new the appearance may be, one can still trace back through time the events and dislocations of its gathering. Nonetheless, one must admit that in this age of observation, it has remained largely hidden from sight or has stood in such plain sight that seeing it truly is simply impossible; it would be dismissed as "eccentric" or with proper temporal bite "anachronistic." In some ways, it is an echo or a repeat of the surprising birth of the modern age that it works with fury to supplant. The close observer and chronicler of that birth, Alexis de Tocqueville, was always struck by how the forces undoing the *ancien regime* had been "gathering almost as if in secret" for decades and even centuries prior to any event that would monumentalize the fact. People are "daily advancing into an unknown future, and when we think they are stationary, that is because we do not see their movements."[77] The world made "quite new" was in many regards not new at all. Only the sheer impossibility of not acknowledging it was. We must trace the contours of contemporary secrets backward in time to understand the eruption of eschatological illiberalism in American political life today.

## *Apocalyptic Time Versus Constitutional Time*

Two cities will serve symbolically as starting and centering points: Hiroshima and Jerusalem. In his early lectures on biopower, Michel Foucault identified atomic power as a paradoxical limit point in differing modalities of power.[78] On the one hand, there was nothing new in the sovereign "right to kill," even if it was now on a scale of tens of millions. The limit point for Foucault is that a nuclear barrage could terminate the logic of power in a biopolitical age and extinguish the underpinnings of a "right to make live."[79] What this formulation overlooks is how different the nuclear moment was with regards to the old sovereign right to kill. The newness was not in the numbers killed per se but in the strange asymmetry that produced them. And this is something much more than the ebb and flow of power in a war of duration, of the superiority of numbers of men, of planes, of oil, of naval ships, and so on. Prior to the bombing of Hiroshima, war had always been an affair of people on earth, and this was no less true even in the most religious of wars. One might invoke God, but one still had to mobilize and deploy men.

The mechanized slaughters of the twentieth century were no different. Consider, for example, the grim novelistic account by Remarque on the conclusion of a battle in World War I, a war in which 15 + million perished in the teeth of modern technology: "Still the little piece of convulsed earth in which we lie is still held. We have yielded no more than a few hundred yards of it as a prize to the enemy. But on every yard there lies a dead man."[80] By World War II, the bonds had begun to fray between man and earth with the supremacy of air power in ascent. Yet even here, for most of the war, it appeared as trench warfare in the sky. Mass against mass: one nation's pilots wrapped in armor confronted another nation's pilots wrapped in armor. When the bombs fell on cities, as with the German blitz of London, it was recognizable as a familiar state of siege against a political center. And in the singular horror of the Nazi Holocaust across the continent of Europe, where a near monopoly of power confronted a near nakedness of humanity, the actors nonetheless moved along at least some familiar lines: armies advancing across frontiers, troops securing occupations, cruelty moving house by house and block by block and then town by town. Such cruelty almost always bore a unique human face. The nausea induced upon reflection of the vastness of the cruelty is in many respects worsened by the intimacy of its delivery.[81] One phrase in particular is used with great frequency to describe the Nazi Holocaust and to give the slaughter a meaning that functions as a warning to the present of what rests in the realm of possibility: it was the epitome of "man's inhumanity to man."[82]

By contrast, part of what so puzzled the residents of Hiroshima in the aftermath of the American atomic attack in August 1945 (Auschwitz had been liberated by the Red Army in January 1945) was the feeling of near-total disconnect from all other previous expectations and experiences of war. The United States had been bombing Japanese cities with traditional weaponry for many months prior to August, and residents in Hiroshima were expecting to encounter a similar fate. Air raid sirens had sounded in the city for weeks, and the sound of planes flying overhead to other targets was a familiar one. It was the sound of warfare between two totally militarized societies. On August 6, 1945, the air raid sirens in Hiroshima sounded early in the morning, but soon after the "all clear sounded at eight o'clock" much to the "relief" of the city's inhabitants.[83] Japanese radar had detected a weather plane flying overhead and two or three other planes that could certainly pose no major threat to the city. For many residences, the sound of the "all clear" would be one of the last sounds they would ever hear. Not long after the "all clear," a survivor of the atomic attack would report that suddenly "everything flashed whiter than any white she had ever seen."[84]

The flash of white light that came from nowhere, that in fact came from the "all clear," killed nearly 100,000 people. Those who survived could not understand what had hit them, what kind of power had been unleashed, or from where it had come. Rumors of the weapon "were vague and incomprehensible" to the survivors in the aftermath.[85] A German Jesuit living in Hiroshima, Father Wilhelm Kleinsorge, describes how in thinking of "the terrible flash," he was later reminded of "something he had read as a boy about a large meteor colliding with earth."[86] Another survivor of the atomic blast, Hatsuyo Nakamura, confronted the wreckage of her city with a phrase of resignation: *Shikata ga-nai* (translated as "it can't be helped").[87] The white light that came from nowhere simply slipped out of previous grids of thinking and knowing about power. Father Kleinsorge had to make recourse to extraterrestrial phenomena and objects to accurately grapple with the experience; Hatsuyo Nakamura would likewise locate understanding outside of the affairs of humanity: "The hell she had witnessed and the terrible aftermath unfolding around her reached so far beyond human understanding that it was impossible to think of them as the work of resentable human beings, such as the pilot of the *Enola Gay*, or President Truman, or the scientists who had made the bomb . . . the bombing seemed a natural disaster—one that it had simply been her bad luck, her fate (which must be accepted) to suffer."[88] The break between "man's inhumanity to man" reaching its apex in Auschwitz and a hell in Hiroshima "so far beyond human understanding that it was impossible to think" of it as the "work of resentable human beings" represents an epochal rupture in political and historical time. With Hiroshima, a difference in kind and not just scale emerges in the old sovereign "right to kill." Foucault saw only an escalation of numbers on this particular point, and in fact, numbers have long dominated thinking about Hiroshima with an entire industry devoted to defending the American attack on the city with Benthamite precision and logic. However, it was more than a shift in scale (although the radical shift in scale is a subcomponent of the shift in kind) as now the power of asteroids, of nature, of gods, of God all at once fell into the hands of the leaders of leading nation-states. No political theory of sovereignty had ever contemplated such an event. *Shikata ga-nai*: an attitude once reserved for divine events enters into political life, whereas political life now busies itself with assuming the labors once thought divine.

This historical break was so profound that it could only really be captured in the absurd hyperbole common to American television talk shows. In 1955, the television show *This Is Your Life* invited a survivor of the atomic blast onto the show, and the host introduced him to the audience amid a cacophony of showbiz bells and whistles with this: "*This* is Hiroshima . . . and in that fateful second on August 6, 1945, a new concept of life and death was given its baptism. And tonight's principal subject—you, Reverend Tanimoto!—were an unsuspecting part of that concept."[89] We today are still a part of that concept and, in some regards, still without suspect. Ironically, Faulkner of all people, Faulkner who is still being cited for the proposition that the past is never past,[90] grasped the enormity of the break with the past in that moment of new baptism. Speaking in Stockholm, Sweden, in 1950 while accepting his Nobel Prize in literature, Faulkner spotted the chasm that stood between the few ticks of time separating the before and after of the fateful second: "Our tragedy today is a general and universal physical fear so long sustained by now that we can even bear it. There are no longer problems of the spirit. There is only one question: When will I be blown up? Because of this, the young man or woman writing today has forgotten the problems of the human heart in conflict with itself which alone can make for good writing because only that is worth writing about, worth the agony and the sweat. He must learn them again. . . . Until he learns these things, he will write as though he stood among and watched the end of man."[91] The new concept of life and death baptized at Hiroshima effects then not only a break with the past but also a collapse of the future into the present. The previous certainties undergirding human life have been blown to bits and will not be easily retrieved. They will have to be *learned* again. The young writer writes "as though" she stood at the end of history because the writer today in fact writes when such possibilities loom as manifestly and materially *imminent*. But this space of the "as though" is also the content of "life" after the baptism of light. It is what makes it such a "new concept."

Life and death thus reconceived, we can begin to understand what it might mean at present to be "pro-life." Faulkner divorced the problem of the spirit from the problem of being blown up. He insisted that the omnipresent threat of annihilation blotted out the spirit of man, the peculiarities of the human heart. It seems to never have occurred to Faulkner that such a nightmarish vision could be greeted not with dread but with the sound of men's hands clapping. And while the antique categories of political philosophy dissolved in the face of these new powers on and over and against earth, contemporary conceptualizations within the tradition of constitutional thought would prove likewise incapable of reckoning with the sound of those hands clapping. That tradition remains incapable of even hearing them and so frets not about the consequences of not reckoning. If we could hear, with what would we reckon?

We would reckon with the Revelation of John or, more precisely, with the political animation of the Revelation of John: the end of the earth as an earthly political project. For the new concept of life and death opened the door to a timely realization of "a new heaven and a new earth."[92] And by this, I mean a disposition toward life and earth not confined to a theology, although the theology will be indispensable to the disposition. Hiroshima was only one door in a set of doubles: Jerusalem too would soon swing open. Echoing if not mirroring the historical split within Jewish Zionism, between a secular project for nationality irrespective of geographic location and a nationalist project unimaginable absent a divinely ordained location, Christian supporters of the founding of Israel also split between liberal desires for justice in the wake of vicious (and, after 1940, genocidal) anti-Semitism and theological longings for a return of Jews as a people to the lands of Jerusalem.[93]

President Truman recognized the State of Israel on May 14, 1948, the same day that the provisional government of Israel declared statehood. The recognition was brief, a few sentences devoid of religious perspective.[94] However, as early as 1932, American political figures articulated their support for the Zionist project in explicitly scriptural terms. For example, the American Palestine Committee, chaired by New York senator Robert Wagner, viewed the possibility of a nation of Israel in Palestine as the potential "fulfillment of the millennial hope for the reunion of the Jewish people with the land of its ancient inheritance, a hope that accords with the spirit of biblical prophecy."[95] In contradistinction to Faulkner's questions of the spirit, the spirit of biblical prophecy summoned the end of man, or the end of the world in which man lived, beyond all "agony and sweat," in the name of "hope." Most critically, this hope no longer required a patient and pious faith in the return of the Christian's savior. As Rabbi Dan Cohn-Sherbok has observed, deliverance was no longer a divine affair; "it required labor."[96]

Christian thought that is otherworldly is not new. Many religious scholars locate the origins of Christian thought with Augustine, describing him as the "real founder of Western Christendom." [97] Augustine reformulated Aristotle's original demarcation between the life of politics and mere life.[98] In Aristotle, the ethical dilemma emerged at the pivot of "difference," but in Augustine, that dilemma was "solved" through Christian universalism. Animal life and the life of man have, to crucial extent, merged: "[M]an, who would have become spiritual even in his flesh had he kept the commandment [in Paradise], now became fleshly even in his mind; and he who, in his pride, had pleased himself, was now, by God's justice, handed over to himself."[99] But for Augustine, man over to himself must be against himself: Aristotle's distinction again holds, but now as no distinction at all. Politics, no longer the preserve of rational animal, is now the shelter of sinful animal: irredeemable here on earth. Otherworldliness is thus not just a devotion to another world but devotion set in opposition to this one. The turn is against, not away. Here is Augustine: "[T]he 'animal' man is not different from the 'fleshly' man. Rather, they are one in the same: that is, man living according to man."[100] This distinction that no longer is a distinction carries theological significance: "[W]hen a man lives according to man and not according to God, he resembles the devil." And again, it stands directly against life on earth: " '[I]f any man love the world, the love of the Father is not in him.' "[101] If life itself (the life of man that is already in its entirety "fleshly") signals the absence of the Holy Father (an absence that is/resembles the devil, evil itself), the good Christian possesses a certain duty toward the world: "a duty of perfect hatred."[102] This duty of perfect hatred rests in and emerges from the politically impotent space of refuge and exile, and here one can reconcile it with life on earth as it stands removed from it, but when it enters the life of the world and the politics of man (as with Constantine's conversion)—and when it is joined with Augustine's blurring of death and life (as in the *Confessions*)—the logical end of politics shifts from the Aristotelian management of "mere life" with the telos of a "good life" to the total annihilation of life itself.

Of course, to be fair to Augustine, the usurpation of God's power by men would be the most sinful thing imaginable. But then, such a thought was, even in extremis, completely unimaginable for Augustine. His outlook remained deeply spiritual. This is what enables Arendt to say that "Augustine's attitude toward secular history is essentially no different from that of the Romans, albeit the emphasis is inverted: history remains a storehouse of examples, and the location of events in time within the secular course of history remains without importance."[103] So we must not blame the Bishop of Hippo for the madness of our time. That would be cruel. He wrote before the baptism of light, after which religious concepts would proliferate throughout political life but now completely void of their original bearings.

Today the Augustinian inversion of Roman history is in a state of collapse. Increasingly large and important sectors of American Christianity now locate the spirit contra the flesh within the river of historical time and events. Augustine's otherworldly spiritual faith is converted into labor and toil. The director of the International Christian Zionist Center in Jerusalem explains the breakdown of the inversion: "The Bible, revered by true Christians as the inerrant Word of God, is really 'just' the history of the land and people of Israel. Of course, I am not here dismissing the sacredness of the Scriptures. My purpose is simply to emphasize a basic truth that has all but evaporated during 2000 years of Christian teaching, teaching which has successfully managed to 'spiritualize' in our thinking the very physical realities penned on the Bible's pages."[104] Such thinking is challenged in some of the mainline Protestant denominations, but the divines of the New Right almost wholly embrace this view. Jerry Falwell instructed his flock that it was their "Christian duty to God to support the Jewish state in fulfillment of biblical prophecy," and Pat Robertson has stated that the political goal is nothing less than the fulfillment of "end time prophecy."[105] In addition to speeding up the time of the end of time, many also see the tribulations of Revelations as no longer the work of God but authored by man. Hal Lindsey, author of the *Late Great Planet Earth* (a work of Christian apocalyptic "nonfiction" that has sold over 30 million copies since being published in 1970),[106] read the history in the Bible to read the Bible in history and predicted that Israel will be the "Ground Zero in the end times events . . . there will be a full-scale exchange of nuclear weapons, and it is at this time that 'the cities of the nations will fall.'"[107]

Far from being fringe views, these prophets have been at the seat of political power in the Republican Party since the election of Ronald Reagan in 1980. And aside from this or that particular policy decision, the New Right's understanding of the future has made deep cultural inroads in the wake of the dawn of the atomic age and the return of Jewish sovereignty to ancient lands. By 1984, four out of ten Americans believed that "when the Bible speaks of the Earth being destroyed by fire, this means that we ourselves will destroy the earth in a nuclear Armageddon."[108] And this apocalyptic vision is the telos at the end of *a*, and the end *of*, political desire. In the place of reason's Truth, labor's Emancipation, or fellowship's Community stands only the "worthless rock hanging tideless in the last red and dying evening."[109]

This future that is no future is the temporal axis around which the law that is no law spins. In the previous chapter on torture, we saw that the return of the "rule of law" (already backward gazing in the very desire for a "return") offered slim grounds for justice given that the return promised a campaign of depoliticization at a moment when racial, class, and imperial powers work through the law to secure their continuity. Legality sans politics is a political position. But does this mean that justice stands hopelessly estranged from the law? In her reading of Derrida's *Specters of Marx*, Wendy Brown highlights the temporal dimension of Derrida's thinking about justice. Justice is "less institutional or spatial than temporal . . . not only must justice have futurity—it is what *makes* futurity, insofar as it generates the future's relationship to the present as a 'living on' of present efforts and aims."[110] But for Derrida and Brown, the law lacks the capacity to transmit the present into the future, to mobilize the forces to make the future so. This inability to project futurity stems from the fact that "justice cast in legal terms repeats the fundamental practices of the current order of justice and thus condemns us to the out-of-jointedness of our time."[111]

Hewing to the terminology of Brown and Derrida, it appears at first glance that Marx haunts their thinking about the law and justice. After all, it was Marx who leveled devastating critiques of the "rights of man" that burst forth with the American and French Revolutions.[112] Moreover, it was also Marx who directed our gaze away from the state and its official vocabulary to the circuitries of value at the heart of production as the primal scene of domination and unfreedom.[113] However, the turn away from the law by Brown and Derrida in this instance is in terms not particularly Marxist in their provenance: "What conventionally sets time right again is the law; but in Derrida's account, law's traditional connection with vengeance, and even with blood revenge, can do no more than perpetuate the out-of-jointness of the times . . . [a] formulation of justice intended to rectify that disjointedness must rely on something other than the law; for Derrida, it must be beyond right, debt, calculation, and vengeance."[114] It appears now that the haunting of Brown reading Derrida reading Marx is Nietzsche. With Nietzsche, they castigate the backward gaze of the debtor and the future-denying longing for revenge.[115] Yet Nietzsche understood the law as being originally the home of those *not* mired in guilt or paralyzed by a hunger for vengeance. Here is Nietzsche: "From a historical point of view, law represents on earth—let it be said to the dismay of the above-named agitator [Eugen Duhring] (who himself once confessed that: 'the doctrine of revenge is the red thread of justice that runs through all of my efforts')—the struggle against the reactive feelings, the war conducted against them on the part of the active and aggressive powers."[116] In a sense, the *repoliticization* of the law is made possible by Nietzsche's rediscovery of war at the center of law's founding and being. And if today the law is "sickly" and incapable of futurity, then surely it is because the "will to power" of the meek has overrun this original citadel of the strong. Here, still keeping with Nietzsche, we might say that what is needed is a revaluation of values, the revaluation of the value of law in our political thinking.

In so doing, we will have to reevaluate and revalue the idea of law without letting it become a historically empty concept (this is a mistake Derrida often makes that Brown almost never does). Both Marx and Nietzsche situate the law within the struggles for power in history. In Marx, the constitutional revolutions of the democratic capitalist age signaled and sustained the arrival of new modes of production and the new class formations and societies that emerged with them. They epitomized futurity in that they broke the older land-based feudal orders. In addition, the law was to assist in securing the *future* of capital. This was true not in any particular decision but in the very frameworks within which decision making would transpire. And bourgeois society (and here we must include its law) was neither static nor nostalgic. Indeed, Marx argued that its very existence was predicated upon "constantly revolutionizing the instruments of production, and thereby the relations of production, and with them the whole relations of society."[117] And without being too reductive, we can look to the great transformations of public and private law in the United States to see this revolutionary process: the disintegration of the constitutionally sacrosanct right to contract, the emergence of welfare state jurisprudence with regards to national regulatory power, the centering of cost-benefit analysis in the shifts of burden and liability in modern tort law, the reconceptualization of the corporate entity as an organism capable of "political speech," and so on.

Nietzsche's view of the democratic age was far dimmer than Marx's (who critically saw the bourgeois revolutions as "progress"). Consequently, his vision remained blind to the great creative energy unleashed by those revolutions. This world-making energy is what Marx thought could be harnessed and what Tocqueville thought needed to be tamed.[118] Our reevaluation and revaluation of "law" will hinge, in part, upon where one ultimately stands in this divide between Nietzsche, on the one hand, and Marx and Tocqueville, on the other.

## Conclusion

The revolutionary character of the United States' constitutional heritage is difficult to deny. It is embedded in the very notion of a written constitution. In a brief address to the Association of American Law Schools, political theorist Hanna Pitkin proposed that we consider the "idea of a constitution" in two senses of its use. The first sense relates to the constitutive elements of a whole, as in Aristotle's "shared way of life in the *polis*."[119] The second sense refers to the "human capacity to act, to innovate, to break the causal chain of process and launch something unprecedented."[120] In addition to launching, that capacity must realize itself across time and into the future. As Pitkin put it, "To constitute, one must not merely become active at some moment but must establish something that lasts, which, in human affairs, inevitably means something that will enlist and be carried forward by others."[121] If justice makes futurity (per Brown and Derrida) and if futurity is the indispensable element to the idea of a constitution (per Pitkin), then the frayed connections between law and justice must begin to be restitched. For it is the refusal to "carry forward" that defines so much of the anti-constitutionalist Right in American politics and is in fact what makes that force anti-constitutionalist. Their future that is no future threatens to rob all of us of any possibility of forging one and as such stands against both justice in time and freedom in life. Recognizing this entails a certain refusal to accept a binarized choice between a turn toward/turn away from the law. Indeed, it seems that deconstruction would undo the neatness of an inside/outside "law" wherein/without justice might find home. In this hyperephemeral age, when "economic, social, and technological transformations occur so rapidly that they often do not even achieve solidity before metamorphosizing into something else,"[122] we must see in the law something other than a set of codes tied logically to a specific order of rule and instead (or in addition) see it as a critical place of memory, a reminder that the capacity to break causal chains and to carry new things forward in political life on earth is forever possible.

*Chapter 4*

# Sovereign Power and Life Amid New Kings and Old Tutors

> *The whole affair is a* felo de se.
>
> —Thomas Paine, *Common Sense*

If the emergence of "the people" and their sovereignty fits within the first part of Hanna Pitkin's definition of a constitution (as acting to "launch something unprecedented"), the question remains whether that power established itself as "something that lasts."[1] The question posed here is a question rooted in the historical and political specificity of the U.S. constitutional tradition and is not a generalized theoretical inquiry into constituent/ constituted power per se. The dual specter of lawlessness and politics haunted the founding generation as well, but it emerged from a worry about constitutional power rather than a response to anti-constitutional politics. A question to consider: to what extent does the Constitution itself represent or carry within it a certain kind of anti-constitutional logic? To enter these questions, it may be useful to turn the assertion—"the Constitution is not a suicide pact"—into a question.

## Is the Constitution a Suicide Pact?

At the midpoint of the past century, in the Supreme Court case of *Terminiello v. Chicago* (1949), Justice Robert Jackson issued a dissenting opinion that introduced a consequential maxim of constitutional interpretation and thus a theory of constitutional order: "There is danger that, if the Court does not temper its doctrinaire logic with a little practical wisdom, it will convert the constitutional Bill of Rights into a suicide pact."[2] The case involved a public speech at an assembly hall by a right-wing agitator, Father Terminiello. Terminiello's speech denounced "Communist Jewish Zionism" while also hurling insults at the crowd protesting his speech outside of the hall. The protesting crowd replied with cries of "Fascists!" and surged into the hall, causing a small melee: broken windows, stink bombs, and scuffles between foes. The City of Chicago charged Father Terminiello with breach of the peace, and the jury instructions "permitted conviction of petitioner if his speech stirred people to anger, invited public dispute, or brought about a condition of unrest."[3] The jury convicted. The majority of the Supreme Court (it was a 5–4 decision) overturned this conviction and held that this jury instruction violated the Constitution.[4]

Justice Jackson accused the majority of skirting the messy particulars of the tumultuous facts for the calm abstractions of First Amendment theorization. The chastisement in full: "The Court reverses this conviction by reiterating generalized approbations of freedom of speech with which, in the abstract, no one will disagree. Doubts as to their applicability are lulled by avoidance of more than passing reference to the circumstances of Terminiello's speech and judging it as if he had spoken to persons as dispassionate as empty benches, or like a modern Demosthenes practicing his Philippics on a lonely seashore."[5] This turn to circumstance unwittingly generates its own abstraction through which to think the particular. Justice Jackson's hypothetical instances of when a First Amendment situation would be most easy to judge is strangely no First Amendment situation at all. "Political" speech has long resided at the apex of speech protected by the First Amendment. Yet Jackson gives us scenes without people (plural) and speech without listeners (even in the singular): they are void of either disagreement or consent, as either fact or potential. In the place of exchange, we find soliloquy. If Terminiello had preached to empty benches or endless seas, there would have been nothing to judge at all.

This production of an ideal speech situation that is no speech situation thus suggests the possibility that Jackson has performed the very act he feared: he has produced a political dead space, a perfect political void. It is a suicide act converted from a jurisprudence of stillness rather than one too sympathetic to discord. Dispassionateness, the condition coterminous with emptiness, is heralded as a communicative virtue rather than the antidemocratic wonder it is. Here is Jackson elaborating on the reason for his dissent:

"[W]e must bear in mind also that no serious outbreak of mob violence . . . or public disorder is likely to get going without help of some speech-making to some mass of people. A street may be filled with men and women, and the crowd still not be a mob. Unity of purpose, passion and hatred, which merges the many minds of a crowd into the mindlessness of a mob, almost invariably is supplied by speeches. It is naive, or worse, to teach that oratory with this object or effect is a service to liberty. No mob has ever protected any liberty, even its own, but, if not put down, it always winds up in an orgy of lawlessness."[6] If unity and passion are wedded together into an orgy of lawlessness, then the rule of law must produce the antithetical couple of individuation and dispassion. But again, the logic of this formula produces both the empty bench and the lonely shore as *ideal*. Jackson may have been intentionally absurd, but the marking of an outer limit is quite often the opening of a window into inner thought.

The majority opinion of Justice William O. Douglas did not simply weigh the "risks" slightly differently than Justice Jackson and then decide they were worth taking. Rather, Justice Douglas challenged the fear of sui-cide with a theory of life that reconceived the danger and thus offered a rival political value and vision. Contrary to Justice Jackson's assertion that the majority chose abstraction to fact, the majority embraced the facts to guide the abstraction. In short, the majority did not flee the orgy; they sanctified it as the heart of democracy and thus paradoxically (as the orgy was one of "lawlessness") deserving of legal protection. Even more, Justice Douglas argued that the "vitality of civil and political institutions" did not simply require a begrudging tolerance of rancor and debate; instead, vitality flowed from precisely these actions. The "function of free speech under our system of government is to invite dispute," Douglas insisted.[7] But he also pressed well beyond this Millian framing and claimed that free speech "may indeed best serve its high purpose when it induces a condition of unrest, creates dissatisfaction with conditions as they are, or even stirs people to anger."[8] To translate into Jackson's vocabulary, the vitality of political life depends, at least in part, on the passionate rousing of a mob from the crowd.

The art and science of distinguishing between the crowd and the mob, the anxieties of not being able to do so, the worries of not properly policing the demarcation once drawn, all of this is as old as the republic.[9] Justice Jackson's dissent thus carries forward almost two centuries of hard-won knowledge and deeply embedded fears. The disagreement between Justice

Jackson and Justice Douglas on a jury instruction in a misdemeanor case in Chicago reveals fissures and factions in political life and thought that are as enduring as they are profound. On this point, they both agree. For Jackson, the decision threatens to transform the Constitution into a suicide pact. What is in jeopardy of being nullified by the "most extravagant hopes of both right and left totalitarian groups" is local democratic governance and public order.[10] For Justice Douglas, the *vitality* of political life is at stake. And here we might take into account two meanings and temporalities of vitality. Vitality signals strength, vigor, exertion, and development; it is future oriented. But in medical discourse, vitality is also an immediate and existential question, for vitality is the "peculiarity distinguishing the living from the nonliving."[11] Potentiality presumes existence, but existence also requires potentiality. And it is the tumultuousness of politics rather than the orderliness and prestige of local authority that ensures both and also that which "sets us apart from totalitarian regimes."[12]

One might read this exchange as a set of argumentative moves interesting and relevant only to historians of Cold War liberalism and of no import to political theorists of the present. However, Justice Jackson's argument has survived and thrived out of that original context. It has, as is said, "taken on a life of its own." His pithy admonition that the Constitution must not become a "suicide pact" has endured because it so perfectly flatters the age. Unmoored from the particular case, it floats freely as an ideal adjudicatory supplement in an age of cost-benefit rationality, state authoritarianism, and ongoing imperial crisis.[13] It carries and facilitates violence and domination within the "rule of law" and in the most lawyerly fashion. Its real magic is that it seems nearly incapable of locating firm limits while nonetheless professing them the sine qua non of law.[14]

Arguments put forth by Alan Dershowitz (a leading "liberal" lawyer) on the legalization of preemptive and preventive torture offer a glimpse into this legal order. Dershowitz concedes that "the rule of law requires that all governmental action be subjected to legal constraints."[15] But the constraint is necessarily loosened by the need for a balancing act, although it is the balancing act that is supposed to produce the constraint. Dershowitz continues, "Democracies seek to operate within the rule of laws, and laws must realistically reflect the desirable balance between the legitimate needs of security and the equally legitimate claims of human rights."[16] However, the needs of security are so infinite that they threaten to outstrip the capacities of the law entirely: "'[T]he survival of states is not a matter of law.' "[17] So the survivability of the state trumps the survivability of the rule of law even as the latter is allegedly the sign of democracy itself. As such, the law must perform its own self-negation to "survive" along with the state it now serves under rather than over. Unsurprisingly, Dershowitz concludes his argument with this: "[T]o paraphrase Robert Jackson . . . the law must not be 'a suicide pact.' "[18]

As we just saw, however, suicide has not been avoided; for the state to live to its potential, the law must potentially perish. And because the law desires nothing other than the survival of the state in the final instance, it will suffer auto-immolation to ensure it. Everything must be balanced, and at the end, we discover decisive and true values. But because the law endured into the final hour, because it was not suspended but enveloped, we can attest that the rule of law was never violated. And since the law has made a pact to follow the state until the end of time, there is no time without the law, and this time of law is what grounds the violence waged in the name of the state: it is an ultimate virtue that is ultimately sacrificable. Here, we have the absolute nullification of vitality; it is now Justice Douglas's position that is forced into the dissent.

But the question now really is: the vitality of what? The self-sacrificial capacity of the law turns Justice Jackson's dictate that the law must not be a suicide pact into a riddle: who was/are the self-preserving subjects of the forbidden pact? If the state is that which must be not be sacrificed by the law, that which may ultimately sacrifice the law, then what pact binds the state? Or what binding pacts produce the state? Now we have wandered into the well-tilled fields of social contract. But even here (or especially here), the law that must not be a suicide pact is predicated on the very potentiality of such an act at any and every moment of enforcement. This is what leads Hobbes to say that "he that attempteth to depose his Soveraign, be killed, or punished by him for such attempt, he is the author of his own punishment."[19] This is not lessened by Hobbes's argument that no subject may be forced to harm himself as it runs counter to the "[e]nd for which the Soveraignty was ordained." That one may justly disobey a sovereign's command to "kill, wound, or mayme himself" is to only claim that the *end* of the pact logically is not suicide, but that does not mean that the law ever escapes its potentiality (as opposed to end; in paradoxical realization of ends) as a suicide pact.

Nonetheless, Hobbes's qualification is a critical one. It forces the question: what is the difference between a pact with the end of suicide and a pact with the omnipresent risk of suicide? Hobbes views the former as a logical impossibility when it comes to the covenants of sovereignty since the only motive and aim of sovereign pacts is "the foresight of their own preservation, and of a more contented life thereby; that is to say, of getting themselves out of that miserable condition of Warre."[20] After all, the sword is hitched to the covenant to "secure a man" who desires not political freedom but freedom from worry. And the bonds of political life dissolve when that protection wavers: "The Obligation of Subjects to the Soveraign, is understood to last as long, and no longer, than the power lasteth, by which he is able to protect them."[21] Man is thus not a political animal; he is an anxious one.

Dershowitz's liberalism inverts Hobbesian protoliberalism in one aspect and apparently realizes it in another. In order for the state to act, to produce the conditions of its action, it must saturate the life of the commonwealth with fear, not of certain punishment and awe, but of an open-ended "condition of Warre." Today, Dershowitz explains, we cannot simply hold prisoners "until the end of the war, because this is a war that will never end."[22] Dershowitz empowers the Leviathan on the basis of unending war, but it was only on the promise of the cessation of that "miserable condition" that men covenanted to produce its power. Moreover, the state now has an existence divorced from its aim of protection: "States will do what they deem necessary, not only to ensure their own survival, but also to protect the lives of their citizens from catastrophic threats."[23] We must rest for a moment with this "but also."

The disjunction between the existence of the state and the life of the citizen by Dershowitz echoes an observation that Sheldon Wolin made on the withdrawn and radical atomization of political life in Hobbes's thought: "The epitaph of the political community was that 'the individual existence has little embodiment in political existence.'"[24] It is this disjunction between the life of the state and the life of the citizen that bifurcates the inquiry into the parties of the (non)suicide pact. The bifurcation intensifies even more when Dershowitz altogether drops the figure of the citizen for the profoundly depoliticized life of the "civilian." In this new order (where the laws of war have merged with the laws of governance), we have nothing but belligerent combatants and innocent civilians. And the "innocent life" of the civilian is treasured insofar as it never wanders off that conceptual reservation. This explains, in part, why any political dissent or mobilization against the War on Terror was so quickly swept into a division of for/against this or that belligerent and why this then crisscrossed any actual formal barriers or boundaries of inside/outside the nation-state.

If the citizen is severed conceptually from participation in political life, and if the citizen decomposes further into the innocent civilian (his innocence as an a priori can only be such in a situation where the life of the polity and the life of the citizen have been constitutionally reconfigured as strangers; that is, when the most vital of vital signs in democratic life are not present, not even faintly), then the penultimate adjudicatory rule of law in the rule of law (for the ultimate will not be adjudicatory) has killed the imagined authorizing subject of the law in the United States' constitutional system: the people as a People (however conceived or construed as partial or aspirational or fictive or hegemonic).[25] We are thus confronted with either a homicidal act or a suicidal pact and must determine which. Or is it both—in that the coup d'état performed a coup de grâce on the self-wounded creature?

### Individualism and Slavery

The establishment of the Constitution in 1787 presupposed the existence of the people in contradistinction to persons. The people were new as both a political power but also a simple sociological fact: memories of arrival in the New World were fresh. Moreover, despite the racial exclusions and dominations at the constitutional core of the people, they bore the traces of differential origins. Thomas Paine, who did perhaps more than any other thinker in the eighteenth century to conjure and bind the people into a people, extolled those differences in both repudiating the fantasy of England as the "mother country" and finding common ground and "common sense" in political values rather than origin fables. These two moves were intertwined. Paine wrote in 1776, "[N]ot one third of the inhabitants, even of this province [Pennsylvania], are of English descent. Wherefore I reprobate the phrase of parent or mother country applied to England only, as being false, selfish, narrow and ungenerous."[26] Paine saw in the people's differences the shared experience of flight and shared political basis for flight: "This new world hath been the asylum for the persecuted lovers of civil and religious liberty from *every part* of Europe. Hither they have fled, not from the tender embraces of the mother, but from the cruelty of the monster."[27]

This reading of Paine is in accord with Jason Frank's argument that "the people are a political *claim*, an act of political subjectification, not a pregiven, unified, or naturally bounded empirical entity."[28] With the emphasis on "claim," Frank works to center the contestation and incompleteness in any and all invocations of the people. To paraphrase Frank, no representation can ever represent the people in full. Unlike Frank, my interest is less in the "claim" (who is and is not in the people, who does and does not represent the people, etc.) and more in the "political" values in the subjectification as such.[29]

The Constitution by the People[30] required first the constitution of the people. Or, at the very least, the Constitution by the people would have to simultaneously have been the constitution of the people.[31] In fact, the people that emerged were already ascendant before and during the Revolution. And this political ascendancy was so entrenched by the time of the 1787 Constitution that there was no going back to, or constituting anew, feudal or aristocratic orders. This political change was also a social change, and there was no corner of society that remained untouched by this ascendancy. All boundaries of rank were eroding. Lower orders trampled upon old distinctions: "Farmers called themselves yeoman and gentleman at the same time."[32] Historian Gordon Wood has described the republican revolution of the eighteenth century as inaugurating "nothing less than new ways of organizing society."[33] It "offered new conceptions of the individual, the family, the state, and the individual's relationship to the family, the state and other individuals."[34] Thomas Jefferson argued that this world-remaking force was invigorating to the individual and the polity. Equality was vitality for both: " '[T]he sickly, weakly, timid man fears the people . . . the healthy, strong and bold, cherishes them.' "[35]

The individual's relationship to other individuals appeared as nothing more than a relationship between individuals. Individuals made history by abolishing it. If history was a majestic stage, the primary actors had exited. There were to be only private dramas now. Our time is thus not the first time that imagined it stood at history's end. This conceit, of course, was the basis and target of Marx's critique of the epoch. Looking at the French Revolution, Marx found it perplexing that "a nation which has just begun to liberate itself, to tear down all the barriers between different sections of the people and to establish a political community, should solemnly proclaim (*Declaration* of 1791) the rights of egoistic man, separated from his fellow men and from the community."[36] He also spied an inversion of revolutionary practice and natural-right theory. In practice, "the right of liberty ceases to be a right as soon as it comes into conflict with political life, whereas in theory political life is no more than the guarantees of the rights of man. . . . But practice is only the exception, while theory is the rule."[37] The contradiction between the exception and rule is resolved in the establishment of the law and the birth of the constitutional state: "The *formation of the political state*, and the dissolution of civil society into independent *individuals* whose relations are regulated by law, as the relations between men in the corporations and guilds were regulated by privilege, are accomplished by *one and the same act*."[38]

Marx throws light on the movement of power from the nakedly despotic state into the naturalized society of liberty in the very act of establishing the professed neutrality of the state in matters of despotism in the name of liberty. The protection of despotism from the reach of a politics is ensured and regulated by the rule of law. The rule of law is the cause and consequence of the cleavage between freedom in the state and freedom from the state. That is to say, the rule of law in the age of constitutionalism is not a guarantee of life as such but is always and inextricably tied to the production and protection of a particular way of life. That particularity is a political project, and consequently the rule of law is already something more than a pact of self-defense even in its most purely atomized articulation.

The simultaneous action of rooting the public law in the imagined natural life of man *and* the naturalization of the life of man as apolitical in the political act of lawmaking is not a peculiar move of the French Revolution. Marx tracked it back to the many constitutions of the American states in the late eighteenth century. However, this order of thought swept up thinking beyond the formalities of this or that particular constitution. It defined the age and found its fullest realization in the writing of the great propagandist for that age, Thomas Paine. Paine believed that where the rule of law was absent, "freedom" was in a "fugitive" condition.[39] It was fugitive in two senses: it was on the run from "tyranny" but also ephemeral in every instant if not constituted in and as law. Without law, there was only power "granted by courtesy," and courtesy was the opposite of right, the enemy of right. Law thus became nearly synonymous with freedom and the necessary and proper telos of political revolt. Paine diagnosed the rapidly deteriorating colonial situation as being governed by "legislation without law," and this left the "mind of the multitude" with no "fixed object before them."[40] The rule of law would both banish the capriciousness of courtesy and focus the minds of the many on proper objects. The multitude would be commonly aligned, an alignment that was the first task and precondition of the rule of law, without being perfectly unified. Paine argued, "For as in absolute governments the King is law, so in free countries the law *ought* to be King."[41]

The new law-king arose from the sum power of individuals and aimed at preserving the prepolitical preconditions of that power: "[E]very man wishes to pursue his occupation, and to enjoy the fruits of his labours, and the produce of his property in peace and safety . . . when these things are accomplished, all the objects for which government ought to be established are finished."[42] The people were enshrined into sovereignty in a double sense: individually and collectively. And at the same moment, a fissure appeared in sovereignty between law, on the one side, and the people, on the other. This fissure in some ways tracks with Marx's mapping of a series of disjunctions that signal the impossibility of freedom in the new age (without an account of the duality of the people beyond the exception/rule contradiction in revolutionary/theoretical extremis). Because Paine could never really get beyond a trustee-delegation mode of constitutional imagining, the constitutional subject of the people as a collective force could not endure beyond the moment of founding. The law would trump the people (and again, the content is not of concern at this moment) in the name of individual sovereignty. Here is Paine describing this transfer of power and the crowning of the law-king: "But where says some is the King of America? I'll tell you Friend, he reigns above, and doth not make havoc of mankind like the Royal Brute of Britain. Yet that we may not appear to be defective even in earthly honors, let a day be solemnly set apart for proclaiming a charter; let it be brought forth placed on the divine law, the word of God; let a crown be placed thereon, by which the world may know, that so far as approve of monarchy, that in America THE LAW IS KING. . . . But lest any ill use should afterwards arise, let the crown at the conclusion of the ceremony be demolished, and scattered among the people whose right it is."[43] The smashing of collective sovereignty at the revolutionary moment of an insurgent collectivity in revolt is the decapitation of the people in the name of a law that presumes and produces the sovereign individual. It is the self-inflicted wound Marx saw so clearly.

This wound haunts Paine's thinking, and he exhibits something of a desire to undo it or a regret for having done it or a magical thinking of not having done it at all. Today it is the still-open wound that so many of our legal theorists spend careers rubbing salt into; they imagine it as ointment.[44]

But again to Paine. After securing the right of now-sovereign, now-divine individuals to pursue their own paths of commerce and enjoy the minor fruits of their labor, Paine frets, "[C]ommerce diminishes the spirit, both of patriotism and military defense."[45] Moreover, he revalues the law as now a good in itself and not simply a means to an end; it is its own end when it is *ours*.[46] This is why patriotism must not be deflated by an ethos of commerce. And it is why the breaking of the bonds of political solidarity is a crime far greater than even a military action against independence. Paine writes that a "distinction should be drawn, between, English soldiers taken in battle, and inhabitants in America taken in arms. The first are prisoners, but the latter traitors. The one forfeits his liberty, the other his head."[47] There are no calculations of summed happiness here. The politics of friendship and equality establishes a new measure of freedom. It is the same revaluation that a decade later led the French revolutionaries to declare that the existence of Louis XVI represented a crime per se. "The people's victory made him alone a rebel," Robespierre said, and the French reached the same verdict on treason as the Americans did.

If Hobbes thought individual life was inalienable in the logic of contractual sovereignty, the theorists of the American Revolution pledged life itself in the name of an emergent popular sovereignty. Hannah Arendt famously celebrated what she took as the principles of American Revolution (in sharp distinction to the French) and thought the Declaration of Independence was one of its signatures. Arendt thought the "principle" of the republic was "present in the 'mutual pledge' of life, fortune, and sacred honour, all of which, in a monarchy, the subjects would not 'mutually pledge to each other,' but to the crown."[48] But the mutuality of the pact, a pact between citizens or subjects, could certainly be present in a monarchy as well as a republic. Hobbes taught us that an implied horizontal contract could ground a vertical and total monarchical power. Thus, mutuality is not what distinguishes the American effort: political vitality is. In this sense, Arendt is correct in spying the importance of a *double* dimension in the "happiness" pursued in the Declaration of Independence.[49] And in so doing, she (perhaps unintentionally) reminds us that the division of the political (the realm of chimerical rights for Marx, the space of action and freedom for Arendt) and civil society (the true zone of human unfreedom for Marx, the place where political freedom was nonsensical and mute for Arendt) had not been fully established and perhaps never has (contra Marx and Arendt).

To continue onward with our inquiry into the jurisprudential maxim that the law is not a suicide pact, let us look more closely at life and law in the Declaration of Independence. As noted, the original pledge was one of life, fortune, and honor (even as the Declaration declares "certain unalienable Rights" such as "Life, Liberty, and the Pursuit of Happiness"). The sacrificial pledging was the opposite of both the apocalyptic nihilism of the contemporary anti-constitutionalist Right as well as the innocent-civilian rationalization of today's torture-proceduralism liberals. The Declaration argued that it was the "Right of the People" (and even their "duty") to slough off despotism and institute a new government to "provide new Guards for their *future* security."[50] But the security was not so much for the individual person as it was for the people and their political constitution and thus their capacities as law-kings. This difference is certainly not categorical, absolute, or relentlessly maintained in the Declaration; it was, however, real.

The Declaration justified itself with a recitation of the "long train of abuses" suffered by the people at the hands of the king of Great Britain. The Declaration lists twenty-seven specific indictments against the king. The first: "He has refused his Assent to Laws, the most wholesome and necessary for the public good." Second: "He has forbidden his Governors to pass Laws of immediate and pressing importance, unless suspended in their operation till his Assent should be obtained; and . . . he has utterly neglected to attend them." Third: "He has refused to pass other Laws for the accommodation of large districts of people, unless those people would relinquish the right of Representation in the Legislature." Fourth: "He has called together legislative bodies at places unusual, uncomfortable, and distant from the depository of their Public Records, for the sole purpose of fatiguing them into compliance with his measures." It is not until much, much later in the litany of monarchical criminality do we read this as indictment number twenty-four: "He has plundered our seas, ravaged our coasts, burnt our towns, and destroyed the lives of our people." All combined, the conclusion is this: the king is "unfit to be the ruler of a free people."

This valuation of freedom has become alien to our present-day thinking. Today, we have abandoned both the future and the freedom that in tandem defined the political vision of the Declaration. The primacy of the innocent civilian—whose life is precious enough to overturn a constitutional order, to in fact refashion the constitutional order so as to place its "protection" at first rank (as life has been read backward into the fetal, the fetal has been read forward into life)—is the most radical inversion of the values of the Declaration imaginable. The twenty-fourth indictment has become the first and last value. That those who trumpet originalism do this revaluation is a mockery; that this is also done by those committed to a "living" constitution is an unnoticed irony.

Whatever glory found in the political life of the Declaration must be held side-by-side to the unfreedoms it presumed and foretold. And as the Declaration announced the arrival of the people as a political force and tethered that force to the rule of law, we will need to consider the distinction between terror/tyranny on the one side and law/justice on the other. The Declaration praised legislative assemblies that resisted the dictates of the Crown for their surplus of "manly firmness." The manliness of a vibrant political life was both a metaphor carrying a subordinating norm and a brute literal fact of spatial production. Alexis de Tocqueville made this observation on republican political life in the latter days of the early republic: "Almost all men in a democracy pursue a political career or practice a profession, whereas the women are forced, because of the limitations upon their income, to stay every day inside their houses to preside in person very closely over the details of domestic affairs."[51] A "woman's independence is irretrievably lost"[52] in this scheme, and the irretrievable loss of independence was the original loss of the Declaration of Independence and the opening political move in the modern emergence of the "rule of law." All the charges leveled against the king could be leveled against the domestic patriarch. Kingship was not abolished in the republican order; it was simply relocated and subjected to calculations of utility rather than freedom. Tocqueville believed that women accepted this "yoke" willingly, in which case, we can say that the law is in fact a suicide pact. But being unpersuaded by Tocqueville, one might say the law is not a suicide pact; it is a murder-suicide: in destroying half the population's political freedom, it destroyed political freedom as such. The utility calculation misfired.

Hannah Arendt lavished praise on the early Americans and their revolution, and she did so in systematic contrast to the failures of the French and their revolution. A critical distinction she drew was the sustained respect for the law by the former. It kept men in check and its dissolution in the French Revolution opened the door for The Terror. The "American Revolution remained committed to the foundation of freedom and the establishment of lasting institutions, and to those who acted in this direction nothing was permitted that would have been outside the range of civil law."[53] By contrast, the French Revolution was defined by the "lawlessness of the 'all is permitted.' "[54] To properly think through this alleged historical and theoretical chasm, we should turn to Thomas Jefferson. Three years after authoring the Declaration of Independence, Jefferson was serving as the second governor of the state of Virginia. As an almost symbolic ratification of the new source of political sovereignty and legitimacy in the era of the rights of the people, Jefferson replaced a chair of divinity with a chair of law at the College of William and Mary. He selected his teacher, good friend, and legal mentor, George Wythe, as the first holder of the chair of law.[55] George Wythe was a distinguished patriarch of the legal and political world of Virginia. He was "a lawyer, a signer of the Declaration of Independence, and a teacher of law . . . the first and most influential of American law professors."[56]

The first law professor, along with his brilliant pupils (Jefferson et al.), both before and after the Revolution, had to wrestle with the question of slavery. The dilemma confronting these bright legal minds was this: what kind of property, precisely, was the slave? In Arendt's terminology, with regards to enslaved Africans on American soil, what was permissible within the range of the civil law? These were not easy questions. Judge John T. Noonan explains the delicate task the law assumed in acting as a stern and clear teacher to the slaves who were conceived of as a form of property. Statutes "measured the amount of violence that masters might employ" because " 'without force, the alienability of the title to the human capital of blacks would have been worthless.' "[57] The body would be broken but broken with precision, precision in the form of a legal rule: ears could be nailed to pillories but for no more than one hour; then, in succession, each ear could be sliced off the head, after each hour nailed; the naked back would then be lashed, but not more than thirty-nine lashes.[58] In the awful silence following the thirty-ninth lash, one can almost hear liberal torture-proceduralists clapping and saying, "Yes, see: constraints, limits, *law*."

But the dilemma of what kind of property the slave was remained a difficult legal question to resolve. Were slaves real estate and thus tied to the laws of landed property? Or were they personal property transferable according to laws geared more toward the easy circulation of wealth? From 1776 to 1779, Jefferson and Wythe worked in committee to reform the laws so as to, as Jefferson put it, "render property certain."[59] However much the law wavered in producing with certainty the *type* of property the slave was, there was no uncertainty as to the status of the enslaved *as* property. When George Wythe was later sitting as a judge in the 1790s on cases involving the disputed transfer of slaves, he rendered judgment without any "need to ask about the slaves" and in fact did not even "bother to record their names."[60] And this area of the civil law was of momentous importance to the polity as a polity: of the roughly 750,000 inhabitants of Virginia in the 1790 census, approximately 290,000 of them were enslaved.[61]

Now to France, with Arendt, by contrast. . . . At the historical moment George Wythe was busy judging enslaved "property," the French Revolution was unfolding with increasing ferocity. Among the many to fall under the blade of "The Terror" was Alexis de Tocqueville's great-grandfather (and lawyer for Louis XVI at the Convention), Malesherbes. Tocqueville's parents were also imprisoned and avoided the guillotine by the sheer luck of the timing of the fall of Robespierre. Alexis's father, Hervé de Tocqueville, recounts the shattering of the normality of their lives in 1793: "On 17 December we were at the table when the concierge of the chateau came in with consternation on his face and, employing unusual language said: 'Citizen Rosanbo, outside are some citizens from Paris asking for you.' We all turned pale. M. de Rosanbo left the room at once, and our anxiety was extreme when it became clear that he was not coming back."[62] Without denying or justifying (or condemning) the "terror" this scene evokes, and even assuming for the sake of argument that Arendt is correct in identifying this scene (in its particularity and in its representative capacity) as ultimately a *lawless* one, it could not begin to compare to the organized and *lawful* violence and degradation—*the terror*—experienced by the enslaved persons of the state of Virginia. The unusual language that startled the concierge and bewildered Hervé de Tocqueville was the language of an attempted equality: "Citizen Rosanbo." He was marked for death as an individual, a recognized being, a fellow member of political life. He lost his life, but his humanity was not in doubt; his loyalty was.[63] In France, the high were brought low and it was called lawless terror; in the United States, the low disintegrated into "property" and it was called civil law. We might also note the sheer difference in scale, but I do not think terror is ultimately an empirical question. The question is, what is more terrifying: losing one's life or being abolished while still living?

## Classed Sovereignty and Tutored Subjects

If shattered individualized sovereignty and codified racialized slavery stood as the totemic twins of the rule of law, then the textual and historical recourse to "the people" as a unified force and source of fundamental law appears hopelessly out of place—not simply fictitious, but absurd. Yet, as we have seen, these precise orders sprang forth from antithetical origins: sovereignty was something shared prior to being scattered, and that sharing (like the scattering) was between equals even if and when equality rested upon foundational exclusions. Moreover, that equality only came from the sharing, and so that power making the new world of "commons" and its "sense" operated prior to the rights it secured. But the right was understood as now more precious than the power and hence was to be, if not abolished, exiled back to the place it was imagined to have derived, in the home and the heart of the singular man. Power and right rested together, and Paine could be perhaps seen as at one with Rousseau but in reverse: centrifugal rather than centripetal in the force and source of law. This might be why Paine was at once so at home during the French Revolution, as a *citoyen* and member of the Convention, and also so obviously doomed to oblivion within it, as ultimately a prisoner in the Luxembourg Prison, condemned to death and saved by fate alone.

Rousseau had sought to overcome faction via the formation of a "general will" that required and secured a division between private interests and public power, in both the individual and the body politic. In *The Social Contract*, Rousseau insisted that in a world of multiple interests, "it is what is common to those different interests which yields the social bond."[64] The common bond, that "act which made a people a people,"[65] was not a collection of interests but a new thing altogether: a *public* interest in which each and every individual was to take part and to be partly refashioned by. Crucially, the common bond of the people did not abolish distinction but simply prioritized that element within each individual that tilted toward the common good. Humans are creatures with multiple desires, and "every individual as a man may have a private will contrary to, or different from, the general will that he has as a citizen."[66] The grand task of political life for Rousseau was to anchor the republic from the potential storms of private interests, in the individual and in the polity, without in any manner denying or abolishing private interests as such. It is this element that the conservative liberalism of Alexis de Tocqueville will venerate sixty years after *The Social Contract* as "self-interest properly understood."[67]

At first glance, the U.S. Constitution appears to be a close and comfortable cousin within this family of thought. The preamble is worth reconsidering in full: "We the People of the United States, in Order to form a more perfect Union, establish Justice, insure domestic Tranquility, provide for the common defense, promote the general Welfare, and secure the Blessings of Liberty to ourselves and our Posterity, do ordain and establish this Constitution for the United States of America." Despite the opening by the people as a "we," the chief theoreticians, political advocates, and architects of the U.S. Constitution departed radically with the unifying tendencies of Rousseau without entirely following the hyperindividualized inclinations of Paine.[68] Famously, by contrast, Madison in *The Federalist Papers* conjured the people through the permanence of "faction." The people as a people was already a people divided and thus ironically never a people, and the collective was divided by "interests" as defined by relationships to, and in particular ownership of, property. If the unity of the people disappeared, so too did the individuality of its members: "Unequal faculties of acquiring property . . . ensues a division of the society into different interests and parties. The latent causes of faction are thus sown in the nature of man."[69] The nature of man was tethered to the organization of interests and factions; the ontological ground of the Republic of Interests is therefore class based. Different people find political home within different genuses of accumulated property, and it is where political thinking begins and returns consistently as well.

Thus understood, the people must itself be conceived as some kind of accumulation and a question for accounting. Consequently, "the people" works politically as the source of laws when it works in some majoritarian form; majorities exercise power, and minorities possess rights (those with property, not those who were it). The particular numbering of that majority is not of concern here. Yet, whatever the numbering (50.1 percent, 64 percent, 70 percent), the majority as a majority was also the principal *object* of the rule of law. The majority was that which must be forever "checked" by an intricate labyrinth of constitutional "balances." Understood abstractly, it is the enduring and mysterious paradox of liberal constitutionalism; understood materially, it is the victory of certain classes of white men over and against others. The paradox at the heart of the Constitution of 1787 is not that "[w]e cannot have democracy *with* constitutionalism, and we cannot have democracy with*out* constitutionalism either."[70] Instead, there is another double paradox: a propertied interest in a Republic of Interests is understood to have no interest at all, and the majority interest in a Republic of Interests shall be the one interest whose interest shall not be accounted for at all. The former is included in the meaning of American constitutionalism, the very heart of the rule of law, whereas the latter is banished as the true sign of lawlessness, the disorder and "confusion of the multitude." To return to the Preamble of the Constitution, it is the People who now threaten Justice, Tranquility, and Liberty. One might even say that Justice and Liberty hinge on the production of Tranquility and the domestication of the People. Justice Jackson's political theory in *Terminiello* thus has an originalist basis as well as a textualist hook.

It has been approximately a century since Charles Beard radically challenged the predominant belief (in being both reverential and divorced from standards of fact) that "the Constitution is not only the work of the whole people, but it also bears in it no traces of the party conflict from which it emerged."[71] Without following the path of economic history and biography that Beard took and without taking too literally the political economics of particular votes and individual interests (in some ways, Beard lost all account of ideology in Marx and took direct representation of world into law to be the register of power and critique), one may start from a similar position but look in a different direction in reading *The Federalist Papers* on the rule of law and the two paradoxes of interest sketched above. Madison explained that the fundamental division in society is between "those who hold and those who are without property . . . those who are creditors and those who are debtors, fall under a like discrimination."[72] Property itself subdivided into a multitude of types: landed, manufacturing, mercantile, and moneyed. Within each of these, further subdivisions abounded as well.[73] As noted, these divisions were the fonts of faction, and faction was the inextinguishable energy of the nation.

Real schisms existed between the forms of property and the men of "different sentiments and views" derived from them (as the sectional tariff crisis in the early nineteenth century would make clear),[74] yet a terror bound them together in common cause and defense. They confronted "common threats on the frontier"[75] and remained a trivial power vis-à-vis the great ones of Europe. In the South, the fear of slave uprisings haunted the white imagination and also bound a collective psyche across economic division.[76] But the omnipresent threat to law and order was the specter of "*popular rights*"[77] made manifest in assembly. Political science would need to be developed and deployed to break the connection between popular will and constitutional assembly because that swelling and surplus majority faction of debtors and the propertyless might legislate in their self-interest (as understood by the authors of the *Federalist Papers*). At no place is this concern more explicit than at the close of *Federalist #10*: "Democracies have ever been spectacles of turbulence and contention; have ever been found incompatible with personal security or the rights of property . . . theoretic politicians, who have patronized this species of government, have erroneously supposed that by reducing mankind to a perfect equality in their political rights, they would, at the same time, be perfectly equalized and assimilated in their possessions, their opinions, and their passions." The explosion of material cleavages into the political realm via the perfect equality of political rights in the practices of democracy had to be fore-stalled. A contentious and tumultuous majority within one state "may kin-dle a flame" for a "rage for paper money, for an abolition of debts, for an equal division of property, or for any other wicked project,"[78] but if "a popular insurrection happens in one state, the others will be able to quell it"[79] with the newly empowered Union. Should the Union fail, the result would be nothing less than the erection of a "tyranny on the ruins of law and order."[80]

The "civil war" in Massachusetts of 1786–87, precipitated by "desperate debtors" in revolt, presented a harbinger of what awaited the minority fac-tions with the confederative status quo.[81] Critically, the means of rebellion disturbed them far less than the ends. After all, these were all men of revolu-tionary experience, and the authors of the *Federalist Papers* did not deny the right to revolt in principle. More alarming than the taking up of arms was the capacity of majorities to seize legislative powers for their wicked projects. Without sound constitutional design, the terror would move through the assemblies. So, the new Union would require the power to put down such revolts when they occurred outside the confines of legal formality and would need to be structured so that this majority power would be thwarted from assemblage and power. In response to the "terrorist" attacks of September 11, 2001, eminent constitutional scholars debated whether or not the United States allows for emergency measures in times of imagined existential crisis.[82] What is overlooked in this debate is that the Constitution is already an emer-gency response to a perpetual terror: the terror of the people as a people emerging into history and politics with interests all their own.

Here is the remedy provided by the Constitution to the politicized "tumors" threatening the social body with lawless ruin: "Whilst all author-ity in it will be derived from and dependent on the society, the society itself will be broken into so many parts, interests and classes of citizens, that the rights of individuals, or of the minority, will be in little danger from inter-ested combinations of the majority."[83] There is a performative circularity to the constitutional order: it breaks society as a deliberate political act, and brokenness is the presumptive, natural, and apolitical ground of the constitutional order. In short, the interest that is no interest has produced the conditions of its permanence, and its permanence is seen as the mark of its justness and rightness. Madison reconfigured the political clash between those without property and those with it, between those who labored under debts and those who issued it, as a battle between passion and interests, on one side, and "the rules of justice . . . [and] the permanent and aggregate interests of the community," on the other.[84] The people are rendered transitory in contrast to the timelessness of property, even as the authority of the People must be drawn upon to secure the new regime. One is thus led to a partial agreement with Justice Jackson. As conceived by *The Federalist Papers*, and from the perspective of the people as a sovereign force, the Constitution is *not* a suicide pact; the futurity of a pact becomes the fact of the present: it is, instead, a suicide *act*. And from the perspective of a propertied oligarchy: *tranquility*.

Alexis de Tocqueville sought, in a fashion, to weld the vitality of the people with the life of the law, each supplementing and suffusing the other. This required a "new political science" to break the barriers of egoism (in Marx's terminology), abolish singularized sovereignty (of Paine's variety), and resist the logics of commercialized protocapitalist class society (presumed and championed by Madison). At the same time, Tocqueville sought to "educate" and channel the youthful energies of democracy. Like the *Federalist* men of law and order at the end of the eighteenth century, Tocqueville worried about the emerging new power of the people. Unlike the men of reaction on both sides of the Atlantic, Tocqueville understood the spreading egalitarian sentiment to be an "irresistible revolution." In sum, the vitality of the people, the body and spirit of the republic, had to navigate two extremities or excesses emanating from the historical swell of egalitarianism that also produced their political capacities. First, one must stand guard against the excesses of self-interests whereby liberty degenerates into license, and man comes to exist "in and for himself" alone. Conversely, the excesses of men coming together, of working in collection, haunt Tocqueville too, as here the "disorderly passions" and "wild instincts" of the people open up and usher in revolutionary moments.[85] As possible and partial antidote to these two tendencies, Tocqueville suggested that we look to the organization of the judicial power in the United States as institutional order and sociopolitical practice.[86] The rule of lawyers now stood at the heart of the rule of law.

Tocqueville viewed the constitution of American judicial power as not only exemplary but also singular. No other "nation in the world has organized judicial power in the same way as the Americans."[87] It does, however, share some "traditional attributes" of judicial power with other national systems: the power rules upon the law with reference to a particular case, the power attends first to that particularity and only derivatively to general principles, and lastly, the power must be called upon rather than itself independently solicit the particularity on which it rules.[88] The central difference Tocqueville identified between the American judiciary and other nations, what made it unique, is that the judiciary may ground its decision-making power on constitutional grounds and thus render moot laws it interprets as unconstitutional. Tocqueville recognized that this configuration of judicial power had invested the judicial branch of the government "with immense political power."[89] Two things could temper this immense power: the traditional attributes of judicial power delineated above and the ability of the constituting sovereign power, the people as a People, to amend the Constitution and thereby ultimately "reduce the judges to obedience." With such an immensity of power residing in the judiciary, one finds a political culture in which the "judicial authority is invoked in almost every political context."

It is the ubiquity of this invocation that must generate an immense tension with Tocqueville's notion of "liberty" and political vitality. For Tocqueville, liberty is not mere license to be left alone for purely private pursuits, a regime of "negative liberty"[90]; rather, it is an invitation and incitement, perhaps even a demand, to relocate and reconceptualize interest in and through a politics of participation and shared self-governance: it is a *political* liberty. Such an intertwining of interests makes a "man care for his fellows, and, in a sense, he often finds his self-interest in forgetting about himself."[91] Liberty thus understood flourishes from bringing "men constantly into contact, despite the instincts that separate them."[92] And this too is critical for understanding liberty in the Tocquevillian sense. Our instincts in modernity run toward separation once the antique bonds of self and place dissolved with the feudal order, and thus liberty is a practice to be constantly performed in order to create and nurture democratic subjects. Without the constant exercise of these practices, without these "daily duties performed," one might find order but one will not find freedom. This is why Tocqueville places such hope in administrative decentralization and the life of the township. It permits the handling and circulation of power throughout the sociopolitical body and places liberty "within the people's reach."[93] Here we have power "broken into fragments" so that it can be handled and shaped and transformed by the "maximum number of people."[94] Power is broken, but the people are tethered together; power circulates in the name of liberty rather than being blocked in the name of right.

One must now ask: to what extent can Tocqueville's thesis—that the organization of the judicial power in the United States is the best way to preserve order and maintain political liberty—survive an interrogation through Tocqueville's own theoretical formulations about liberty and order? Recall that a defining characteristic of judicial power is that it is seized of the particular case and that the judge's decision is intended "just to affect some private interest." If judicial authority is, as Tocqueville tells us, invoked constantly in political contexts (it could *not* be not invoked constantly given the power residing there) and if that authority may be seized of a matter only through the articulation of the particular case, the private interest at hand, then there exists a structural incentive to disaggregate political claims and interests into private ones. And this practice ultimately runs counter to Tocqueville's insistence that the "knowledge of how to combine is the mother of all forms of knowledge; on its progress depends that of all others."[95] Rather than locating private interest in participation in a common project, a common good, the judicial organization of power tempts us into a reversal and lays the groundwork for one of Tocqueville's feared excesses: the disintegration of political life into the uncivilized luxe of a privatized and commercial one, a world of unchecked rivalry and unknown fraternity.

Further, judicial power operates in a highly formalized and professionalized space, a space clouded with the mystery of its "judicial attributes and procedures," where the derivative attacks on general principles transpire within "obscure arguments," thus serving to "partly hide the importance of the attack from public observance."[96] This is the antithesis of Tocqueville's celebrated township form of power; here is not the circulation of fragmented power wielded and handled by the maximum number of peoples: the democratic subject does not exercise power; the administered subject instead appeals to it. The space is now wide open for the supplanting of participation with spectatorship. True, Tocqueville informed us that the judicial power may be tamed, that the judges may be brought to "obedience" by the people, but the problem here is not that the judiciary has too much power in the scheme of things. It is rather that the judicial power so organized and set into motion stands to undermine and even eviscerate the political liberty Tocqueville championed, the liberty, incidentally, which would be a prerequisite for taming this or that particular cluster of governmental power.

Nonetheless, even assuming that the organization of judicial power in the United States preserves liberty, what shall we make of the claim that it safeguards order as Tocqueville imagines? Liberty and order are closely linked for Tocqueville: "Daily duties performed or rights exercised keep municipal life constantly alive. There is a continual gentle political activity which keeps society on the move without turmoil."[97] Tocqueville harbors no longing for revolutionary activity or mass political action; surplus tumultuousness is to be carefully guarded against. It threatens vitality as much as atrophy but from the opposite direction. How, then, does he imagine checking the overreach of judicial power without excess? As Tocqueville reminds us, the Constitution "rules both legislators and simple citizens."[98] It is not open to revision by the everyday politics, the simple legislative act; nor, however, is it immutable: the constituting power, the people, may change the Constitution.

If it involved only everyday politics, then the statement that the Constitution "rules both legislators and simple citizens" would lose its theoretical and political bite. Now, we might ask generally and cannot not ask our theorist of liberty as practice, what is a theory without a practice? That is, to render obedience, must not this power of rendering be not simply theorized but *practiced*? And if it is so practiced, what then of certain stabilities required by a conservative, yet liberal, order? We would in fact be a society on the move, but how could it be without certain degrees of turmoil, almost by definition? Tocqueville in fact understood the instability of the law in the ancient regime of France to have been an important source of its downfall. He argued that "contempt" for the law grew from the fact that the "eighteenth century government seems to have made a fetish of tinkering with the laws of the land."[99] In many ways, the practice of popular sovereignty seemed to carry within it the almost inevitable logic of the institutionalization of its very excess by the uncertain duration of basic law: "[T]he danger [is] that revolutionary instincts will mellow and assume more regular shape without entirely disappearing, but will gradually be transformed into mores of government and administrative habits."[100]

The survival of the life of the law and the republic therefore required a long view, which the people as the people constitutionally lacked in Tocqueville's thinking. His worry about the impulses and instincts of democracy led him to reintroduce the aristocratic element into the center of his theorizing and thus unleashed an order antithetical to a people ruling: they would instead be ruled by the "sovereignty of the law."[101] In the United States, devoid of old families connected across generations to land and place, "it is at the bar or bench that the American aristocracy is found."[102] The power of this aristocracy constituted the "strongest barriers against the faults of democracy" because the lawyers by training and temperament "conceive a great distaste for the behavior of the multitude and secretly scorn the government of the people."[103] Even this strong counterpower to the democratic age could not overturn or reverse it, however, and in some strange flash of self-interest, the people as a power would not resist that which distrusted it. Each would find its interest in the other. So, in relationship to the demos, lawyers receive "power through it and over it."[104] In contrast to edicts and constraint, the power of the law is subtle. The counterdemocratic aristocracy, that which is in fact sovereign as a practice, "enwraps the whole of society, penetrating each component class and constantly working in secret upon its unconscious patient, til in the end it has molded it to its desire."[105] On the one hand, the law is a tutor, a guide, a gentle brake; on the other, the law is a master, a foe, a domination. In both instances, inequality configures the relationship and reverses the order of obedience as conceived in popular sovereignty as Tocqueville himself conceived it. The submission is desired, and the desire is produced by the practices of submission: a "new political science for a world itself quite new."

## Conclusion

In 1958, almost a decade after the decision in *Terminiello*, Justice William O. Douglas appeared on the nationally broadcast *Mike Wallace Show*. The interview was one of a series entitled "Survival and Freedom." In tones infused with the lingering paranoia and fright of a receding McCarthyism, Wallace pressed Justice Douglas to consider the dangers of communism, the threat of espionage, the enemies here and there, and the risk to survival with the expansion of freedom. At one point, Justice Douglas stated simply, "Being alive is quite a risk!"[106] Risk was that which life carried with it. Today, the divide of the life of the law and the life of "the people" is increasingly breaking down; ironically, it is the deterioration of both, paradoxically in the name of both risk elimination (in the age of terror) *and* in the abandonment of all sense of risk (in the time of apocalypse), that repositions them as close together as at any point since their joint arrival as *political* powers at the end of the eighteenth century. But it is a mistake to forget the confusions and even antagonisms that shaped them as well from the beginning. If this chapter's analysis pressed to the fore one view of that relationship, it is for cause: to insist that at the twilight of a particular tradition, we recall with reason why we might not cling too tightly to it. That position no doubt carries with it a variety of risks, but then it also carries with it the promises of life.

*Coda*

# Constitutional Power Against
# Constitutional Government

The ascension of Donald Trump to the presidency triggered an avalanche of analysis about the radicalization of the American Right. Trump and Trump-ism has been figured as the arrival of something quite new on the political scene, a break from the traditional norms of conservatism and, more generally, from postwar "consensus" politics. But the new is also understood as the reemergence of the old: the return of the vitality and viability of prewar fascism. Yale historian Timothy Snyder offers the citizenry precisely this lesson by urgently issuing "twenty lessons from the twentieth century, adapted to the circumstances of today."[1] For Snyder, Trump and Trump-ism signals a potential "new dawn of tyranny," and Americans today stand in a potentially parallel position to "Europeans who saw democracy yield to fascism" in the 1930s.[2] Others see Trump's victory as the eruption of something that has been churning below the surface of conservatism for several decades. Rick Perlstein, a historian who has traced the rise of the Right from the ashes of Goldwater's electoral defeat in 1964, argues that the rise of Trump compels a revision of the traditional historical narrative about modern conservatism. The traditional story centers "respectable" conservatives banishing the conspiratorial John Birchers from the movement; William F. Buckley becomes a hero, and Ronald Reagan becomes the president. Perhaps you "had run-ins with the Ku Klux Klan, and white supremacists, and crazy conspiracy theorists, but they were seen as marginal to the story."[3] Trump unsettles this story. Perlstein believes that Trump exposes an "alternate, angry, violent, right-wing genealogy" that is, in fact, central to conservatism's history. Perlstein concludes, "I thought I understood conservatism, but Trump proved me wrong."[4]

The shadow of Trumpism looms over any thinking about the processes of right-wing radicalization and its entry into power, but I want to suggest that the most important event in 2016 on this front occurred not in Trump cobbling together 304 Electoral College votes (one must keep in mind the population delivered him neither a majority nor a plurality of the popular vote) but instead transpired in the U.S. Senate. The Senate's refusal to hold any hearings or votes on Judge Merrick Garland's nomination to fill Justice Scalia's seat on the Supreme Court is something of a theoretical analogue and historical bookend to *Bush v. Gore*. More exactly, the Senate's refusal to entertain *any* nominee put forth by President Obama after Scalia's death represents yet another example of anti-constitutionalism on the Right and illuminates yet again the widespread misdiagnosis of the phenomena. Senate Republicans launched a campaign unprecedented in modern times to strip the elected president of a constitutionally delegated power and rested this action upon a constitutional principle conjured up for this specific instance and no other. In response, those opposed to this serious erosion of constitutional norms could only dream once more of rising above politics, as if there in the thinnest air they could find a sturdy refuge for the rule of law.

On February 13, 2016, Justice Antonin Scalia died in his sleep. A month later, President Obama nominated Judge Merrick Garland of the D.C. Circuit Court of Appeals to fill the seat. Most observers agreed that Judge Garland represented a kind of "centrism" that, in normal times, would produce bipartisan support for his nomination in the Senate. Here is how the president introduced the nominee to the public and educated the public about the process as he viewed it:

> Now, I recognize that we have entered the political season—or perhaps, these days it never ends—a political season that is even noisier and more volatile than usual. I know that Republicans will point to Democrats who've made it hard for Republican Presidents to get their nominees confirmed. And they're not wrong about that. There's been politics involved in nominations in the past. Although it should be pointed out that, in each of those instances, Democrats ultimately confirmed a nominee put forward by a Republican President.
>
> I also know that because of Justice Scalia's outsized role on the Court and in American law, and the fact that Americans are closely

divided on a number of issues before the Court, it is tempting to make this confirmation process simply an extension of our divided politics—the squabbling that's going on in the news every day. But to go down that path would be wrong. It would be a betrayal of our best traditions, and a betrayal of the vision of our founding documents.

At a time when our politics are so polarized, at a time when norms and customs of political rhetoric and courtesy and comity are so often treated like they're disposable—this is precisely the time when we should play it straight, and treat the process of appointing a Supreme Court Justice with the seriousness and care it deserves. Because our Supreme Court really is unique. It's supposed to be above politics. It has to be. And it should stay that way.[5]

The president demands congruence between means and ends: a political confirmation process can only produce a political Court, and because the envisioned end is an apolitical ideal, the means to achieve it must be through relentless depoliticization. Political thinkers like Max Weber and Martin Luther King Jr. also sought to bind together means and ends to guide politics, but here the president sought not to guide but to banish politics by fusing nonpolitical means with antipolitical ends. Constitutional meaning becomes alien to politics as politics is dismissed as the noise of the ignorant wrestling over trivial matters or imaginary slights: "squabbling."

By contrast, the opposition mostly labored under no such illusions and, in fact, developed both a radical political theory and a practice of installing Supreme Court justices. In doing so, Senate conservatives and their intellectual supporters set conservatism ablaze. As the previous chapters have illustrated, this is not without precedent, and it is not without consequence for constitutional law and norms. There are two simultaneous but distinct moments of conservative rupture present in the case of Judge Garland. First, the Senate Republicans (in unison, without dissent) broke with longstanding Senate tradition in denying any hearing on Garland's nomination or for any nominee that the president might put forth and thus overturned the foundations of U.S. conservative thought by suggesting that "the people" should decide whom the next justice on the Court would be. Second, the emergent quasi-plebiscitary principle dissolved beyond its application in the particular case, so the radicalism of the constitutional principle turned at once into the radicalism of an anti-constitutional nonprinciple.

Justice Scalia's death prompted an outpouring of reflections on his life and legacy. Senator Mitch McConnell and Senator Chuck Grassley, Republican Senate majority leader and Senate judiciary chair, respectively, penned this encomium: "Supreme Court Justice Antonin Scalia was a towering figure whose sharp wit and formidable intellect were rivaled by a decades-long fidelity to our founding document and an enduring commitment to the rule of law. His death stands as a tragic loss for our country. Finding the right person to take the seat he occupied will clearly be a monumental task."[6] The leitmotifs of contemporary judicial conservatism are all present: an expressed devotion to the "founding" document, the conflation of fidelity to the document's allegedly singular founding with the "rule of law" itself, and the imagined embodiment of these virtues in the intellect and career of Justice Scalia.

Senator Grassley also issued an individual statement after Garland's nomination that reiterated faithfulness to originalist designs. The turbulent present would be governed by the solidity of the past: "When they structured our nation, the founders placed trust in three separate but equal branches of government. Co-equal authorities are throughout the Constitution, including Article II, Section 2, where the power to nominate an individual to the Supreme Court is granted to the President and authority is given to the Senate to provide advice and consent."[7] All true. But immediately after expressing this commitment to the founders and their wisdom, the senator declares the past to in fact be no guide at all for "[n]owhere in the Constitution does it describe how the Senate should either provide its consent or withhold its consent."[8] Absent explicit textual provision, the senator finds himself in political and theoretical free fall and elects to abdicate the advice and consent responsibility. Or perhaps paradoxically, he claims the "majority of the Senate has decided to fulfill its constitutional role of advice and consent by withholding support for the nomination during a presidential election year. . . . The American people shouldn't be denied a voice."[9]

Throwing the nomination and confirmation process of Supreme Court justices to the American people is a provocative idea. A proper genealogy of this position would likely track back to FDR's "court packing" plan in 1937, the Socialist Party's call under Eugene Debs in 1912 to curb Supreme Court power and "elect all judges," and further back to the anti-Federalists' opposition to the federal judicial power for being "independent of the people, of the legislature, and of every power under heaven."[10] Bracketing the

merits of the proposition, one struggles in vain to find support for it anywhere in the two primary fonts of American constitutional conservatism:
traditionalism and originalism. To put this in the language of traditionalism, can we say that there is a longstanding, deeply rooted right of the
people to select the next Justice (again, suspending for the moment the
question of *should* there be such a right)? And can the assertion that "today
the American people . . . should be afforded the opportunity to replace
Justice Scalia" be nestled comfortably within original understandings of
"advise and consent" as conceived by "the founders"?[11] It is not simply the
absence of support in conservative thinking for this theory of popular selection of a Supreme Court justice; it is instead that this theory stands in *stark
contradistinction* to the theories of traditionalism and originalism.

It is of course Edmund Burke who most famously defended tradition
as the principal source of authority in Anglo-American constitutional
thought, and for this reason, his thought is considered foundational to
Anglo-American conservatism. For Burke, infidelity to tradition snaps the
bonds of allegiance and connection across generations and dissipates the
inherited wisdom that has slowly accrued over time. The "chain and continuity of the commonwealth" rested centrally (though not exclusively) in
the common law. In the "science of jurisprudence . . . is the collected reason
of ages, combining the principles of original justice with the infinite variety
of human concerns."[12] Revolutionary enthusiasms threaten to extinguish
the tradition and indeed tradition as such. Self-confident declarations of
first principles would replace the labors of learning from, inhabiting, gently
modifying, and transmitting the past into the present and future. Burke
worried that the past wisdom embodied in the traditions of the law would
evaporate and the old cases would be viewed as nothing more than a "heap
of old exploded errors . . . no longer studied."[13]

Although Burke defended American independence while excoriating the
French Revolution, the American Revolution was indeed revolutionary, as
discussed in the previous chapter. The revolutionaries cast aside monarchy
rather than a particular monarch. As a consequence, one might anticipate
a somewhat ambivalent reception of Burke by American conservatives
given the simultaneous veneration of origins and a commitment to return
to them via originalism in constitutional theory and politics. In the United
States, revolutionary origins (there's a written constitution rather than
beginnings shrouded in the mists of time) and the revolutionary implications of originalism (one may overturn decades of precedent to return to

the original truth) rest uneasily with Burkean political commitments. Nonetheless, Burke has been assigned founding father status to American conservatism. Edwin J. Feulner, the founder and longtime president of the Heritage Foundation (a leading institution in the world of conservative "think tanks"), created a genealogy of modern U.S. conservatism from Russel Kirk back to Edmund Burke, arguing that both were bound by a commitment to "ordered liberty."[14] Feulner believes "the modern conservative stands with Burke" because of Burke's "abhorrence of ideology and radicalism," his attachment to "policies of prudence," and his idealization of "custom, tradition, and faith."[15] All of these alleged conservative virtues would ultimately be cast aside in the case of Judge Garland.

The Republican refusal to consider any nominee to fill Justice Scalia's vacated seat on the Court constituted a radical break with the customs and traditions of the Senate. Some made a wan effort to invoke tradition for the action. Senator Ted Cruz, for example, claimed that there existed a "long tradition" of such refusal. But this so-called tradition only made sense in the highly circumscribed manner that Cruz articulated it, by excluding the Senate's vote for Justice Kennedy in an election year because the vacancy opened slightly prior and by selectively choosing the length of the tradition ("it has been 80 years since a Supreme Court vacancy was nominated and confirmed in an election year") so as to exclude other relevant cases.[16] Framed so narrowly, the actual tradition disappeared from view, which is why Senator Cruz framed it so narrowly. As one political scientist correctly pointed out, it is "certainly not a norm or tradition by presidents refraining from nominating in a presidential election year or by senators refusing to consider such nominations."[17] Indeed, there is simply no example in modern Court history of a blanket refusal to consider any nominee, as opposed to opposition to particular nominees. The latter case, opposition to a particular nominee in an election year, is represented by the case of Abe Fortas, who was denied elevation to chief justice in 1968 for ethical concerns (he was already a justice of the Court), a case that can hardly constitute a tradition and in any case not the tradition as imagined by Senator Cruz.

In fact, the U.S. Senate confirmed Supreme Court nominees in the election years of 1912, 1916, 1932, 1940, and 1988. And in 1956, President Eisenhower placed William Brennan on the Court via a recess appointment (the Senate confirmed him the following year). To find the most recent parallel, one would have to venture back to the tumult of Reconstruction when the Senate majority, in implacable opposition to President Andrew Johnson, reduced the size of the Court and thus abolished the seat of appointment. Abandoning tradition for such an exceptional precedent is precisely what Edmund Burke rejected when he admonished English supporters of the French Revolution for attempting to connect the revolutionary principles of the French with the example of the English Glorious Revolution a hundred years earlier: "The gentleman of the Society for Revolutions see nothing in that of 1688 but the deviation from the constitution; and they take the deviation from the principle for the principle."[18]

Overturning tradition in every possible sense, the Republican majority converted the deviation into the principle (at least for a fleeting moment as the new principle was established on quicksand and thus not much of a principle at all). Here it is worth more clearly contrasting President Obama's failed nomination of Judge Garland to the Court with President Lyndon Johnson's failed elevation of Justice Fortas to chief justice of the Court in 1968. As already noted, opposition to Justice Fortas was first and foremost opposition to the man. The opposition ranged from the ideological (primarily by those who thought Justice Fortas too liberal) to the ethical (involving speaking fees tied to private businesses) to the reaction of pure bigotry (naked anti-Semitism). As an example of anti-Semitic opposition, the chair of the Senate Judiciary Committee, Mississippi senator James Eastland, said to a fellow senator, "You're not going to vote for that Jew to be Chief Justice, are you?"[19] And even if some political factions perhaps wanted to deny President Johnson the right to nominate anyone, they remained fringe actors or they denied their intent and instead aimed a laser-like focus on Fortas the individual. Everett Dirksen, Senate Republican leader in 1968, rightly noted, "There's nothing about lame ducks in the Constitution."[20] By contrast, Republican leaders in the case of Judge Garland would say again and again that the particular nominee was utterly irrelevant to the issue at hand. House Speaker Paul Ryan said of Republican opposition to Garland, "This has never been about who the nominee is. It is about a basic principle. . . . We should let the American people decide the direction of the Court."[21] Echoing the speaker, Senate Majority Leader McConnell assured those following the spectacle that the refusal of the upper chamber to vote in either committee or on the floor for any nominee "remains about a principle, not a person."[22]

This constitutional "principle," that the Court should be directly influenced by "the people" and therefore no nominations to the Court should occur during an election year, would be a most curious one to the architects of the U.S. Constitution. Senator Everett Dirksen's observation that there is no lame-duck clause in the Constitution highlights the textual point: if the writers of the Constitution had wished to deny the president this particular appointing power during his final year in office, surely they could have expressed this in the document. Nothing in the text states or suggests that the powers of the president wax or wane while in office. Article II, section 1 of the Constitution provides that "[t]he executive power shall be vested in a President of the United States of America. He shall hold his office during the term of four years," and Article II, section 2 of the Constitution states that the president shall have "power, by and with the advice and consent of the Senate, to make treaties, provided two thirds of the Senators present concur; and he shall nominate, and by and with the advice and consent of the Senate, shall appoint ambassadors, other public ministers and consuls, judges of the Supreme Court." In the real world of politics, the persuasive powers of the president do of course ebb and flow, and the ideological composition of the Senate can shift across a president's term in office and contour the parameters of acceptable nominees to the Court, but neither of these facts can establish a "principle" emanating from the text, as originally understood, that eliminates any of the president's powers in year four of his electoral term in office.

The originalist screw turns even more when one looks to practices during the founding period, practices that confirm the plain meaning of the text. Or, more precisely, the historical record of the early republic offers little support for sunsetting the president's power during his term and transferring it to the electorate as matter of constitutional principle.[23] In March 1796, an election year, President George Washington nominated, and the Senate unanimously confirmed, Oliver Ellsworth as the third chief justice of the Supreme Court. If there existed a principle of the constitutional system that compelled the Senate to wait until after the upcoming election, it was lost on all senators in 1796. And senators in 1796 were not strangers to rejecting Supreme Court nominees as they had rejected Washington's nomination of John Rutledge to chief justice in December 1795. An even more discomforting case for an originalist is presented by the appointment of Chief Justice John Marshall. Marshall had been serving as John Adams's secretary of state during the election year of 1800. In that election, Adams lost. In the period between the election and the assumption of the executive office by Jefferson (a true "lame-duck" period), Chief

Justice Ellsworth resigned from the Supreme Court. Desperate to fill as many federal vacancies as possible before the new president took power, Adams appointed numerous judgeships and sent the nomination of John Marshall for chief justice to the Senate. As with Ellsworth, the Senate unanimously confirmed John Marshall, and they did so on February 4, *1801*. So, both text and practice cut against an originalist effort to justify the Senate majority's position that Justice Scalia's open seat should not be filled by *any* Obama nominee.

The true scope of the departure from an originalist understanding of the Constitution comes most clearly into view when considering not only the plain wording of the text or the understanding of that meaning via the practices of the founders but also in the political theory behind both. As noted in the previous chapter, Hamilton and Madison intentionally removed "the people" in the everyday electoral sense from participation in constitutional politics and, via Article V, sought to limit the mobilization of a sovereign constitution-making "people" from appearing except in the most extraordinary of circumstances. In the originary moment, the people were explicitly and deliberately excluded from the selection of federal judges in general and Supreme Court justices in particular. The president possessed the appointment power, but between him and the people stood the Electoral College. The Senate possessed the confirmation power, but between the Senate and the people stood the state legislatures—prior to the ratification of the Seventeenth Amendment in 1913, the state legislatures elected U.S. senators.

Conspicuously absent from the appointment and confirmation process is the House of Representatives. The House of Representatives was designed to be most in accord with the wishes and desires (and dreaded "passions") of the people. Madison argued that the House "should have an immediate dependence on, and an intimate sympathy with, the people."[24] It was precisely this immediacy and dependency that rendered the House unfit for confirmation power. By contrast, the Senate represented the sovereignty of the states. More importantly, the six-year terms for senators in conjunction with the staggered terms of election—the entire House is up for election every two years, but no more than a third of the Senate is subjected to popular judgment in an election year—created distance from the people in their electoral capacity. The authors of *The Federalist Papers* viewed this as a virtue of the Senate and, more precisely, lodged the confirmation power in the Senate as a consequence. As the people were prone to "temporary

errors and delusions,"[25] the Senate would stand guard against such mala-
dies. Granting the Senate the power of advice and consent would also check
a president who may suffer from related moments of weakness. "To what
purpose then require the co-operation of the Senate?" Alexander Hamilton
queried. "I answer, that the necessity of their concurrence would have powerful, though, in general, silent operation. It would be an excellent check
upon a spirit of favoritism in the President, and tend greatly to prevent the
appointment of unfit characters from State prejudice, from family connection, from personal attachment, or *from a view to popularity*."[26] In the case
of the president's appointment of Judge Garland, this theory translated into
practice: no one suggested Garland possessed an unfit character—indeed,
after Trump's election, Senator Mitch McConnell suggested Garland as a
possible head of the FBI as he embodied the virtue of an "apolitical professional."[27] But in the Senate's principled inaction on the nomination, the
originalist vision crumbled because the newly articulated principle hitched
the selection of the next justice to a view toward popularity and an immediacy to the electoral people. The joint statement of Senator Grassley and
Senator McConnell could not be further from an originalist understanding
of the Senate's role in the confirmation process: "[T]he American people
have a particular opportunity now to make their voice heard in the selection of Scalia's successor. . . . How often does someone from Ashland, KY
or Zearing, Iowa get to have such an impact?"[28]

Such a radically anti-originalist argument (ironically made in tribute to
the imagined originalism of Scalia) raises a host of vexing questions for
conservatives. If the people are to have voice, then on what grounds does
the advice and consent power remain in the Senate? Should there be a
constitutional amendment to relocate this power to the House of Representatives? On what basis could Senators Grassley and McConnell oppose an
amendment that proposed precisely this? Their radicalism does not simply
thwart Judge Garland but destabilizes the theoretical foundation of a key
Senate power. If the voice of the people is most authentic and clear in a
presidential election, shouldn't the distortion of the Electoral College be
abolished in favor of direct, nationwide popular vote? And if the quadrennial national vote is the site and source of the people's voice, why would
the then-upcoming election of 2016 carry so much weight at the expense
of the previous election in 2012 when President Obama won a clear majority of the popular vote and a near-landslide majority of the Electoral College vote? At what point in a president's term may the Senate annul the

appointment power vis-à-vis the Supreme Court? How as a matter of constitutional method or justification would one demarcate this lame-duck
annulment period with support from neither text nor tradition in this case?
And how can any theory of a unilateral Senate right to partially annul the
previous presidential election be squared with Hamilton's observation that
a president's "nomination may be overruled: this it certainly may, yet it
can only be to make place for another nomination by himself. The person
appointed must be the object of his preference, though perhaps not in the
first degree."[29]

The Senate checks the president with "advice and consent" power, but
the president's nominating power doubles back and also serves as a check
on the Senate's advice and consent power. If one power could defeat the
other absolutely, there would be nothing to check and nothing to balance.
Although the Senate may reject a particular nominee of a president, Hamilton believed it "not very probable that his nomination would often be overruled" because the senators in opposition "could not assure themselves that
the person they might wish would be brought forward by a second or by
any subsequent nomination. They could not even be certain that a future
nomination would present a candidate in any degree more acceptable to
them."[30] Confronting the inevitability of future nominations, it was viewed
as unlikely that the Senate's "sanction would often be refused, where there
were not special and strong reasons for that refusal."[31] The refusal of the
Senate to even entertain the nomination of Garland was special precisely
because the reasoning reversed the thinking of the founders by negating in
principle the futurity of the nominating power of the executive. Here there
was no check on excessive power; instead, there was more fundamentally a
profound reordering and redistribution of power by the Senate and to the
Senate.

This new constitutional principle hinged upon invalidating the presumption of futurity in the equilibrium between Senate and executive
power, but the collapse of futurity continued to unfold so as to render the
new principle no principle at all. Although the senators in the majority
party cited over and over that their action emanated from constitutional
sources (Article II, section 2), the political forces behind it revealed their
hand and showed that what was being engineered was not a radically new
constitutional principle but an assault on constitutional principle as such.
The editorial board of the *New York Times* described it as "A Coup Against
the Supreme Court,"[32] but it went beyond that singular body—it was also a

coup against the 2012 election and electorate, a coup against the underlying rationale of the senatorial power enumerated in Article II, and ultimately a coup against the futurity underlying constitutionalism. For no sooner had the primary political thinkers and actors of the Right unveiled the theory of popular voice in selecting a Supreme Court justice than they abandoned it. This unprecedented action would not extend beyond the immediate case at hand, even though, paradoxically, the immediate case at hand was rationalized as a matter of principle that by definition would have to govern beyond it.

In February 2016, when Obama nominated Garland, few predicted the strange rise of Donald Trump. Many in the Republican Party and beyond dismissed his demagoguery as nothing more than distracting buffoonery. And even after he secured the party's nomination in May, his path to the presidency appeared unlikely as murmurings about a convention challenge or an independent conservative candidate swirled throughout the summer months. The prospect of a victory by the Democratic candidate Hillary Clinton loomed on the horizon. And faced with that possibility, the specter of a prolonged constitutional crisis emerged. Leading Republicans who had embraced and enabled and enacted the nullification of Obama's appointment powers in the name of "the people" began to argue that no Democrat would be permitted to fill Justice Scalia's seat. On the eve of the 2016 election, Senator Burr of North Carolina said, "I am going to do everything I can do to make sure four years from now, we still got an opening on the Supreme Court."[33] Senator Cruz of Texas cited precedent of the Court having fewer than nine justices, suggesting that an indefinitely open seat would perhaps be ideal. Senator McCain, campaigning in the fall, promised that the Republicans would be "united" in blocking confirmation of a nominee proffered by a Democrat after yet another electoral victory.[34] And days prior to the election, a leader of the Heritage Foundation "signaled that this year's Republican blockade of President Obama's nominee, Merrick Garland, is just the beginning of a fight that could last the entire first term of a Clinton Presidency."[35] So-called moderate senators on the Right, those celebrated for being "more willing to compromise," suggested a rushed confirmation of Garland during the lame-duck Congress if Clinton won the election—thus excluding the people from their supposed role in deciding the next justice.[36]

As has been seen throughout the previous chapters of this book, one confronts here not rival or conflicting constitutional interpretations or visions. Instead, we witness an increasingly emboldened and ascendant anti-constitutional politics. The Garland event showed a radicalized Senate invoking a form of law to eviscerate the norm of law: a constitutional principle that proved to be not a constitutional principle. Further, many observers and participants failed to accurately grasp the underlying cause of the situation. Reproducing the logic of the other cases considered in this book, the opponents of this anti-constitutional coup cast themselves as defenders of the rule of law against the invasion of the scourge of politics. First and foremost, President Obama imagined that one could win a political battle by rising above politics. It was, in a way, the same failed gamble he made in legally absolving the architects of the torture regime. By nominating a justice who inspired almost no political passions and represented no real discernible political positions, who indeed was touted as an excellent choice for precisely this reason, the president had ruled politics out of bounds. And academic critics of the Senate echoed this concern about mixing law and politics. Writing in the *NYU Law Review*, Professors Bradley Kar and Jason Mazzone criticized the Senate's inaction and expressed their concern that the end result would be a "more politicized Court" and that as a result "the rule of law will suffer."[37]

Quite appropriately, the Editorial Board of the *New York Times* turned to *Bush v. Gore* to make sense of the event. We can rightly think of the cases being linked and bound together; they are something like bookend events of American political history in the early twenty-first century. The editors castigated the Senate for "tossing out all political norms"[38] but then curiously turned to Al Gore as inspiration for resistance. More exactly, Gore's concession speech to the coup of *Bush v. Gore* is celebrated as "one of the most important speeches in American history" because his speech affirmed the orderly work of honorable institutions "under the rule of law."[39] It is, to put it mildly, perplexing to speak in the same breath of the destruction of all political norms and then idolize a concession to those very transgressions. Gore's concession speech the day after *Bush v. Gore* was indeed one of the more important moments of American history but for different reasons: it taught the wrong lesson. The quiet and dignified acquiescence of Gore did not restore constitutional normality; it normalized its antithesis. At precisely the moment when political resistance is called for, politics is cited as the source rather than the cure to the illness.

Of course, the constitutional crisis of a multiyear Senate refusal to entertain a Clinton nominee evaporated when she won the popular vote but lost the Electoral College vote. This perfectly constitutional and perfectly antidemocratic outcome should spur some skepticism about unnuanced invocations of the rule of law: the negation of democracy was not a negation of constitutionality or law but its smooth operation in accord with its original principles. This too is a missed lesson from the case of *Bush v. Gore*, one studiously evaded in the ritual celebration of Gore's concession speech. A democratic critique of the Constitution compels a commitment to political thinking and political action within the field of the law. Being beholden to apolitical professionalism both saps and discredits the energies necessary for constitutional revision and reimagining. It is also a type of politics that definitionally (rather than cynically and dishonestly) solicits the voice of the people.

Donald Trump lost the people but nonetheless won, and thus so did the Senate coup. As one news headline put it: the Senate majority leader won his bet. Given that, why imagine a chastened return to constitutional normality? Interestingly, President Trump also dwells almost exclusively in the language of winning and losing—it's the basic grammar of his political thinking. Asked if he had any regrets about using "divisive campaign rhetoric," rhetoric that normalized the demonization of entire populations and fused the incitement of violence with the illegality of persons, he replied, "No, I won." If constitutional commitments like equal protection or freedom of the press stand in the way of Mr. Trump winning, it will be equal protection and freedom of press that will lose. This is the logic of the new regime, but it did not arrive unannounced. We might even say it had precedent.

In political theory, the antecedent for this kind of thinking is not James Madison or Edmund Burke. Its roots lie elsewhere. Writing not much later than a decade after World War II, George H. Sabine attempted to summarize the political theory of fascism and to place it within the history of political theory. Although fascism and national socialism were "philosophically valueless," they nonetheless "indubitably happened, and since there can be no guarantee that their like will not happen again, they must be recorded as parts of twentieth century political philosophy."[40] Although these movements demonstrated a variety of attachments and grievances that differed across national frontiers or even between different sects within each nation, a few core convictions held them together. Two are most apt for the present. The first was that "both fascism and national socialism were before everything governments of men, with a minimum of dependable legal rules."[41] Second, the movements elevated, in almost inverse relation to the devaluing of the law, the concept of the will or, as the German Führer would say, "will and determination."[42]

During the confirmation impasse, one often heard in the press and from the floor of the Senate that the Supreme Court had previously had fewer than nine justices on the Court and that nothing in the Constitution stipulated a set number of justices. This is true. However, the number of justices is established as a matter of law, not senatorial discretion. It is a federal statute, 28 U.S. Code section 1, that provides that the "Supreme Court of the United States shall consist of a Chief Justice of the United States and eight associate justices, any six of whom shall constitute a quorum." When Senator Ted Cruz, a senator with an absolutely sterling legal pedigree, casually states that there is historical precedent for a Court with fewer than nine justices to justify the Senate's circumvention of normal legal means to alter the number of Court seats established as a matter of law, one is reminded of a fact from the darker recesses of twentieth-century European history that "it is hard to subvert a rule-of-law state without lawyers."[43] In the place of the normal procedures of law but still clinging to the text of Article II for legitimacy, the paradox of a constitutional principle against constitutional principle governs through no other basis than the power of "will and determination." The vice president of government relations at the Heritage Foundation stated plainly that blocking any nominee by a Democrat to fill Scalia's seat would require "an immense amount of willpower" once the principle of the people's voice had been exposed as nothing but a delaying ruse.[44] Thus, a central think tank of the modern American Right, which had only years earlier attempted to track its historical, political, and theoretical origins back to Edmund Burke, now replaced a respect for tradition with a devotion to anti-constitutional willpower, a condition in which Burke warned, "Men would become little better than the flies of a summer."[45]

Echoes of the fascist past are not the self-same replication of the events of the historical past. Earlier chapters of this book drew distinctions with previous fascist regimes and theories. Again, the movements mapped in this book do not ultimately revolve around a great leader, and neither do they presuppose the suspension of the entire legal order. In taking stock of the valueless values of fascism and national socialism, the theorist Sabine imagined that a "similar movement in the future would probably tap quite different sources of irrationality" than those of pre–World War II Europe.[46]

And this is key: similar but different. The similarities must not be allowed to blot out the differences, and the differences should not prevent the similarities to shine. What sources of irrationality provide sustenance to today's anti-constitutional Right?

Quite surprising in one sense but also perfectly logical in another, the theologians of the Vatican rather than the self-styled "scientists" of American politics provide the answer to the query. For insight, one must turn to *La Civilita Cattolica*, a journal with the imprimatur of the Holy See, rather than the *American Political Science Review*, the flagship journal of American political science. The clerics see clearly how precarious the U.S. constitutional order has become and have ably diagnosed the forces shearing at its foundations. Writing in the wake of Trump's rise to power, Father Antonio Spadaro and his coauthor, Marcelo Figueroa, warned that a "strange form of surprising ecumenism is developing between Evangelical fundamentalists and Catholic Integralists."[47] Rejecting an eschatology of "the future," the "strange ecumenism" relocates that future-coming into the "here and now," applying "its own law and logic in the political sphere," whereby "every process (be it of peace, dialogue, etc.) collapses before the needs of the end, the final battle against the enemy."[48] This is neither the traditionalism of Burke nor the originalism of Madison; it is instead a political reality defined however irrationally through a "cult of the apocalypse." Such heights has it reached in the United States that intellectuals around the current pontiff feel the need to remind Americans that Pope Francis radically opposes any such "apocalyptic hope." The political sphere cannot survive this rival logic. To put it simply, law's future requires a future.

*Notes*

## Preface

1. Fernanda Santos, "Outside Jail, a Vestige of Joe Arpaio's Tenure, Is Closing," *New York Times*, April 4, 2017.

2. Stephen Lemons, "Joe Arpaio: Tent City a 'Concentration Camp,'" *Phoenix New Times*, August 2, 2010.

3. Melendres v. Arpaio, 989 F. Supp. 2d 822 (D. Ariz. 2013).

4. "The Arpaio Pardon," editorial, *Wall Street Journal*, August 28, 2017.

5. Corey Robin, *The Reactionary Mind: Conservatism from Edmund Burke to Donald Trump*, 2nd ed. (Oxford: Oxford University Press, 2018), 51.

6. U.S. Const. art. II, § 2.

7. Ex Parte Garland, 71 U.S. 333, at 380 (1866) (emphasis added).

8. This brief summary of the pardon power is from Harold J. Krent's informative "Conditioning the President's Conditional Pardon Power," *California Law Review* 89, no. 6 (December 2001): 1672–76.

9. *Garland*, 71 U.S. at 380.

10. "President Trump Pardons Sheriff Joe Arpaio," August 25, 2017, https://www.whitehouse.gov/briefings-statements/president-trump-pardons-sheriff-joe-arpaio/.

11. "President Trump Pardons Sheriff Joe Arpaio."

12. Gerald R. Ford, "Proclamation 4311—Granting Pardon to Richard Nixon," September 8, 1974, *The American Presidency Project*, http://www.presidency.ucsb.edu/ws/?pid=4696.

13. Ford, "Pardon to Richard Nixon."

14. Ford, "Pardon to Richard Nixon."

15. Amicus curiae brief submitted by Erwin Chemerinsky, Michael E. Tigar, and Jane B. Tigar, filed September 11, 2017, p. 13, https://assets.documentcloud.org/documents/3990431/Chemerinsky-Amicus-Arpaio-20170911.pdf. It must be noted, however, that President George H. W. Bush's pardons of the leading figures in the Iran-Contra affair did celebrate the service of those he pardoned. However, Bush's pardon situated the behavior of the pardoned within a framework of a then-concluded "Cold War struggle": "When earlier wars have ended, Presidents have historically used their power to pardon to put bitterness behind us and look to the future." He also argued

that the pardoned had "already paid a price" for their "misdeeds or errors." George Bush, "Proclamation 6518—Grant of Executive Clemency," December 24, 1992, *The American Presidency Project*, http://www.presidency.ucsb.edu/ws/?pid = 20265.

16. ACLU, "ACLU Comment on Trump Pardon of Joe Arpaio," August 25, 2017, https://www.aclu.org/news/aclu-comment-trump-pardon-joe-arpaio-0.

17. "Statement of ABA President Hilarie Bass Re: Pardon of Former Arizona Sheriff Joe Arpaio," August 25, 2017, https://www.americanbar.org/news/abanews /aba-news-archives/2017/08/statement_of_hilarie0.html.

18. "The Arpaio Pardon."

19. "A Bad Pardon," editorial, *National Review*, August 28, 2017.

20. "A Bad Pardon."

21. Adam Liptak, "Why Trump's Pardon of Arpaio Follows Law, yet Challenges It," *New York Times*, August 27, 2017.

22. "The Arpaio Pardon."

23. Laurence H. Tribe and Ron Fein, "Trump's Pardon of Arpaio Can—and Should—Be Overturned," *Washington Post*, September 18, 2017.

24. Bonnie Honig, *Emergency Politics: Paradox, Law, Democracy* (Princeton, NJ: Princeton University Press, 2009), 35.

## Introduction

Note to epigraph: Quoted in Murray N. Rothbard, "The Reagan Phenomenon," *Free Life: The Journal of the Libertarian Alliance* 4, no. 1 (1984): 2.

1. Konisberg v. State Bar of California, 353 U.S. 252 (1957). In fact, the issue was not fully resolved until Baird v. State Bar, 401 U.S. 1 (1971).

2. Rosalie M. Gordon, *Nine Men Against America: The Supreme Court and Its Attack on American Liberties* (New York: Devin-Adair 1958), opening quotations are from 3–8.

3. Gordon, *Nine Men Against America*, 40, 43.

4. Gordon, *Nine Men Against America*, 45.

5. Gordon, *Nine Men Against America*, 150.

6. Robert H. Bork, *The Tempting of America: The Political Seduction of the Law* (New York: Free Press, 1990), 1.

7. Bork, *Tempting of America*, 1. See esp. chap. 3, "The Warren Court: The Political Role Embraced."

8. John M. Broder, "Have a Seat, Your Honor," *New York Times*, July 10, 2005.

9. David Kairys collapses the "separate" and the "above" in a manner that obscures the full power of the latter in a political culture of "rights." On the significance of the latter, see Wendy Brown and Janet Halley, "Introduction," in *Left Legalism/ Left Critique*, ed. Wendy Brown and Janet Halley (Durham, NC: Duke University Press, 2002), 1–37. Nonetheless, Kairys's point that the ideal of separation is linked with the ideal of objectivity and neutrality is a correct diagnosis. See David Kairys, "Introduction," in *The Politics of Law: A Progressive Critique*, 3rd ed. (New York: Basic Books, 1998).

10. Karl Marx, "On the Jewish Question," in *The Marx-Engels Reader*, 2nd ed., ed. Robert Tucker (New York: W. W. Norton, 1978). I am not using the word "politically" here in the theoretically specific sense that Marx did in the essay.

11. Marx, "On the Jewish Question," 45.

12. Marx, "On the Jewish Question," 32.

13. Karl Marx and Friedrich Engels, "Manifesto of the Communist Party," in Tucker, *Marx-Engels Reader*, 482. This critique of law has been extended beyond the negative rights and liberty of the eighteenth-century constitutional state and to distributions of the twentieth-century welfare state. See, for example, Jill S. Quadango, "Welfare Capitalism and the Social Security Act of 1935," *American Sociological Review* 49, no. 5 (October 1984): 632–47.

14. For an intellectual survey of the critical legal studies movement, see Alan Hunt, "The Theory of Critical Legal Studies," in *Explorations in Law and Society: Toward a Constitutive Theory of Law* (New York: Routledge, 1993), 139–81.

15. Harold J. Spaeth and Jeffrey A. Segal, *Majority Rule or Minority Will: Adherence to Precedent on the U.S. Supreme Court* (Cambridge: Cambridge University Press, 1999), 288.

16. Spaeth and Segal, *Majority Rule*, xv.

17. Louis D. Brandeis, "The Opportunity in the Law" (address before the Harvard Ethical Society, 1905).

18. Catharine A. MacKinnon, *Toward a Feminist Theory of the State* (Cambridge, MA: Harvard University Press, 1989), 161–62.

19. Ken Kress imagines the unraveling of the power of the judiciary with such a demystification: "The debate about judicial activism within the nonlegal academy, the political community, and popular culture rests upon a similar presupposition that a judicial decision is legitimate if it accurately applies the law, but it is open to question, if not downright immoral, if it reflects nonlegal factors such as the judges' personal preferences or political ideology." Ken Kress, "Legal Indeterminacy," *California Law Review* 77, no. 2 (March 1989): 285.

20. Catharine A. MacKinnon, "Feminism, Marxism, Method, and the State: Toward Feminist Jurisprudence," *Signs* 8, no. 4 (Summer 1983): 658.

21. Spaeth and Segal, *Majority Rule*, xv.

22. Senator Specter was attacked on the Right for elevating adherence to precedent over fealty to constitutional originalism with a symptomatic article title: see George Neumayr, "The Law of Lawlessness," *American Spectator*, November 2, 2005. Senator Specter had been key to the Senate's rejection of President Reagan's nomination of Robert Bork to the Supreme Court.

23. Benjamin Barber, *Fear's Empire: War, Terrorism, and Democracy* (New York: W. W. Norton, 2014), 88.

24. Lida Maxwell, "Toward an Agonistic Understanding of Law: Law and Politics in Hannah Arendt's *Eichmann in Jerusalem*," *Contemporary Political Theory* 11, no. 1 (2012): 105.

25. Although Lida Maxwell has offered a thought-provoking and different interpretation of Arendt's thought in a rereading of *Eichmann in Jerusalem*. Maxwell suggests an Arendtian "agonistic approach" to law that highlights the "non-juridical (political) conditions of law's authority." Maxwell, "Toward an Agonistic Understanding of Law," 105. In *On Revolution*, where Arendt discusses the American Revolution in contrast to the French Revolution, I find that Arendt rests the foundation of U.S. law less on unpredictable action and more on the predictable and preexisting rule of the townships. I discuss Arendt's view of the American Revolution in greater detail in Chapter 4.

26. Gordon Wood, "A Note on Mobs in the American Revolution," *William and Mary Quarterly* 23, no. 4 (October 1966): 635.

27. Bruce Ackerman, *We the People: Transformations* (Cambridge, MA: Harvard University Press, 1998), 102. Ackerman argues that "[f]or Americans, law breaking does not necessarily imply lawlessness" (14). Rather than draw a distinction with the French Revolution, Ackerman contrasts the American experience with the Bolshevik Revolution of 1917. The Bolsheviks entered into a realm of lawlessness because they, unlike Americans of any generation, sought to "destroy the entire matrix of preexisting institutions" (12). Ackerman helps us recover a tradition of "naked violations of Article Five" (111) and "irregularities" such as the "revolutionizing of the South's political class" during Reconstruction.

28. Here it is worth reading together Martin Luther King Jr.'s "Letter from Birmingham Jail," in *A Testament of Hope: The Essential Writings and Speeches of Martin Luther King, Jr.*, ed. James M. Washington (New York: HarperCollins, 1986) and Akinyele Omowale Umoja's *We Will Shoot Back: Armed Resistance in the Mississippi Freedom Movement* (New York: New York University Press, 2013).

29. Charles Ogletree, *All Deliberate Speed* (New York: W. W. Norton, 2004), 143.

30. Phillipe Sands, *Lawless World* (New York: Viking, 2005), 3. "Actions taken in the aftermath of 9/11 were now raising serious questions about American commitment to basic rules of international law" (3).

31. Gregory M. Huckabee, "The Politicizing of Military Law—Fruit of the Poisonous Tree," *Gonzaga Law Review* 45, no. 3 (2009/2010): 612.

32. Owen Fiss, *A War Like No Other: The Constitution in a Time of Terror* (New York: New Press, 2015), 124.

33. Carl Schmitt, *Political Theology: Four Chapters on the Concept of Sovereignty* (Chicago: University of Chicago Press, 2006), 13.

34. Linda Meyer, " 'Nothing We Say Matters': Teague and New Rules," *University of Chicago Law Review* 61, no. 2 (1994): 423.

35. Teague v. Lane, 489 U.S. 288 (1989).

36. Meyer, " 'Nothing We Say Matters,' " 423.

37. Susan Bandes, "Taking Justice to Its Logical Extreme: A Comment on *Teague v. Lane*," *Southern California Law Review* 66, no. 6 (September 1993): 2461.

38. Meyer, " 'Nothing We Say Matters,' " 443–44.

39. Meyer, "'Nothing We Say Matters,'" 492.

40. William E. Connolly, *Capitalism and Christianity, American Style* (Durham, NC: Duke University Press, 2008), 4.

41. Connolly, *Capitalism and Christianity*, 40.

42. Bandes, "Taking Justice to Its Logical Extreme," 2462.

43. Judith N. Shklar, *Legalism: Law, Morals, and Political Trials* (Cambridge, MA: Harvard University Press, 1964), 144.

44. Shklar, *Legalism*, 17. Although Shklar rightly read the adaptability of legalism, she misread the political ends to which it has been historically hitched in U.S. history. Writing in the same year in which the Democratic Party would not recognize Fannie Lou Hamer and the Mississippi Freedom Democratic Party at its national convention, Shklar oddly asserted that "in the Constitutional order" of the United States, "class domination is relevant neither in theory nor in practice" (144).

## Chapter 1

1. The five conservative justices had issued an injunction on December 9 to halt the recount until a decision in the case was reached. Justice Scalia justified this on the grounds that counting the votes could pose a threat to the "legitimacy" of Bush's victory (oddly still an open question of law and fact as of December 9). Linda Greenhouse, "Bush v. Gore: Special Report. Election Case a Test and a Trauma for the Justices," *New York Times*, February 20, 2001.

2. Bush v. Gore, 531 U.S. 98 (2000).

3. *Bush*, 531 U.S. at 104–5.

4. Akhil Amar, "Bush, Gore, Florida, and the Constitution," *Florida Law Review* 61, no. 5 (December 2009): 962.

5. Owen Fiss, "The Fallibility of Reason," in *Bush v. Gore: The Question of Legitimacy*, ed. Bruce Ackerman (New Haven, CT: Yale University Press, 2002), 89.

6. Laurence H. Tribe, "eroG .v hsuB: Through the Looking Glass," in Ackerman, *Bush v. Gore*, 50. There is also an important element of class discrimination in that poorer counties are less able to afford newer and more reliable technology. Unfortunately, the courts have been resistant to incorporating class analysis into the jurisprudence of equal protection even as class chasms have been radically widening. The republic that once provoked Tocqueville's analysis of a democracy born of a relative equality of conditions has become the living embodiment of Marx's critique about the unbridgeable distance between constitutional law and constitutive political fact.

7. *Bush*, 531 U.S. at 104.

8. Justice Breyer and Justice Souter agreed that the recount procedure generated equal protection problems, but they insisted that Florida be given time to remedy the infirmities.

9. *Bush*, 531 U.S. at 109.

10. *Bush*, 531 U.S. at 104.

11. Jack M. Balkin, "The Use That the Future Makes of the Past: John Marshall's Greatness and Its Lessons for Today's Supreme Court Justices," *William and Mary Law Review* 43, no. 4 (2002): 1338.

12. Balkin, "Lessons for Today's Supreme Court Justices," 1327 and 1338.

13. Kathryn Abrams, "Extraordinary Measures: Protesting Rule of Law Violations After *Bush v. Gore*," *Law and Philosophy* 21, no. 2 (2002): 189. See also Margaret Radin, "Can the Rule of Law Survive *Bush v. Gore*?" in Ackerman, *Bush v. Gore*, 110–28. On pp. 118–19, Radin writes, "It's not based on legal principles applicable to other cases and presumably will not serve as precedent for other cases" and thus is a "naked affront to the rule of law."

14. Harold J. Spaeth and Jeffrey A. Segal, *Majority Rule or Minority Will: Adherence to Precedent on the U.S. Supreme Court* (Cambridge: Cambridge University Press, 1999), xv.

15. Abrams, "Extraordinary Measures," 189–90.

16. Spaeth and Segal, *Majority Rule*, xv (emphasis added).

17. Martin Shapiro, *The Supreme Court and the Administrative Agencies* (New York: Free Press, 1968), 40.

18. See generally Milton Friedman, *Capitalism and Freedom* (Chicago: University of Chicago Press,1962), esp. chap. 2, "The Role of Government in a Free Society."

19. See West Coast Hotel v. Parrish, 300 U.S. 379 (1937) overturning Adkins v. Children's Hospital, 261 U.S. 525 (1923).

20. This is in accord with the observation of Jack Knight and Lee Epstein: precedent works as a "norm" and social science researchers are "unlikely to detect its presence by conventional examinations of the vote." Jack Knight and Lee Epstein, "The Norm of Stare Decisis," *American Journal of Political Science* 40, no. 4 (November 1996): 1018. Of course, sustained shifts in the judiciary and changes in the facts and value underlying precedents do open up old decisions for new challenges. Precedents of course fall, but they fall to new precedent-setting cases.

21. To be clear, these three interpretative commitments do not necessarily imply right-wing consequences. For example, liberal justice Hugo Black could have been called a "textualist," white plaintiffs opposing affirmative action via the Equal Protection Clause will find cold comfort in "originalism," and proponents of same-sex marriage and marijuana legalization might themselves find shelter in the nouveau vogue jurisprudence of the Tenth Amendment.

22. Antonin Scalia, *A Matter of Interpretation: Federal Courts and the Law* (Princeton, NJ: Princeton University Press, 1997), 38.

23. Scalia, *A Matter of Interpretation*, 138–39.

24. The First Amendment was not incorporated in its entirety in a single decision. Rather, from the late 1920s to the early 1940s, the Supreme Court began applying the various provisions of the First Amendment to the states. For a mapping and discussion of this process, see Laurence H. Tribe, *American Constitutional Law*, 2nd ed. (Mineola, NY: Foundation Press, 1988), 772–74.

25. John Hart Ely, *Democracy and Distrust: A Theory of Judicial Review* (Cambridge, MA: Harvard University Press, 1980), 15.

26. Texas v. Johnson, 491 U.S. 397 (1989).

27. Daniel Farber, William Eskridge Jr., and Philip Frickey, eds., *Constitutional Law: Themes for the Constitution's Third Century*, 3rd ed. (St. Paul, MN: West Group, 2003), 428.

28. Spaeth and Segal, *Majority Rule*, xv.

29. See *Federalist*, no. 51 (James Madison), in James Madison, Alexander Hamilton, and John Jay, *The Federalist Papers*, ed. Isaac Kramnick (1788; Harmondsworth, UK: Penguin, 1987). In *Federalist*, no. 62, Madison wrote, "In a compound republic, partaking both of the national and federal character . . . no law can be passed without the concurrence, first of a majority of the people, and then of a majority of the States."

30. *Federalist*, no. 62 (Madison).

31. Marbury v. Madison, 1 Cranch 137 (1803).

32. The original political hope of judicial review was driven by a desire to move power away from the immediate grip of the people and their majorities.

33. Robert G. McCloskey, *The American Supreme Court*, 3rd ed. (Chicago: University of Chicago Press, 2000), 25.

34. Jeffrey Segal and Harold J. Spaeth, *The Supreme Court and the Attitudinal Model Revisited* (New York: Cambridge University Press, 2002), 118.

35. Gordon Silverstein, "The Last Conservative," *New Republic*, May 1, 2009 (commenting on the decision in *Bush v. Gore*).

36. Richard L. Hasen, "*Bush v. Gore* and the Lawlessness Principle: A Comment on Professor Amar," *Florida Law Review* 61, no. 5 (December 2009): 980 (asserting that the consensus against lawlessness is informed by a disagreement over which court was acting lawlessly, the Florida Supreme Court or the U.S. Supreme Court).

37. Brown v. Allen, 34 U.S. 443, at 540 (1953) (concurring).

38. The full concession speech was published in the *New York Times*, December 14, 2000.

39. Chad Flanders, "Please Don't Cite This Case! The Precedential Value of *Bush v. Gore*," *Yale Law Journal Pocket Part* 116 (2009): 143.

40. Michel Foucault, *This Is Not a Pipe* (Berkeley: University of California Press, 2008), 20.

41. Radin, "Survive *Bush v. Gore*?" 125.

42. Abrams, "Extraordinary Measures," 190–91.

43. It is unclear how broad and deep the initial revolt was. Abrams thought that most of the critiques that highlighted the rule of law violation rejected or ignored any possible turn toward novel forms of resistance to the "lawlessness" of the Court. Radin, by contrast, thought that many in the legal community shared her desire to move beyond legal argument for some kind of direct action.

44. Bruce Ackerman, "Off Balance," in Ackerman, *Bush v. Gore*, 195.

45. Radin, "Survive *Bush v. Gore*?" 125.

46. Radin, "Survive *Bush v. Gore*?" 125.

47. Jurgen Habermas, "On the Internal Relation Between Law and Democracy," in *The Inclusion of the Other*, ed. Ciaran P. Cronin and Pablo de Greiff (Cambridge, MA: MIT Press, 1998).

48. Habermas, "Internal Relation," 254.

49. Habermas, "Internal Relation," 254.

50. For an excellent historical survey of the institution, see Robert Caro, *The Years of Lyndon Johnson*, vol. 3, *Master of the Senate* (New York: Knopf, 2002), esp. chap. 1, "The Desks of the Senate," and chap. 3, "Seniority and the South."

51. Sanford Levinson offers a more sustained argument of this proposition in *Our Undemocratic Constitution* (Oxford: Oxford University Press, 2006).

52. Data are available at www.fec.gov.

53. The states included Georgia, Idaho, Indiana, North Carolina, Oklahoma, Wyoming, and South Dakota.

54. They were challenged by the Brennan Center at NYU (www.brennancenter .org). The Brennan Center argues that "the right to vote is more valuable when citizens are able to vote for the candidate of their choice." But we should insist that there is another value beyond the individual and his or her choice and that value consists of the multiplication of associational opportunities and the emergence of new groups and claims into political life. That is, there is a collective and cultural dimension to democracy that is jeopardized by the exclusion of parties.

55. Timmons v. Twin Cities Area New Party, 520 U.S. 351 (1997).

56. The Green Party ticket in 2000 was headed by Ralph Nader. Nader's running mate was Winona LaDuke.

57. Police blocked the Green Party candidates from entering into the debate hall in Boston in 2000 under threat of arrest. Over thirty prodemocracy protestors were imprisoned for attempting to gain entry. In 2012, Green Party nominee Jill Stein was arrested and handcuffed to a chair for eight hours for attempting to enter into the debate arena at a university in New York. In 2016, Jill Stein was removed by police from the debate venue and several of her supporters were arrested.

58. See Arkansas Educational Television Commission v. Forbes, 532 U.S. 666 (1998).

59. Richard H. Pildes, "Democracy and Disorder," *University of Chicago Law Review* 68, no. 3 (2001): 714.

60. See Richard Posner, *Breaking the Deadlock: The 2000 Election, the Constitution, and the Courts* (Princeton, NJ: Princeton University Press, 2001). Posner's pragmatist defense ultimately rests upon the claim "that it is a function of law in general . . . to *produce* order" (61), and the Court successfully halted further confusion and tumultuousness with its decision.

61. Cass Sunstein, "Order Without Law," in *The Vote: Bush, Gore, and the Supreme Court*, ed. Cass R. Sunstein and Richard A. Epstein (Chicago: University of Chicago Press, 2001).

62. Amar, "Bush, Gore, Florida, and the Constitution," 953–54.

63. Richard A. Epstein, "'In Such a Manner as the Legislature Thereof May Direct': The Outcome in *Bush v. Gore* Defended," in Sunstein and Epstein, *The Vote*, 15.

64. Florida Advisory Committee to the United States Commission on Civil Rights, *Ex-Felon Voting Rights* (August 2008), p. 2, http://www.usccr.gov/pubs/EX-FelonVRFL.pdf.

65. Christopher Uggen, Ryan Larson, and Sarah Shannon, *6 Million Lost Voters: State-Level Estimates of Felon Disenfranchisement* (The Sentencing Project, 2016), http://www.sentencingproject.org/publications/6-million-lost-voters-state-level-esti mates-felony-disenfranchisement-2016/.

66. Uggen, Larson, and Shannon, *Six Million Lost Voters*, 6, 18.

67. *Voting Rights Restoration Efforts in Florida*, report from the Brennan Center for Justice at the NYU School of Law (July 14, 2017), https://www.brennancenter.org/analysis/voting-rights-restoration-efforts-florida.

68. Martin Luther King Jr., "Letter from Birmingham Jail," in *A Testament of Hope: The Essential Writings and Speeches of Martin Luther King, Jr.*, ed. James M. Washington (New York: HarperCollins, 1986), 293.

69. See Angela Behrens, Christopher Uggen, and Jeff Manza, "Ballot Manipula-tion and the 'Menace of Negro Domination': Racial Threat and Felon Disenfranchise-ment in the United States, 1850–2002," *American Journal of Sociology* 109, no. 3 (November 2003): 563.

70. *Ex-Felon Voting Rights*, 6. For a rich political and theoretical interrogation of this exclusion, see generally Andrew Dilts, *Punishment and Inclusion: Race, Member-ship, and the Limits of American Liberalism* (New York: Fordham University Press, 2014).

71. Richardson v. Ramirez, 418 U.S. 24, at 77 (1974) (quoting Reynolds v. Simms, 377 U.S. 533 [1964]).

72. *Richardson*, 418 U.S. 24, at 86 (Marshall, J. dissenting).

73. Johnson v. Governor of the State of Florida, 405 F.3d 1214 (11th Cir. 2005).

74. On the processes and implications of the transformation of diverse acts into the sure-sign grounds of the being behind and beneath them, see generally Michel Foucault, *The History of Sexuality*, vol. 1, *An Introduction*, trans. Robert Hurley (New York: Random House, 1978).

75. Dominant groups in a society organize around democratic norms while sub-ordinating other groups with antidemocratic and exploitative practices. Cheryl Harris, "Whiteness as Property," *Harvard Law Review* 106, no. 8 (June 1993): 1744.

76. Jeff Manza and Christopher Uggen, "Democratic Contraction? Political Con-sequences of Felon Disenfranchisement in the United States," *American Sociological Review* 67, no. 6 (December 2002): 778 and 792.

77. "Law Professors for the Rule of Law," cited by Radin, "Survive *Bush v. Gore*?" 113.

78. Jeffrey Toobin, "Precedent and Prologue," *New Yorker*, December 6, 2010. According to Toobin, *Roe v. Wade* generated sixty-five citations in the decade following the ruling in 1973. Some lower courts, notably the Sixth Circuit, have cited *Bush v. Gore* as precedent; however, the very act of citing the case becomes grounds for dissent. As example, in the case of Stewart v. Blackwell, 444 F 3d 843 (2006), the dissenting opinion responded to the majority's invocation of *Bush v. Gore* with this: "[W]e should heed the Supreme Court's own warning and limit the reach of Bush v. Gore to the peculiar and extraordinary facts of that case." On *Stewart v. Blackwell* and the lower courts' dilemma with *Bush v. Gore*, see Flanders, "Please Don't Cite This Case!" Commenting on recent election law cases, Professor Richard L. Hasen noted that "18 years after *Bush v. Gore*, the case remains radioactive." Richard L. Hasen, "Supreme Court Avoids Bush v. Gore II in Ducking Pennsylvania Redistricting Controversy," *Harvard Law Review Blog*, March 22, 2018, https://blog.harvardlawreview .org/supreme-court-avoids-bush-v-gore-ii-in-ducking-pennsylvania-redistricting-con troversy/. If a future Supreme Court majority revives the decision, it will be a most noteworthy event. That it would be noteworthy is itself noteworthy.

## Chapter 2

1. President Obama's former UN ambassador Susan Rice reaffirmed the position explicitly: "We don't negotiate with terrorists, that's the policy of the United States." "Transcript of Interview by John King with Susan Rice," *State of the Union with John King*, August 9, 2009, http://transcripts.cnn.com/TRANSCRIPTS/0908/09/sotu.01 .html. A refusal to negotiate with those people from some other time helps to shore up what Wendy Brown calls the "stories constitutive of modernity." "Modernity is not only premised on the notion of *emergence* from darker times and places, it is also structured *within* by a notion of continual progress." Wendy Brown, *Politics Out of History* (Princeton, NJ: Princeton University Press 2001), 6. The very possibility of negotiation or consideration is foreclosed because the presence of the men with beards who live in caves unravels the constitutive narratives that sustain the position from which one would negotiate. A rival *within* the present is different from a rival *with* the present.

2. By "hypernationalist ideologues," I mean that the exertion of national force outside of any constraints of multinational or international agreement is understood as being a good in and of itself, to be affirmed and entrenched via practice/repetition. A result and example of this is found in assertions that the Geneva Conventions do not apply to the sui generis category of prisoners labeled by the American executive power as "enemy combatants" and in the enthusiastic development of a doctrine of "preemptive unilateralism" in relation to other sovereign states in the context of international law.

3. Contemporary polling techniques indicate that the base of support for torture is in white, evangelical, and fundamentalist Christian populations, also a central base of support for the Right in general. A recurring tale from detainees within the American-run camps (and confirmed by independent reports) is the denigration of the

Quran by interrogators and guards combined with religiously infused verbal abuse. The "theoconservative" Catholic response is summarized and criticized in Damon Linker, *The Theocons: Secular America Under Siege* (New York: Anchor Books, 2006), esp. chap. 4, "Theocons at War."

4. See generally John Cooley, *Unholy Wars: Afghanistan, America, and International Terrorism* (London: Pluto Press, 2002).

5. The relevant sections of the UN Charter include Chapter VII, "Actions with Respect to Threats to the Peace, Breaches of the Peace, and Acts of Aggressions," read in tandem with Chapter I, "Purposes and Principles." Violations of these principles stood at the heart of the Nuremberg Trials as "crimes against peace."

6. Judith Butler, *Precarious Life: The Power of Mourning and Violence* (London: Verso, 2004), 65. Butler's sentence concludes, "[A]nd this means that the state of emergency is potentially limitless and without end, and that the prospect of an exercise of state power in its lawlessness structures the future indefinitely" (65). This book works, in part, to problematize that assertion regarding "lawlessness," and thus the elliptical break is theoretically intentional. Further, the flip side of Butler's claim—that the discretionary powers of "petty sovereigns" is a rupture with the rule of law and that the separation of powers constitutes a sound basis for securing justice, individual dignity, and/or political freedom—troubles me as well. I will return to all of these points.

7. Senator Dianne Feinstein, "Foreword," in the *Senate Intelligence Committee Report on Torture* (Brooklyn, NY: Melville House, 2014).

8. Antonio Taguba, "Preface," in Physicians for Human Rights, *Broken Laws, Broken Lives: Medical Evidence of Torture by US Personnel and Its Impact* (Cambridge, MA: Physicians for Human Rights, 2008), viii.

9. Laurel Fletcher and Eric Stover, *Guantánamo and Its Aftermath: U.S. Detention and Interrogation Practices and Their Impact on Former Detainees* (Berkeley: University of California, Berkeley, Human Rights Center and International Human Rights Law Clinic, 2008), 23 (hereinafter *Detention and Interrogation Practices*).

10. Ron Suskind, "Faith, Certainty, and the Presidency of George W. Bush," *New York Times Magazine*, October 17, 2004.

11. *Detention and Interrogation Practices*, 54. In 2017, there remained prisoners in Guantanamo Bay who had been held there for over a decade without any formal charges levied against them.

12. *Detention and Interrogation Practices*, 30. In addition, the UN Commission on Human Rights has reported that the primary objective of indefinite detention is not the prevention of renewed battle, but rather it is "to obtain information." UN Economic and Social Council, Commission on Human Rights, Sixty-Second Session, "Situation of Detainees at Guantanamo Bay," February 15, 2006, 13. The UN commission also held that medical officials at Guantanamo systematically violated international ethical standards in conspiring to turn medical knowledge into a weapon of interrogation (33).

13. *Detention and Interrogation Practices*, 34.

14. *Detention and Interrogation Practices*, 50.

15. "Guantanamo Suicides 'Acts of War,'" BBC News, June 11, 2006, http://news
.bbc.co.uk/2/hi/americas/5068606.stm. Life is strangely precious in the camps. Sanction *does* land upon those who fail to prevent the death of the detainees. As a matter
of technique, in the practice of interrogation and in the application of the "law" governing it, death constitutes failure. A guard from Guantanamo describes the *professionalism* at stake: "It is totally understood in the camp that if a detainee dies on your
shift, you are done. I mean that's it! You are going to be so in trouble that you don't
even want to have to deal with it." *Detention and Interrogation Practices*, 55. Or, more
succinctly from a CIA lawyer, "If the detainee dies, you're doing it wrong." This order
of things thus differs from Giorgio Agamben's theorization of *homo sacer* tethered to
and produced via the allegedly paradigmatic camps of modernity. The two primary
features of Agamben's theoretical claim, that *homo sacer* may be killed by anyone
without law's sanction and the rites of law shall not govern his death, are undermined
by the detail with which the camp law works at Guantanamo. Giorgio Agamben,
*Homo Sacer: Sovereign Power and Bare Life*, trans. Daniel Heller-Roazen (Stanford, CA:
Stanford University, 1998), 100–115. Legal charges *can* be levied against those who do
it wrong, and after the "facts," a death sentence can be issued by the tribunal/appellate
system. The asymmetry between "doing it wrong" in killing outside of procedure and
the commission of an "act of war" in dying by one's own hand is deeply colonial; the
admiral's lament carries a profound if unintended truth, a truth unseen and thus
exacerbated in Agamben's critique of the camps. Assertions that the suicides were in
fact covered-up homicides only buttress this point. Scott Horton, "The Guantanamo
'Suicides': A Camp Delta Sergeant Blows the Whistle," *Harper's Magazine*, March
2010.

16. Karen Greenberg and Joshua Dratel, eds., *The Torture Papers: The Road to
Abu Ghraib* (Cambridge: Cambridge University Press, 2005), 418 (emphasis added).

17. Greenberg and Dratel, *Torture Papers*, 504. General Taguba's report found
that Private Granier received active and direct support and encouragement from those
above him.

18. The ACLU, for example, thinks "our commitment to the rule of law is tested"
by the new regime and frets that "we may be failing this test." William Fisher, "The
Other GITMO: Bagram Air Base," *Public Record*, January 12, 2009.

19. As an example, the *New York Times* editorial page argued, "That is the real
nature of Mr. Bush's grotesque legacy: abuse and torture at an outlaw prison." Editorial, "Closing Guantanamo," *New York Times* (New York edition), January 17, 2009,
WK12. Correcting this legacy, the editorial continues, is "essential to restoring the rule
of law," and this return of the law will allow Americans to again "have faith in themselves and their government."

20. Phillipe Sands, *Lawless World: America and the Making and Breaking of Global
Rules from FDR's Atlantic Charter to George W. Bush's Illegal War* (New York: Viking,
2005).

21. This imagined "break" works implicitly as the natal point for narratives of new orders of governance, a narratological break that can work justly only if that newness does not signal the facticity of imperial violence, the violence omnipresent in the law, and/or violence devoid of the law's presence.

22. Neal R. Sonnett, "Guantanamo: Still a Legal Black Hole," *Human Rights* 33, no. 8 (Winter 2006): 8–9.

23. See generally Leila Brannstrom, "How I Learned to Stop Worrying and Love the Legal Argument," *No Foundations* 5 (2008), 22 (also pushing against this dominant narrative).

24. On the failure to extend jurisdiction to Bagram, see Al-Maqaleh v. Hagel, 738 F. 3d 112 (D.C. Cir. 2013).

25. This kind of violence is different from the violence normally associated with the law. Robert Cover, "Violence and the Word," *Yale Law Journal* 95, no. 8 (July 1986), 1601–29.

26. Andrew Gumbel, "Justice, Bush-style," *Nation*, October 20, 2008.

27. The lawyer in question is John Yoo, now the Emanuel S. Heller Professor of Law at UC Berkeley. Yoo served as deputy attorney-general in the Office of Legal Counsel from 2001 to 2003, and in that position, he took an active role in generating the conditions mapped out above as an author of the authorizing "torture memos." Responding to mobilizations against his tenure at Berkeley, his membership in the profession of law, and his status as a free man, Yoo has stated that those challenges must all fail because they are "political rather than legal." Adam Liptak, "The Reach of War: Penal Law; Legal Scholars Criticize Memos on Torture," *New York Times*, June 25, 2004.

28. Christopher Edley Jr., "The Torture Memos and Academic Freedom," Berkeley Law, University of California, April 10, 2008, http://www.law.berkeley.edu/news/2008/edley041008.html.

29. Thus, I am unsure of Agamben's turn to Derrida's "force of law" lecture to think the space of "exception." Or rather, I find both misapplied if applied to the appearance of the torture camps within American imperial jurisdiction. Agamben's mobilization of Eichman's defensive assertion in Jerusalem that " 'the words of the Fuhrer have the force of law' " (Giorgio Agamben, *State of Exception* [Chicago: University of Chicago Press, 2005], 38) seems inapt to capture and indeed will lead us to miss the fact that even our American Führer must *turn* to the law; without the law, he does not have words. If the law is what the law does, then the metaphysical antihistoricism of Agamben falters. Or, if I've misread the position, then what he takes as genealogical terrain needs elaboration beyond the curious deployment of "the West," which he sometimes confuses with "humanity."

30. Greenberg and Dratel, *Torture Papers*, 219. Formally, the memo was sent from then assistant attorney general (and now a federal appellate judge of the Ninth Circuit) Jay Bybee to presidential counsel Alberto Gonzalez. It is now known that John Yoo

authored it. Jack Goldsmith, *The Terror Presidency: Law and Judgment Inside the Bush Administration* (New York: W. W. Norton, 2007).

31. Greenberg and Dratel, *Torture Papers*, 175.

32. *Senate Intelligence Committee Report on Torture*, 6.

33. Jeremy Waldron, "Torture and Positive Law: Jurisprudence for the White House," *Columbia Law Review* 105, no. 6 (October 2005): 1701. Waldron compares two hypothetical situations to illustrate this point: (1) a taxpayer looking to claim maximum deductions under the code and (2) a man in a domestic relationship with a woman trying to determine how far he may push with bullying, intimidation, and force before it triggers the laws of domestic violence. Waldron argues that the very seeking of limits in the second hypothetical is misplaced and a reading of the law that negates its design. In this vein, one must recall that the American military previously had a policy requiring soldiers to imagine that they were the ones being held captive and enduring the interrogation. From that angle, the indeterminacy of the text suddenly becomes more determinate and far, far closer to Waldron than to Yoo. Perspectivality in theaters of equality is precisely what the Yoo position aims to abolish and what the camps work furiously to undo.

34. Greenberg and Dratel, *Torture Papers*, 176 (emphasis in original).

35. Greenberg and Dratel, *Torture Papers*, 176.

36. Greenberg and Dratel, *Torture Papers*, 176. In exacting legal *style*, they helpfully provide a string citation: 8 U.S.C. §1369 (2000); 42 U.S.C. §1395w-22 (2000); 42 U.S.C. §1395x (2000); 42 U.S.C. §1395dd (2000); 42 U.S.C. §1396b (2000); 42 U.S.C. §1396u-2 (2000). The aesthetics of the law are in full force and work as a force: they help make it a "legal" analysis. At a glance, there is no confusing these texts for anything else, such as an essay, an editorial, a manifesto, or a poem.

37. Greenberg and Dratel, *Torture Papers*, 176.

38. Greenberg and Dratel, *Torture Papers*, xv (emphasis added). The memo ultimately gives the president nearly unlimited powers once the matter is determined to fall within executive domain: "Congress may no more regulate the President's ability to detain and interrogate enemy combatants than it may regulate his ability to direct troop movements on the battlefield." Greenberg and Dratel, *Torture Papers*, 203. Harold Koh explains the logical outcome of this thinking: "[T]he notion that the President has the constitutional power to permit torture is like saying he has the constitutional power to commit genocide." Sands, *Lawless World*, 215.

39. Youngstown Sheet and Tube, Co. v. Sawyer, 343 U.S. 579 (1952).

40. *Youngstown*, 343 U.S. at 587.

41. *Youngstown*, 343 U.S. at 635.

42. *Youngstown*, 343 U.S. at 637.

43. Former solicitor general and previous director of the OLC, Walter Dellinger, says that the opinion "goes beyond anything the OLC has ever stated" regarding presidential powers and that it does so by ignoring relevant cases, particularly *Youngstown*.

R. Jeffrey Smith, "Slim Legal Grounds for Torture Memos: Most Scholars Reject Broad View of Executive's Power," *Washington Post*, July 4, 2004, A12.

44. Liptak, "The Reach of War."

45. Common and binding ethical cannons hold that a lawyer is expected to have knowledge of those elementary principles of law that are commonly known by well-informed attorneys and to discover additional rules of law that may be readily found by standard research techniques. Metzger v. Silverman, 62 Cal. App. 3d Supp. 30 (1976). For example, Goebel v. Lauderdale, 214 Cal. App. 3d 1502 (1989), held that an attorney is not liable for every mistake he or she may make but is expected to know the elementary principles of law commonly known to well-informed attorneys.

46. Goldsmith, *The Terror Presidency*, 145.

47. Goldsmith, *The Terror Presidency*, 149.

48. Waldron, "Torture and Positive Law," 1687.

49. Waldron, "Torture and Positive Law," 1687.

50. See generally Jonathan Simon, *Governing Through Crime* (Oxford: Oxford University Press, 2007).

51. Lt. Col. Stephen Abraham et al., "Open Letter to Representative Peter Hoekstra," August 27, 2009, https://wikileaks.org/podesta-emails/emailid/21108.

52. William E. Hellerstein, "No Rights of Prisoners," in *The Rehnquist Court: Judicial Activism on the Right*, ed. Herman Schwartz (New York: Hill and Wang, 2002), 71.

53. Hellerstein, "No Rights of Prisoners," 72.

54. "Prison-industrial complex" is not intended here as a rhetorical flourish. Many smaller communities have developed a reliance on the prison system as a jobs program; the prisons become economic "interests."

55. Greenberg and Dratel, *Torture Papers*, 448.

56. Steven C. Caton, "Abu Ghraib and the Problem of Evil," in *Ordinary Ethics: Anthropology, Language, and Action*, ed. Michael Lambert (New York: Fordham University Press, 2010), 177.

57. Charles Sheehan, "MP Investigated in Iraq Was at Pa. Prison During Abuse Scandal, but Not Implicated," *Associated Press*, May 7, 2004.

58. Agamben, *Homo Sacer*, 179.

59. David Oshinsky, *"Worse Than Slavery": Parchman Farm and the Ordeal of Jim Crow Justice* (New York: Free Press, 1996); Saidiya V. Hartman, *Scenes of Subjection: Terror, Slavery, and Self-making in Nineteenth-Century America* (Oxford: Oxford University Press, 1997).

60. Oshinsky, *"Worse Than Slavery,"* 120.

61. Oshinsky, *"Worse Than Slavery,"* 137.

62. Ida B. Wells described lynching as an "unwritten law" that was "cool and calculating" as opposed to an "outburst of uncontrollable fury" or the "unspeakable brutality of an insane mob." Ida B. Wells, "Lynch Law in America," *Arena* 23, no. 1 (January 1900): 15–24. Likewise, Paul Thomas has observed in the photographs of

lynching scenes that the white terrorists exhibit a sense of propriety and matter-of-factness about them and clearly "did not see themselves as lawless." Paul Thomas, "Lovely Day for a Necktie Party," *Film Quarterly* 63, no. 3 (Spring 2010): 82–83.

63. Kendall Thomas, "Beyond the Privacy Principle," *Columbia Law Review* 92, no. 6 (October 1992): 1469.

64. Oshinsky, *"Worse Than Slavery,"* 124.

65. Hartman, *Scenes of Subjection.*

66. Paul Lieberman and Dan Morain, "Unveiling the Face of the Prison Scandal," *Los Angeles Times*, June 19, 2004. The article is a curious piece of portraiture in that the entire narrative is driven by the *slide* of Granier from a "white-collar" future into a lower-middle-class milieu; only *they* could have been so depraved. He is an enigma of evil to the journalists because he did not *come* from there: as a boy, he "mixed daily with the children of doctors and lawyers. Friends assumed a white-collar life would be the destiny" of the boy. A class-based worldview that pathologizes members of the working class helps to situate torture "outside" the law, or at least that element of unguarded delight. It was the grin and the "thumbs-up" in the pictures from Abu Ghraib that did Granier in. Unsurprisingly, the article spends most of its time trying to determine the classed psychology of Granier rather than investigating the prisons where he worked and the law that he applied. The description of the prison and its racial makeup was in passing.

67. On continuities, see generally Michelle Alexander, *The New Jim Crow: Mass Incarceration in an Age of Colorblindness* (New York: Free Press, 2012).

68. Alexander, *New Jim Crow*, 109–19.

69. McCleskey v. Kemp, 481 U.S. 279 (1987).

70. *McCleskey*, 481 U.S. at 287.

71. *McCleskey*, 481 U.S. at 308.

72. Alexander, *New Jim Crow*, 111.

73. United States v. Armstrong, 517 U.S. 456 (1996).

74. *Armstrong*, 517 U.S. at 458.

75. *Armstrong*, 517 U.S. at 470.

76. *Armstrong*, 517 U.S. at 468.

77. In both the technical and social sense.

78. Butler, *Precarious Life*, 64. For Butler, rights are read as law and law is conceived as constitutionally prescribed and derived; the concern is expressed as the executive branch unilaterally "suspend[ing] constitutionally protected rights." More explicitly: "One might conclude with a strong argument that government policy ought to follow established law. And in a way, that is part of what I am calling for. But there is also a problem with the law, since it leaves open the possibility of its own retraction" (86). My point centers on execution and realization rather than retraction. As many have noted, Euro/American conceptualizations of law and legality have been historically linked to colonial plunders and expansions and not simply in the attempted dehumanization of subjects as subjects outside the law (as inconceivable (non)persons

unjustly denied a proper accounting per Butler). As example, one might look to the shift that occurred in the American government's (if we can suspend its plurality for a moment) approach to Native Americans. From the presidency of Andrew Jackson until the 1870s, the policy consisted of expulsion and genocide; after the 1870s, "the war continued" but now "with the weapons of the rule of law." Mark S. Weiner, *Americans Without Law: The Racial Boundaries of Citizenship* (New York: New York University Press, 2008), 37. The explicit aim of the Dawes Act of 1877, writes Weiner, was to spread the "civilizing influence of private property" and thus to "infuse the Indian self with an Anglo-Saxon vision of law and so to destroy the Indian as a social fact" (39). That is, juridical incorporation served as the *mechanism* of genocide.

79. This analogy emerged in the wake of the *McCleskey* decision; see Anthony Amsterdam, "Race and the Death Penalty Before and After McCleskey," *Columbia Human Rights Law Review* 39, no. 1 (Fall 2007): 34–58, and Hugo Bedau, "Someday McCleskey Will Be Death Penalty's Dred Scott," *Los Angeles Times*, May 1, 1987.

80. Brannstrom, "Love the Legal Argument," 25.

81. Greenberg and Dratel, *Torture Papers*, 229.

82. Greenberg and Dratel, *Torture Papers*, 230.

83. Greenberg and Dratel, *Torture Papers*, 232. Colin Dayan has also noted that the "Rehnquist's Court's Eighth Amendment cases prepared the way" for the torture of detainees with the shift from conditions to intent. Colin Dayan, *The Story of Cruel and Unusual* (Cambridge, MA: MIT Press, 2007), 59 (not noted by Dayan is how widespread this jurisprudential standard now extends).

84. U.S. Const. art. 1, § 9.

85. Robinson v. California, 370 U.S. 660 (1962), applied the Eighth Amendment's restrictions to the actions of the state governments.

86. Roper v. Simmons, 543 U.S. 551 (2005), outlawed the use of the death penalty against someone who committed the crime while under the age of eighteen.

87. Kennedy v. Louisiana, 554 U.S. 407 (2008), prohibited the use of the death penalty when the crime is rape, even when the victim is a minor.

88. Velvet Revolution, http://www.velvetrevolution.us/torture_lawyers/index.php.

89. Velvet Revolution, http://www.velvetrevolution.us/torture_lawyers/index.php.

90. Antonin Scalia interview, *60 Minutes*, April 27, 2008.

91. In this, I am in agreement with Judith Butler's point regarding the earlier tribunal mechanisms established at Guantanamo: it is a "law that is no law, a court that is no court, a process that is no process." Butler, *Precarious Life*, 62. See pp. 62–77 for an excellent mapping of this auto-negation. I think this can be distinguished from the earlier theorization by Butler of lawlessness, sovereignty, and the rule of law.

92. Contrast "There is hardly a political question in the United States which does not sooner or later turn into a judicial one" (Tocqueville) with "the state of exception" is "the hidden matrix and *nomos* of the political space in which we are still living" (Agamben). Alexis de Tocqueville, *Democracy in America*, ed. J. P. Mayer, trans.

George Lawrence (New York: Harper, 1988), 270, and Agamben, *Homo Sacer*, 166–67, respectively.

93. Agamben, *Homo Sacer*, 2.

94. Carl Schmitt, *The Concept of the Political*, trans. George Schwab (Chicago: University of Chicago Press, 1996), 31n12.

95. Agamben, *State of Exception*, 9.

96. See generally *Federalist*, no. 10 (James Madison), in James Madison, Alexander Hamilton, and John Jay, *The Federalist Papers*, ed. Isaac Kramnick (1788; Harmondsworth, UK: Penguin Classics, 1987). It is by no accident that Alexis de Tocqueville will claim in his 1848 preface to *Democracy in America* that "the sacred rights of family and property" are preserved in America by the "principles of order, balances of powers, true liberty, and sincere and deep respect for the law." See *Democracy in America*, xiv.

97. We should look to Article V of the U.S. Constitution as a theory and a practice; it is perplexing and unique.

98. Executive Order 13491 (January 2009).

99. This is Owen Fiss's succinct summary of the president's position in *A War Like No Other: The Constitution in a Time of Terror* (New York: New Press, 2015), 118. The precise quotation from President Obama: "[A]t a time of great challenges and disturbing disunity, nothing will be gained by spending our time and energy laying blame for the past." http://www.politico.com/story/2009/04/obama-memo-release-weighty-decision

100. *Senate Intelligence Committee Report on Torture*, xii.

101. *Senate Intelligence Committee Report on Torture*, xi.

102. *Senate Intelligence Committee Report on Torture*, xii.

103. *Senate Intelligence Committee Report on Torture*, xi.

## Chapter 3

1. An Act for the Relief of the Parents of Theresa Marie Schiavo.

2. This observation holds across disagreement about other elements of the legislation. See O. Carter Snead, "The Surprising Truth About *Schiavo*: A Defeat for the Cause of Autonomy," *Constitutional Commentary* 22, no. 3 (2005): 383–404 ("this extraordinary avenue of relief"); Adam M. Samaha, "Undue Process: Congressional Referral and Judicial Resistance in the Schiavo Controversy," *Constitutional Commentary* 22, no. 3 (2005): 505–28 ("Congressional action was both extraordinary and feeble"); and Michael Stoke Paulsen, "Killing Terri Schiavo," *Constitutional Commentary* 22, no. 3 (2005): 585–97 (commending the "extraordinary efforts to save her life").

3. The Schiavo case arose in Florida. For that state's statutory scheme, see Fla. Stat. § 765 (2012) (esp. Part II, Part III, and Part IV).

4. See generally Cruzan v. Missouri Dept. of Health, 497 U.S. 261 (1990); Washington v. Glucksberg, 521 U.S. 702 (1997).

5. Paulsen, "Killing Terri Schiavo," 585. This point is seconded in Edward J. Larson, "From *Cruzan* to *Schiavo*: Similar Bedfellows in Fact and at Law," *Constitutional Commentary* 22, no. 3 (2005): 405.

6. Jill Lepore has argued that the reduction of political thinking to the extremities of "life and death" leads to a public discourse that is "no longer civil, pluralist, and yielding. And when this happens, day after day, year after year, there is no more politics; there is only one sort of impasse or another." See Jill Lepore, "The Politics of Death," *New Yorker*, November 30, 2009, 67. One can decline Lepore's invitation to view "politics" as defined by civility and pluralist yielding (indeed the theater of civil yielding frequently excludes from view the unyielding operations of *political* power that mark off such spaces and practices and shroud the very real "life-and-death" questions at the heart of politics) yet still explore further the logic of the impasse as practice in the present. Such routinization of the "impasse," its always being there to be overcome and thus never really overcomeable, might very well help explain the gathering forces and repeating force of contemporary anti-constitutionalism.

7. I have tried to use facts that even radical critics of the Schiavo decision (and thus staunch supporters of Terri's Law) do not dispute. Therefore, this quote is from Paulsen, "Killing Terri Schiavo," 586. Some supporters of the law, however, resorted to inventing "medical facts" to justify congressional intervention. Majority Leader Bill Frist took the floor of the Senate and issued his own "medical diagnosis" of Terri Schiavo and claimed that she was not in a persistent vegetative state. None of the doctors who treated Schiavo concurred with Frist's fantasy projection, and the autopsy confirmed that Schiavo's brain was "profoundly atrophied" and exhibited "massive and irreversible damage."

8. In Re Quinlan, 70 N.J. 10 (1976).

9. *Quinlan*, 70 N.J. at 24.

10. *Quinlan*, 70 N.J. at 26.

11. *Quinlan*, 70 N.J. at 19.

12. *Quinlan*, 70 N.J. at 40.

13. *Quinlan*, 70 N.J. at 42.

14. None of these cases spoke directly to a right to end life-sustaining treatment. Griswold v. Connecticut, 381 U.S. 479 (1965), overturned restrictive contraception laws and drew a zone of privacy around heteromarital sexual practices in the home; Eisenstadt v. Baird, 405 U.S. 438 (1972), redefined the right in *Griswold* to an individual right unmoored from the marital status; Stanley v. Georgia, 394 U.S. 557 (1969), secured a privacy right within the home to possess (but not distribute) texts the state deemed as obscenity; and Roe v. Wade, 410 U.S. 113 (1973), established a right to abortion as fundamental and rooted it in the privacy right to make family planning decisions. Also, the N.J. Court cited Art. I, paragraph I of the state constitution: "1. All persons are by nature free and independent, and have certain natural and unalienable rights, among which are those of enjoying and defending life and liberty, of

acquiring, possessing, and protecting property, and of pursuing and obtaining safety and happiness (N.J. Const. art. I, § 1)."

15. The quotation is from Chief Justice Rehnquist's majority opinion in *Cruzan*, 497 U.S. at 278 (1990).

16. *Glucksberg*, 521 U.S. at 723n18.

17. *Glucksberg*, 521 U.S. at 724–25.

18. Although *Glucksberg* did not recognize a fundamental constitutional "right to die," nothing in the opinion foreclosed the possibility of states passing laws to permit assisted suicides. The Court held that such a distinction was not an irrational violation of the Equal Protection Clause in Vacco v. Quill, 521 U.S. 793 (1997).

19. Robert A. Burt, "Family Conflict and Family Privacy: The Constitutional Violation in Terri Schiavo's Death," *Constitutional Commentary* 22, no. 3 (2005): 429.

20. This summary of state law is taken from Burt, "Family Conflict," 430.

21. Snead, "The Surprising Truth," 384.

22. Jay Wolfson, "A Report to Governor Jeb Bush and the 6th Judicial Circuit in the Matter of Theresa Marie Schiavo," December 1, 2003, http://news.findlaw.com/hdocs/docs/schiavo/1203galrpt.pdf. Also available at this site is a treasure trove of documents related to this case. See http://news.findlaw.com/legalnews/lit/schiavo/. I thank Etienne Pelaprat for directing me to this source and for guiding my eye to the full proceedings in the state of Florida prior to federal intervention.

23. The Florida Supreme Court declared the law unconstitutional "on its face and as applied."

24. The University of Miami Ethics Program maintains a complete timeline of the case, with relevant orders, motions, opinions, statutes, and press statements. See https://bioethics.miami.edu/research-and-clinical-ethics/terri-schiavo-project/timeline-of-key-events/part-1/index.html.

25. Burt, "Family Conflict," 447.

26. Robert P. George, "Terri Schiavo: A Right to Life Denied or a Right to Die Honored?" *Constitutional Commentary* 22, no. 3 (2005): 421. Constitutional law places the *Schiavo* case squarely in George's "etc."; George seems not to notice and describes the case as one involving "euthanasia." Nowhere in this essay does the professor of jurisprudence even mention the Constitution or the jurisprudence of the Court in the area of substantive due process. He does cite the journal *First Things*, *National Catholic Bioethics Quarterly*, his own interview in *National Review*, and an address by Pope John Paul II.

27. On the absence of constitutional consideration, see Scott E. Grant, "The Contagion of Constitutional Avoidance," *Constitutional Commentary* 22, no. 3 (2005): 497.

28. This has strong echoes of the majority opinion in Bush v. Gore, 531 U.S. 98, at 109 (2000) ("Our consideration is limited to the present circumstances"). Although "precedent" has a different meaning in each institutional context, in both cases the law found itself in a heightened state of present-ism. Political forces seemed incapable of imagining governance beyond the instant.

29. U.S. Const. art. 1, § 9.

30. U.S. Const. art. 1, § 10. The importance of this should not be underestimated as the 1787 Constitution was a constitution of *federalism*.

31. For an argument along these lines, see Steven Calabresi, "The Terri Schiavo Case: In Defense of the Special Law Enacted by Congress and President Bush," *Northwestern Law Review* 100, no. 1 (2006): 151.

32. See the plurality opinion in Planned Parenthood of Pennsylvania v. Casey, 505 U.S. 833 (1992).

33. George, "Terri Schiavo," 421.

34. Paulsen, "Killing Terri Schiavo," 587. Translation: living wills may be ignored. Steven Calabresi also flirts with the position: "I have serious doubts about the morality of starving anyone to death—even a truly comatose person who can never recover and who indicated clearly that he or she wanted to be starved to death." Calabresi, "The Terri Schiavo Case," 156. Translation: living wills may be ignored.

35. Calabresi, "The Terri Schiavo Case," 156. Apparently, hearing alarm bells in that is a sign that one "believes that morality . . . is not an issue" (157). And this then leaves one inevitably in the ideological camp of "the culture-of-death forces" (168).

36. Federal courts refused to issue an injunction to reverse the removal of the feeding tubes because the Schindlers could not show a "substantial likelihood of success on the merits." The courts thus clung to the letter of the law in order to thwart the spirit of the law. However, only Judge Birch of the Eleventh Circuit confronted the constitutionality of the law and argued that it violated the separation of powers. Judge Birch noted that the courts had "hypothetically assume[d] jurisdiction to avoid resolving" the constitutional questions. Schiavo ex rel. Schindler v. Schiavo, 404 F.3d 1270 (11th Cir. 2005).

37. DeShaney v. Winnebago County Dept. of Social Services, 489 U.S. 189 (1989).

38. *Roe*, 410 U.S. 113.

39. *DeShaney*, 489 U.S. at 193.

40. *DeShaney*, 489 U.S. at 193.

41. *DeShaney*, 489 U.S. at 193. Joshua's father was convicted of child abuse and received a sentence of two to four years.

42. In the majority: Chief Justice Rehnquist, Justice Scalia, Justice Kennedy, Justice White, Justice O'Connor, and Justice Stevens. In the dissent: Justice Brennan, Justice Marshall, Justice Blackmun.

43. *DeShaney*, 489 U.S. at 195.

44. *DeShaney*, 489 U.S. at 203.

45. This is also true, to a modified extent, in the line of cases establishing and affirming the right to have an abortion without criminal prohibition. See generally the trimester framework in *Roe* and the "undue burden" standard in *Casey*.

46. A claim has also been made that the right to abortion must be central to any political movement for sexual/bodily freedom broadly and diversely construed. See Ann Scales, "Poststructuralism on Trial," in *Feminist and Queer Legal Theory: Intimate*

*Encounters, Uncomfortable Conversations,* ed. Martha Fineman, Jack Jackson, and Adam Romero (Burlington, VT: Ashgate, 2009), 395–410.

47. Burt, "Family Conflict," 433.

48. *Cruzan,* 497 U.S. 261 (1990) (Scalia, J. concurring opinion).

49. From the official party website www.gop.com: "Kagan's Memos as Clerk Reveal Views Far Left of the Mainstream." Kagan served as clerk to Justice Marshall. As a criticism of Kagan, the GOP contrasted the wise "conservative" ruling in *DeShaney* with Kagan's "Liberal View" on the Fourteenth Amendment that the "Constitutional Guarantee of Liberty Should Be Read Broadly."

50. Ronald Dworkin, *Life's Dominion: An Argument About Abortion, Euthanasia, and Individual Freedom* (New York: Knopf, 1993), 4 ("Abortion is tearing America apart. It is distorting its politics, and confounding its constitutional law").

51. Dworkin, *Life's Dominion,* 10.

52. Dworkin, *Life's Dominion,* 10–11.

53. Dworkin, *Life's Dominion,* 13. Dworkin does not discuss the *DeShaney* case in *Life's Dominion.*

54. Martin Jay, "The Apocalyptic Imagination and the Inability to Mourn," in *Rethinking Imagination,* ed. Gillian Robinson and John Rundell (New York: Routledge, 1994), 31.

55. Valerie Hartouni, *Cultural Conceptions: On Reproductive Technologies and the Remaking of Life* (Minneapolis: University of Minnesota, 1997), 37. Giorgio Agamben thinks that "politicizing" life and death is a threshold moment for biopolitics in late modernity. See Giorgio Agamben, *Homo Sacer: Sovereign Power and Bare Life,* trans. Daniel Heller-Roazen (Stanford, CA: Stanford University, 1998), part 3. Agamben cites the *Quinlan* case as a critical moment in this politicizing turn of events. He makes no mention of abortion. Without denying the importance of the politics of abortion and euthanasia in the biopolitics of "population" management, it seems incumbent to nonetheless create the space for thinking about these moments distinct from anxieties about the "health" of the body politic. In her book *Ourselves Unborn: A History of the Fetus in Modern America* (New York: Oxford University Press, 2011), 189–90, Sara Dubow explains that "there have been many different fetuses in twentieth-century America. . . . The fetus has been the vehicle through which people have wrestled with assumptions about science and religion, anxieties about demography and democracy, beliefs about feminism and motherhood, and ideas about conservatism and liberalism." As distinct from the politics of biopower and race, we must consider a new fetus: the Augustinian one.

56. Dworkin, *Life's Dominion,* 27.

57. Jacob Taubes, *Occidental Eschatology,* trans. David Ratmoko (Stanford, CA: Stanford University Press, 2009), 27.

58. Taubes, *Occidental Eschatology,* 9.

59. In the midst of the Schiavo affair, Congress subpoenaed a brain-dead Terri Schiavo to "testify" before Congress; more recently, a legislative committee in Ohio

invited a nine-week-old fetus to "testify" on behalf of an antiabortion bill. No women who had ever had an abortion were invited to testify. The fetus and the vegetative patient are no longer objects of power; they are now most bizarrely *subjects*.

60. Augustine, *Confessions*, trans. Henry Chadwick (Oxford: Oxford University Press, 1998), book I, chap. 6.

61. William Connolly, *Capitalism and Christianity, American Style* (Durham, NC: Duke University Press, 2008), 4–5.

62. Most prominently, Lee Edelman has issued a call for a queer revolt against "enslavement to the future" in "the name of having a life." Lee Edelman, *No Future: Queer Theory and the Death Drive* (Durham, NC: Duke University Press, 2004), 30. Edelman sees the political mobilization of the fetus as being entirely centered on a "reproductive futurism" and understands a politics of the future as entirely bound up in that futurism (24). However, Edelman's reading of political life through the lens of psychoanalytic theory misses the apocalyptic dimensions of the right-wing "politics of life" and thus (at least rhetorically) unwittingly converges with it in its call for "no future." As well, this queer project is insufficiently attentive to other critical theorists, such as Wendy Brown and Jacques Derrida, who have sought to nurture care for the future without any of the teleological closures Edelman critiques in reproductive futurism. In contrast to the role of apocalypticism on the political Right, this queer theoretical negation of futurity currently finds little purchase on the political Left (a point conceded by Edelman in his critique, a point that in fact prompts the critique).

63. Martin Luther King Jr., quoted in Kenneth L. Smith and Ira G. Zepp Jr., *Search for a Beloved Community: The Thought of Martin Luther King, Jr.* (Valley Forge, PA: Judson, 1974), 125.

64. Wendy Brown, *Politics Out of History* (Princeton, NJ: Princeton University Press, 2001), esp. chap. 7, "Futures: Specters and Angels: Benjamin and Derrida."

65. Brown, *Politics Out of History*, 4.

66. Brown, *Politics Out of History*, 14.

67. Brown, *Politics Out of History*, 138–42.

68. Brown, *Politics Out of History*, 148. . . . true even if "(the *Manifesto*) quickly made itself obsolete even by Marx and Engel's own account" (148).

69. In modern times, "faith in an apocalypse by revelation had been replaced by faith in an apocalypse by revolution." David J. Leigh, *Apocalyptic Patterns in Twentieth-Century Fiction* (Notre Dame, IN: Notre Dame University Press, 2008), 14.

70. Jacques Derrida, "Of an Apocalyptic Tone Newly Adopted in Philosophy," in *Derrida and Negative Theology*, ed. Harold Coward and Toby Foshay (Albany: State University of New York Press, 1992), 53.

71. Derrida, "Apocalyptic Tone," 53.

72. King too thought this a worldly aim: "[T]hough acutely aware that the Beloved Community is 'not yet,' but in the future—perhaps even the distant future— Martin Luther King believed that it would eventually be actualized." Kenneth L. Smith

and Ira G. Zepp Jr., "Martin Luther King's Vision of the Beloved Community," *Christian Century*, April 3, 1974.

73. Brown, *Politics Out of History*, 144.

74. Hannah Arendt, *Between Past and Future* (New York: Penguin, 1968), 52.

75. Arendt, *Between Past and Future*, 66.

76. Arendt, *Between Past and Future*, 68.

77. Alexis de Tocqueville, *Democracy in America*, ed. J. P. Mayer, trans. George Lawrence (New York: Harper, 1988), 175.

78. Michel Foucault, *Society Must Be Defended: Lectures at the College de France 1975 to 1976* (New York: Picador, 1997), 253.

79. Foucault, *Society Must Be Defended*, 253.

80. Erich Maria Remarque, *All Quiet on the Western Front* (New York: Fawcett, 1967), 84.

81. See Primo Levi, *The Drowned and the Saved* (New York: Simon & Shuster 1988), esp. chap. 5, "Useless Violence."

82. Although Elie Wiesel rejected this understanding of the Holocaust as denying the specificity of the Holocaust: "The statement is: 'It was man's inhumanity to man.' No! It was man's inhumanity to Jews." See Elie Wiesel, "Remarks at the Dedication of Yad Vashem" (March 15, 2005).

83. John Hersey, *Hiroshima* (New York: Knopf, 1985), 11 (originally published in the *New Yorker* in 1946).

84. Hersey, *Hiroshima*, 12. In thinking about apocalyptic thinking, Derrida turns to the Book of Revelation, which "dominates the whole of the Western apocalyptic" and argues that "every apocalyptic eschatology is promised in the name of light, of the visionary and the vision, and of a light of light, of a light brighter than all the lights it makes possible." Derrida, "Apocalyptic Tone," 50.

85. Hersey, *Hiroshima*, 82.

86. Hersey, *Hiroshima*, 18.

87. Hersey, *Hiroshima*, 122.

88. Hersey, *Hiroshima*, 122.

89. Hersey, *Hiroshima*, 186.

90. The full quote is: "the past is never dead, it is not even past."

91. William Faulkner, "Address Accepting the Nobel Prize in Literature" (December 10, 1950).

92. Rev. 21:1.

93. Dan Cohn-Sherbok, *The Politics of Apocalypse: The History and Influence of Christian Zionism* (Ann Arbor: University of Michigan Press, 2006), 113–15.

94. "Draft of recognition of Israel," May 14, 1948, Ross Papers, Alphabetical Correspondence File, 1916–1950, Harry S. Truman Presidential Library and Museum, https://www.trumanlibrary.org/whistlestop/study_collections/israel/large/documents/index.php?documentdate = 1948–05–14&documentid = 48&pagenumber = 1.

95. Paul C. Merkley, *The Politics of Christian Zionism, 1891 to 1948* (London: Frank Cass, 1998), 102.

96. Cohn-Sherbok, *The Politics of Apocalypse*, 32.

97. Thomas J. J. Alitzer, *History as Apocalypse* (Albany: State University of New York Press 1985), 81.

98. Aristotle, *The Politics*, ed. Trever J. Saunders, trans. T. A. Sinclair (London: Penguin, 1981), book I; also book III, chap. ix: "But a state's purpose is not merely to provide a living but to make a life that is good. Otherwise it might be made up of slaves or animals other than man, and that is impossible because slaves and animals do not participate in *eudaimonia*."

99. Augustine, *The City of God Against the Pagans*, ed. and trans. R. W. Dyson (Cambridge: Cambridge University Press, 1998), book 14, chap. 15.

100. Augustine, *The City of God Against the Pagans*, book 14, chap. 4.

101. Augustine, *The City of God Against the Pagans*, book 14, chap. 8 (quoting the Apostle John).

102. Augustine, *The City of God Against the Pagans*, book 14, chap. 6.

103. Arendt, *Between Past and Future*, 66.

104. "History and Prophecy," Israel My Beloved: God's Banner to the Nations, https://israelmybeloved.com/history-prophecy/.

105. Cohn-Sherbok, *The Politics of Apocalypse*, 162–63.

106. In addition, the similarly themed *Left Behind* series authored by Moral Majority cofounder Tim LaHaye has sold more than 60 million copies since being published in 1995.

107. Cohn-Sherbok, *The Politics of Apocalypse*, 153–54.

108. Cohn-Sherbok, *The Politics of Apocalypse*, xii.

109. Faulkner, "Nobel Prize Speech." The end of political desire: this becomes all the more true when we read the tideless time in contrast to the riparian imagery of Machiavelli: "I compare fortune [*fortuna*] to one of those violent rivers which, when they are enraged, flood the plains, tear down trees and buildings, wash soil from one place and deposit in another. . . . Yet although such is their nature, it does not follow that when they are flowing quietly one cannot take precautions, constructing dykes and embankments so that when the river is in flood they would keep to one channel or their impetus lees wild and dangerous." Machiavelli, *The Prince*, 2nd ed., trans. Harvey C. Mansfield (Chicago: University of Chicago Press, 1998), chap. xxv. The earthly embrace of Faulkner and Machiavelli represents a clear disagreement with Augustine and a direct repudiation of *Shikata ga-nai* in the face of enormity. And as neither romanticizes the forces on earth and the passions common to humanity, neither (and here esp. Machiavelli) falls into dreaming of postpolitical futures on Earth as Mill, Marx, and King had tendencies to do.

110. Brown, *Politics Out of History*, 147.

111. Brown, *Politics Out of History*, 154.

112. See generally Marx, "On the Jewish Question," in *The Marx-Engels Reader*, 2nd ed., ed. Robert Tucker (New York: W. W. Norton, 1978).

113. See generally Karl Marx, *Capital, Volume I: A Critique of Political Economy*, trans. Ben Fowkes (London: Penguin, 1992).

114. Brown, *Politics Out of History*, 154. Brown suggests that Derrida's claims are "corroborated by the boundless litigiousness of the present age, and especially by the conversion of historical-political claims of oppression to legal claims for rights or reparations."

115. See generally Friedrich Nietzsche, *On the Genealogy of Morals*, trans. Douglas Smith (Oxford: Oxford University Press, 2009), the second essay, esp. §§ 20–23.

116. Nietzsche, *Genealogy of Morals*, second essay, § 11.

117. Karl Marx and Frederick Engels, "Manifesto of the Communist Party," in Tucker, *Marx-Engels Reader*, 476.

118. Looking toward Europe (and France in particular) from America, Alexis de Tocqueville worried that "democracy had been left to its wild instincts; it has grown up like those children deprived of parental care . . . it is worshipped as the idol of strength; thereafter when it is weakened by its own excesses, the lawgivers conceive the imprudent project of abolishing it instead of trying to educate and correct it." Tocqueville, *Democracy in America*, 13. An idol of strength driven by wild instincts is precisely what Nietzsche thought absent in the democratic "herd."

119. The address was published as Hanna Fenichel Pitkin, "The Idea of a Constitution," *Journal of Legal Education* 37, no. 2 (June 1987): 167–69.

120. Pitkin, "Idea of a Constitution," 167, 168.

121. Pitkin, "Idea of a Constitution," 167, 168.

122. Brown, *Politics Out of History*, 139.

## Chapter 4

1. Hanna Fenichel Pitkin, "The Idea of a Constitution," *Journal of Legal Education* 37, no. 2 (June 1987): 168.

2. Terminiello v. Chicago (*Terminiello*), 337 U.S. 1, at 37 (1949).

3. *Terminiello*, 337 U.S. 1, at 5.

4. It violated the First Amendment as incorporated via the Due Process Clause of the Fourteenth Amendment. Justice Jackson spent some time suggesting that the Court should circumscribe the opinion because it was a municipal ordinance and the application of the First Amendment via incorporation was a judicial usurpation of power. The politics of incorporation and interpretation is discussed more fully in Chapter 2 of this book.

5. *Terminiello*, 337 U.S. at 13 (Jackson, J. dissenting).

6. *Terminiello*, 337 U.S. at 32 (Jackson, J. dissenting).

7. *Terminiello*, 337 U.S. at 4 (Douglas, J.).

8. See generally John Stuart Mill, *On Liberty* (1859; London: Penguin, 2007) (on the value of invited dispute); see generally Niccolo Machiavelli, *Discourses on Livy*

(1531; Oxford: Oxford University Press, 2009), book I (on the value of tumultuous-ness). Mill is directly on point; Machiavelli is also on point, even if less directly so.

9. See generally Jason Frank, *Constituent Moments* (Durham, NC: Duke University Press, 2010), chaps. 1–3.

10. Of course, a political theory of life inheres in a jurisprudence of order. Sheldon Wolin teaches that "in the ontology of political thought, order has been the equivalent of being, anarchy the synonym for non-being." Sheldon Wolin, *Politics and Vision: Continuity and Innovation in Western Political Thought* (Princeton, NJ: Princeton University Press, 2004), 218.

11. *Merriam-Webster Medical Dictionary* (2006), s.v. "vitality."

12. *Terminiello*, 337 U.S. at 4 (Douglas, J. dissenting).

13. It might also be seen as working in tandem with an emerging "governmentality of neoliberalism" that "facilitates the dismantling of liberal democracy." See Wendy Brown, *Edgework: Critical Essays on Knowledge and Politics* (Princeton, NJ: Princeton University Press, 2005), 52. Yet its cost-benefit logic still retains an end ultimately irreducible to the values and logics of the market. Perhaps it sutures the two orders together in some odd manner.

14. This happens in part by the production of "value" in the circulations and domains of authoritarianism and Empire. Human beings on the underside of those orders suffer from a deflationary spiral and become worth almost nothing. See Judith Butler, *Precarious Life: The Power of Mourning and Violence* (London: Verso, 2004). By contrast, Empire and state are transfigured into the most precious of all metals. Plugged into the jurisprudential economatrix of "law and economics," we soon discover cruelty has no horizon at the same instant that there is an overproduction of procedure.

15. Alan Dershowitz, "Should We Fight Terror with Torture?" *Independent*, July 3, 2006.

16. Dershowitz, "Fight Terror with Torture?"

17. Dershowitz, "Fight Terror with Torture?" (quoting former U.S. secretary of state Dean Acheson).

18. Dershowitz, "Fight Terror with Torture?"

19. Thomas Hobbes, *Leviathan* (1651; London: Penguin, 1982), chap. XVIII.

20. Hobbes, *Leviathan*, chap. XVII.

21. Hobbes, *Leviathan*, chap. XXI.

22. Dershowitz, "Fight Terror with Torture?"

23. Dershowitz, "Fight Terror with Torture?"

24. Wolin, *Politics and Vision*, 252.

25. An analogous point is made by Hannah Arendt regarding international humanitarian law. Also, the value of "citizen" should be read functionally rather than formalistically here.

26. Thomas Paine, "Common Sense" in Paine, *Common Sense and Other Writings*, ed. George S. Wood (New York: Modern Library, 2003), 22.

27. Paine, "Common Sense," 21.

28. Frank, *Constituent Moments*, 3.

29. Since not all politics theoretically presumes the people, seeks them out as legitimating ground, invokes them rather than demotes and/or disaggregates them, and so on.

30. See U.S. Const. pmbl.

31. Frank says that politics renders the people perpetually "not yet." Frank, *Constituent Moments*, 5, 65.

32. Gordon Wood, *The Radicalism of the American Revolution* (New York: Knopf, 1992), 118. Wood reports that this change was noted with "chagrin" by a young John Adams suggesting that old orders disappearing did not entail ancient antagonisms withering.

33. Wood, *Radicalism of the American Revolution*, 96.

34. Wood, *Radicalism of the American Revolution*, 96.

35. Wood, *Radicalism of the American Revolution*, 97 (quoting Jefferson).

36. Karl Marx, "On the Jewish Question," in *The Marx-Engels Reader*, 2nd ed., ed. Robert Tucker (New York: W. W. Norton, 1978), 43.

37. Marx, "On the Jewish Question," 44.

38. Marx, "On the Jewish Question," 45–46.

39. Paine, "Common Sense," 33.

40. Paine, "Common Sense," 47.

41. Paine, "Common Sense," 31.

42. Thomas Paine, "Rights of Man," in Paine, *Common Sense and Other Writings*, 170.

43. Paine, "Common Sense," 32.

44. For example, Jack Balkin told Occupy Wall Street protestors to "occupy the Constitution" as if such occupation was in any way possible.

45. Paine, "Common Sense," 39.

46. Paine, "Common Sense," 32 ("A government of our own is our natural right"). This is in conflict with his formulation where honor belongs to those who "should discover a mode of government that contained the greatest sum of individual happiness, with the least national expense" (31).

47. Paine, "Common Sense," 46.

48. Hannah Arendt, *On Revolution* (New York: Penguin, 1963), 130.

49. See generally Hannah Arendt, "The Pursuit of Happiness," chap. 3 in *On Revolution*. We need to think of the political vitality in unsettling the demarcations of public/private, freedom/necessity, that Arendt held to.

50. Declaration of Independence, para. 2 (U.S. 1776) (emphasis added).

51. Alexis de Tocqueville, *Democracy in America*, ed. J. P. Mayer, trans. George Lawrence (New York: Harper, 1988), book II, chap. 11.

52. Tocqueville, *Democracy in America*, book II, chap. 11.

53. Arendt, *On Revolution*, 92.

54. Arendt, *On Revolution*, 92.

55. John T. Noonan Jr., *Persons and Masks of the Law: Cardozo, Holmes, Jefferson, and Wythe as the Makers of the Masks* (Berkeley: University of California Press, 2002).

56. Noonan, *Masks of the Law*, 32.

57. Noonan, *Masks of the Law*, 38.

58. Noonan, *Masks of the Law*, 38.

59. Noonan, *Masks of the Law*, 50.

60. Noonan, *Masks of the Law*, 55.

61. U.S. Census Bureau, *Census Data for the State of Virginia*, in 1790 Census Information, http://www2.census.gov/prod2/decennial/documents/1790m.zip.

62. Hugh Brogan, *Alexis de Tocqueville: A Life* (New Haven, CT: Yale University Press, 2008). Two days later, the good citizens from Paris returned to the estate and arrested Malesherbes and Alexis de Tocqueville's parents.

63. Saint-Just had in fact argued that Louis XVI should be judged as an "enemy," as a lower order of humanity, and thus not be "raised to the rank of citizen" deserving of a trial. Saint-Just lost this motion and it was "Citizen Capet" who was put on trial and executed for attacking "the sovereignty of the people." David Andress, *The Terror: The Merciless War for Freedom in Revolutionary France* (New York: Farrar, Straus and Giroux, 2005), 137.

64. Jean-Jacques Rousseau, *The Social Contract*, trans. Maurice Cranston (London: Penguin, 1968), 69.

65. Rousseau, *Social Contract*, 63.

66. Rousseau, *Social Contract*, 63.

67. Tocqueville, *Democracy in America*, book II, chap. 8.

68. Even Paine's redistributive economic plans stayed within this conceptual framework.

69. *Federalist*, no. 10 (James Madison), in James Madison, Alexander Hamilton, and John Jay, *The Federalist Papers*, ed. Isaac Kramnick (1788; Harmondsworth, UK: Penguin Classics, 1987).

70. Bonnie Honig, *Emergency Politics: Paradox, Law, and Democracy* (Princeton, NJ: Princeton University Press, 2009), 27.

71. Charles A. Beard, *An Economic Interpretation of the Constitution of the United States* (1913; New York: Free Press, 1941), 11.

72. *Federalist*, no. 10 (Madison).

73. *Federalist*, no. 10 (Madison).

74. This spurred Calhoun's "nullification thesis."

75. *Federalist*, no. 25 (Hamilton).

76. "[A]n unhappy species of population abounding in some of the States, who, during the calm of regular government, are sunk below the level of men; but who in tempestuous scenes of civil violence, may emerge into human character, and give a superiority of strength to any party which they may associate themselves." *Federalist*,

no. 43 (Madison). In this sense, the "tyranny of the majority" turns doubly frightful to the founders.

77. *Federalist*, no. 26 (Hamilton) (emphasis added). "The circumstances of a Revolution quickened the public sensibility on every point connected with the security of popular rights, and in some instances raised the warmth of our zeal beyond the degree which consisted with the due temperature of the body politic."

78. *Federalist*, no. 10 (Madison).

79. *Federalist*, no. 9 (Hamilton).

80. *Federalist*, no. 21 (Hamilton).

81. *Federalist*, no. 6 (Madison). "If [Daniel] Shays had not been a *desperate debtor*, it is much to be doubted whether Massachusetts would have been plunged into a civil war."

82. See Bruce Ackerman, "The Emergency Constitution," *Yale Law Journal* 113, no. 5 (March 2004): 1029–91, in contrast with Laurence Tribe and Patrick Gudridge, "The Anti-Emergency Constitution," *Yale Law Journal* 113, no. 8 (June 2004): 1801–70.

83. *Federalist*, no. 52 (Madison).

84. *Federalist*, no. 10 (Madison).

85. Tocqueville, *Democracy in America*, 13, 16. Here, the experience of revolutionary France is very much animating Tocqueville's anxieties.

86. The Federalists imagined the judiciary as the "citadel of the public justice and the public security" and "guardians of the Constitution." *Federalist*, no. 78 (Hamilton). The judiciary was twice removed from the people in that its members were appointed by an executive power itself selected by an electoral college and confirmed by a senate not directly determined by popular vote. Moreover, judges served for life tenures. The judiciary stood as calm reason in the face of the "impetuous vortex" of the legislative power. *Federalist*, no. 48 (Madison).

87. Tocqueville, *Democracy in America*, 99.

88. Tocqueville, *Democracy in America*, 100.

89. Tocqueville, *Democracy in America*, 100.

90. Isaiah Berlin, "Two Concepts of Liberty" (lecture, Oxford University, October 31, 1958).

91. Tocqueville, *Democracy in America*, 510.

92. Tocqueville, *Democracy in America*, 511.

93. Tocqueville, *Democracy in America*, 63.

94. Tocqueville, *Democracy in America*, 69.

95. Tocqueville, *Democracy in America*, 517.

96. Tocqueville, *Democracy in America*, 102.

97. Tocqueville, *Democracy in America*, 69.

98. Tocqueville, *Democracy in America*, 102.

99. Alexis de Tocqueville, *The Old Regime and the French Revolution* (New York: Anchor, 1983), 66.

100. Tocqueville, *Democracy in America*, 700.

101. The "sovereignty of the law" produces and protects a "healthy freedom." Tocqueville, *The Old Regime*, 120.

102. Tocqueville, *Democracy in America*, 268.

103. Tocqueville, *Democracy in America*, 263, 264.

104. Tocqueville, *Democracy in America*, 266 (emphasis added).

105. Tocqueville, *Democracy in America*, 270. This stands side-by-side in Volume One of *Democracy in America* with Tocqueville's statement that "in America the sovereignty of the people is neither hidden nor sterile as with some other nations; mores recognize it, and the laws proclaim it" (58). Where should we look: to the celebration or to the secret? It is not always clear with Alexis de Tocqueville.

106. Archived at the Harry Ransom Center for the Humanities at the University of Texas at Austin, http://www.hrc.utexas.edu/multimedia/video/2008/wallace/douglas_william_t.html.

## Coda

1. Timothy Snyder, *On Tyranny: Twenty Lessons from the Twentieth Century* (New York: Tim Duggan Books, 2017), 13.

2. Snyder, *On Tyranny*, 13.

3. Jon Wiener, "Rick Perlstein: Trump Has Exposed the Dark Underbelly of American Conservatism," *Nation*, May 12, 2017.

4. Wiener, "Rick Perlstein."

5. Barack Obama, "Remarks by the President Announcing Judge Merrick Garland as His Nominee to the Supreme Court," March 16, 2016, https://obamawhitehouse.archives.gov/the-press-office/2016/03/16/remarks-president-announcing-judge-merrick-garland-his-nominee-supreme.

6. Mitch McConnell and Chuck Grassley, "Democrats Shouldn't Rob Voters of Chance to Replace Scalia," *Washington Post*, February 18, 2016.

7. Chuck Grassley, "Grassley Statement on the President's Nomination of Merrick Garland to the U.S. Supreme Court," March 16, 2016, https://www.grassley.senate.gov/news/news-releases/grassley-statement-presidents-nomination-merrick-garland-us-supreme-court.

8. "Grassley Statement."

9. "Grassley Statement."

10. Brutus, No. XV *in The Antifederalists*, ed. Ceclia M. Kenyon (Indianapolis: Bobbs-Merrill Company, 1966).

11. The assertion regarding the role of the American people is from McConnell and Grassley, "Democrats Shouldn't Rob Voters."

12. Edmund Burke, *Reflections on the Revolution in France* (Oxford: Oxford University Press, 2009), 95.

13. Burke, *Reflections*, 95.

14. Edwin Feulner, "The Roots of Modern Conservative Thought from Burke to Kirk," Heritage Foundation, July 9, 2008, https://www.heritage.org/political-process/report/the-roots-modern-conservative-thought-burke-kirk.

15. Feulner, "Modern Conservative Thought."

16. Jon Greenberg, "Ted Cruz Overstates Supreme Court Nomination 'Tradition,'" Politifact, February 14, 2016, http://www.politifact.com/truth-o-meter/statements/2016/feb/14/ted-cruz/ted-cruz-supreme-court-nomination-tradition/.

17. Quoted in Greenberg, "Ted Cruz Overstates."

18. Burke, *Reflections*, 23.

19. Bruce Allen Murphy, *Fortas: The Rise and Ruin of a Supreme Court Justice* (New York: William Morrow, 1988), 361.

20. Murphy, *Fortas*, 299.

21. Amita Kelly, "McConnell: Blocking Supreme Court Nomination 'About a Principle, Not a Person,'" NPR, March 16, 2016, https://www.npr.org/2016/03/16/470664561/mcconnell-blocking-supreme-court-nomination-about-a-principle-not-a-person.

22. Kelly, "McConnell."

23. Robin Bradley Kar and Jason Mazzone note three cases prior to the Civil War that might fall into this category, but they note a categorical difference: those cases only involved "Presidents who were originally elected as Vice President and assumed the Presidency upon death of an elected President." Kar and Mazzone, "The Garland Affair," *NYU Law Review* 91 (May 2016): 66. In any event, this can hardly stand as evidence of a principled and consistent tradition in the modern practice of the Senate.

24. *Federalist*, no. 51 (James Madison), in James Madison, Alexander Hamilton, and John Jay, *The Federalist Papers*, ed. Isaac Kramnick (London: Penguin Classics, 1987).

25. *Federalist*, no. 61 (Alexander Hamilton).

26. *Federalist*, no. 76 (Hamilton) (emphasis added).

27. "Judge Garland Not Interested in FBI Job," *Reuters*, May 16, 2017.

28. McConnell and Grassley, "Democrats Shouldn't Rob Voters."

29. *Federalist*, no. 76 (Hamilton).

30. *Federalist*, no. 76 (Hamilton).

31. *Federalist*, no. 76 (Hamilton); see also *Federalist*, no. 66 (Hamilton).

32. Editorial, "A Coup Against the Supreme Court," *New York Times*, November 7, 2016, A22.

33. "A Coup Against the Supreme Court."

34. Mike DeBonis and Paul Kane, "Supreme Court Is an Issue Again After McCain Suggests Clinton Blockade," *Washington Post*, October 17, 2016.

35. Jonathan Swan, "Heritage Calling for a Supreme Court Blockade if Clinton Wins," *Hill*, November 3, 2016.

36. Swan, "Heritage Calling."

37. Kar and Mazzone, "The Garland Affair," 86.

38. "A Coup Against the Supreme Court."

39. "A Coup Against the Supreme Court."

40. George H. Sabine, *A History of Political Theory*, 3rd ed. (New York: Holt, Reinhart and Winston, 1961), 885.

41. Sabine, *History of Political Theory*, 900.

42. Sabine, *History of Political Theory*, 904.

43. Snyder, *On Tyranny*, 38.

44. Swan, "Heritage Calling."

45. Burke, *Reflections*, 95.

46. Sabine, *History of Political Theory*, 885.

47. Antonio Spadaro and Marcelo Figueroa, "Evangelical Fundamentalism and Catholic Integralism: A Surprising Ecumenism," *La Civilita Cattolica*, July 13, 2017.

48. Spadaro and Figueroa, "Evangelical Fundamentalism."

# Index

abortion: Agamben's silence on, 158n.55; anti-, 75, 80; rights, 76, 79–80, 155n.14, 157nn.45–46, 158n.59. *See also* fetal politics; life and death

Abrams, Kathryn, 31, 143n.43. *See also* legal academy

Abu Ghraib prison, 45, 48, 54, 56, 63; Department of Defense report on, 43. *See also* torture camps

Ackerman, Bruce, 9, 32, 14n.27. *See also* legal academy

ACLU, xiii, 148n.18

Act for the Relief of the Parents of Theresa Marie Schiavo, An. *See* Terri's Law

Adams, John, 28, 128–29

advice and consent. *See* Senate, confirmation power

Afghanistan, 42–43. *See also* Bagram Air Base

African Americans, 36–38, 55–60, 108–9, 112, 151n.62

Agamben, Giorgio, 57, 63–64, 148n.15, 149n.29, 153n.92, 158n.55

Alexander, Michelle: *The New Jim Crow*, 58–59

Alito, Justice Samuel, 7

Al Qaeda, 42, 45

Amar, Akhil, 22, 36. *See also* legal academy

American Bar Association, xiii

American Palestine Committee, 89

*American Political Science Review*, 136

American Revolution, 8–9, 17, 105, 107, 125, 140n.25

Annan, Kofi, 42

anti-constitutionalism: and Arpaio's pardon, xiii; of *Bush v. Gore*, 30–31, 39; of the Constitution, 95–119; and culture of life,

17, 77, 81, 155n.6; and fascism, 135–36; and futurity, 11–13, 77, 94, 156n.28; and the Garland case, 18, 122, 123, 131–33; and habeas corpus, 11–12, 13–14; and lawlessness, 14–15; paradoxes of (*see* paradoxes of anti-constitutionalism); and politicization, 14–15; and precedent, 11–12; of Terri's Law, 17, 75–78, 156n.28, 157n.36; and the torture memos, 52, 53

Anti-Federalists, 12, 124

apocalypticism: and Cold War rhetoric, 41; and culture of life, 17, 81; and the Declaration of Independence, 106; and futurity, 13, 17, 83–85, 91–92, 136, 160n.84; and queer theory, 159n.62; as risk abandonment, 119; and torture-proceduralism, 106. *See also* apocalyptic time

apocalyptic time, 85–94. *See also* apocalypticism

appointment power. *See* nominating power

Arendt, Hannah: on the American Revolution, 105, 107; and culture of life, 77; on the French Revolution, 107–8, 109; and futurity, 84; and lawlessness, 8; *On Revolution*, 140n.25

Aristotle, 77, 90, 94

Arpaio, Joe, ix–xiii

atomic age, 81, 85, 86–88, 91. *See also* apocalyptic time

Augustine, 89–91; *Confessions*, 81. *See also* Christian thought

Auschwitz, 58, 86, 87. *See also* Holocaust, Nazi

Bagram Air Base, 43, 44, 46, 50, 65. *See also* torture camps

Balkin, Jack, 164n.44. *See also* legal academy

*Acknowledgments*

This book owes much to the rich intellectual culture at Cornell Law School, a culture that cultivated conversations across disciplinary and professional boundaries during my time there as a student. I had the good fortune to study under Steve Shiffrin, Martha Fineman, Kathy Abrams, Anna Marie Smith, and Austin Sarat, all of whom taught me to understand that the law is always historically situated and informed by political theory.

I found an equally stimulating community at Berkeley. The cross-currents between the law school, the Department of Political Science, and the Department of Rhetoric were particularly nourishing. Many of the ideas in this book were sharpened due to encounters with my wonderful Berkeley colleagues: Yves Winter, Matt Baxter, K-Sue Park, George Ciccariello-Maher, Libby Anker, Tucker Culbertson, Robyn Marasco, Sharon Stanley, Jimmy Klausen, Ivan Ascher, Diana Anders, Leila Brannstrom, Tim Fisken, Yasmeen Daifallah, Sara Kendall, Satielle Larson, Zhivka Valiavicharska, Nina Hagel, and Mi Lee. A seminar with Hanna Pitkin allowed me to rethink the concept of "crisis"—what it means, what it offers—and that rethinking subtly winds its way through this book even if the concept is not explicitly foregrounded in the text. Paul Thomas offered me critical feedback on most of the chapters in this book. Gordon Silverstein's recommendations and advice early in the project shaped its trajectory. Steve Shiffrin and Kathy Abrams provided invaluable commentary on all the chapters, and their scholarship inspired and provoked me to think about law and politics in new ways. I will always be thankful for the many afternoon conversations with Kathy Abrams in the California sunshine at Café Strada; I'm happy we both ended up on the West Coast. And my feline friend, Omar, was a wonderful writing companion during these years.

My colleagues at Whitman College also contributed to the completion of the book. I am thankful to Jeanne Morefield for sharing her thoughts on

Edmund Burke, Tim Kaufman-Osborn for reading a draft of the coda on quite short notice, Paul Apostolidis for enriching conversations on the politics of the religious Right, and Shampa Biswas for helpfully providing guidance on the publishing process when I most needed it. My faculty position at Whitman was created to honor the legacy of Justice William O. Douglas. I hope this book succeeds in that task.

Scholarship cannot exist without institutional support and infrastructure. The Townsend Center for the Humanities at Berkeley provided me a fellowship to research the chapter on torture, and I'm grateful for my Townsend colleagues' engagement with my early thinking and writing on the subject. The Board of Trustees at Whitman College continues to support a quite generous sabbatical program, and this permitted me to finish the book. The Research Group on Constitutional Studies (RGCS) at McGill University extended me warm hospitality for a semester residency where I researched and wrote the coda to this book. The faculty and students at RGCS approached my work with a charitable and critical attentiveness for which I am most appreciative. My semester at McGill was made possible by the Fulbright Program, which awarded me the Fulbright Visiting Research Chair in Constitutional and Political Theory. I'm thankful as well for conversations with colleagues at Emory Law School during my time there as a visiting scholar with the Vulnerability and Human Condition Initiative. I presented drafts of several chapters at conferences at the New School, Keele University, and the University of Minnesota. The annual conferences of the Western Political Science Association and the Association of Law, Culture, and Humanities also provided forums for presenting work from several chapters. I presented the full argument of the book in a public lecture at McGill. An invitation from the *Harvard Civil Rights–Civil Liberties Law Review* to participate in a colloquium on the work of Nimer Sultany gave me a venue to develop ideas that eventually turned into Chapter 4.

Writers need editors, and I am happy to have worked with Damon Linker at the University of Pennsylvania Press. Damon shepherded this book through the review process and extended to me the perfect mixture of freedom and deadlines. In addition, I have found Damon's scholarship and public interventions on religion and politics to be enlightening and thought-provoking. Anonymous peer reviewers for Penn Press took the time to closely read the manuscript and provided me with numerous suggestions. Their reviews made this a better book, and I'm grateful for their labor. Jamie Warren, an independent editor, helped me to meet a tight editing deadline with skill and friendship.

I owe special thanks to Lily Seaman. Lily has read every word of this book. She both pushed and helped me to clarify phrases, sentences, paragraphs, and chapters. When the value of the project slipped from my view, she reminded me of why it mattered. Lily's political, scholarly, and professional work on the psychological impact of climate change has served as an inspiration for my work in thinking about what we owe the future. Lily also reminds me there is life outside of work and that life is an adventure to be lived.

Finally, I would like to thank Wendy Brown for all she has given to me and this book project over the years. It would be impossible to fully capture and enumerate the intellectual and personal debts I owe. It is with admiration, gratitude, and friendship that I dedicate this book to her.